JUST LIKE A GIRL

HOW GIRLS LEARN TO BE WOMEN

From the Seventies to the Nineties

Sue Sharpe

PENGUIN BOOKS

PENGUIN BOOKS

Published by the Penguin Group
Penguin Books Ltd, 27 Wrights Lane, London w8 5tz, England
Penguin Books USA Inc., 375 Hudson Street, New York, New York 10014, USA
Penguin Books Australia Ltd, Ringwood, Victoria, Australia
Penguin Books Canada Ltd, 10 Alcorn Avenue, Toronto, Ontario, Canada m4v 3b2
Penguin Books (NZ) Ltd, 182–190 Wairau Road, Auckland 10, New Zealand

Penguin Books Ltd, Registered Offices: Harmondsworth, Middlesex, England

First published in Pelican Books 1976
Second edition published in Penguin Books 1994
1 3 5 7 9 10 8 6 4 2

Filmset by Datix International Limited, Bungay, Suffolk
Printed in England by Clays Ltd, St Ives plc
Set in 10/12 pt Monophoto Garamond

For my mother,
Mary Sharpe

CONTENTS

The girls who form the central part of this book were originally the focus of research for a thesis in Social Psychology. My interest in feminine ideas and attitudes at this time was intensified by my growing involvement in the women's movement and I had decided to explore the present situation of girls at school and their future ideas about work and marriage. I ambitiously planned not only to look at girls from English families and backgrounds but also to make a comparative study of English, West Indian and Asian girls. (When I refer to 'English girls' this denotes those who are white and whose families are long-established in Britain. For simplicity I have referred to the black girls as 'West Indian' and 'Asian' regardless of whether or not they were born in Britain (most of them were not), or whether or not they classify as British citizens. This may be technically incorrect but it seemed the clearest way of distinguishing between them and implies no denial of status.)* Subsequently, 249 girls from the fourth forms of four schools in the London borough of Ealing gave me information about themselves by filling up a questionnaire, and some were interviewed in depth. Three of the schools were comprehensive, one was secondary modern, and all were mixed. One hundred and forty-nine girls came from English families, fifty-one were of West Indian origin and forty-nine were of Asian origin. Most of them were working class.

By the time I had completed the research and was getting into complex data analysis I had become increasingly alienated from the work. The warm and living nature of the feelings, ideas and hopes of the girls who had participated had been frozen somehow and lost within long computer sheets covered with endless statistics and calculations. Useful as this type of analysis can be in other contexts,

---

* This terminology has been slightly changed in the new edition. See Preface to the Second Edition.

I put it to one side in favour of writing about the girls in a more comprehensive way. I tried to locate their own personal statements within the general situation of girls and women in a way that would be more meaningful. They would then be contributing, not as statistics or as typical examples, but as separate individuals who share patterns of personality and experience through growing up in similar environments and having similar social positions and prospects.

Consequently, this book does not set out to be a definitive sociological or psychological study, nor does it present or test any grand theories. It is intended as a descriptive and analytical account of the situation of young girls in Britain today, set in a historical and social context and illustrated by girls themselves. (Although the characteristics of their situation and the problems they face will be found in many countries outside Britain as well.) It does, however, contain two biases: the first is that I am more interested in the situation of working class girls, because their social and economic position provides fewer alternatives than their middle class and better-off sisters. The reality of their lives is often denied by the freewheeling assumptions of sexual equality and opportunity put over in popular ideology, and neglected in the evaluation of women's progress towards 'emancipation'. The second bias is that my account is intentionally feminist and as such is, of course, no less valid, and may help to counter the opposite bias contained implicitly in so much that has been written about girls and women in the past.

The girls quoted in this book come predominantly from one area of London, and their position should be distinguished from that of girls living in other parts of the country: in industrial cities, provincial towns and rural villages. As the capital and central city of England, London differs in its range and number of opportunities; and in ideology too, it is easier in London to express and distribute new or radical ideas such as those about women and equality. In other areas, limited opportunities and the trenchant hold of traditional views about women leave many girls with little to look forward to outside marriage and motherhood. And in regions such as Lancashire, women's work in the textile industries has always been an economic necessity both for the women themselves and for the continuation of the industry. Women there have no illusions about liberation through working, as the sort of work available is usually tiring and badly paid. Girls growing up around these areas are well aware of this and look with relief towards marriage, unless they have the education, initiative or other means necessary to change their situation.

Nevertheless, girls from different regions share many things in common as a consequence of their sex. Their upbringing in the family prepares them for 'femininity', their education reinforces the sex divisions through school organization, and the curriculum teaches them 'skills' suitable for 'women's work' in which they encounter some measure of discrimination throughout all parts of the occupational structure. Popular ideas and beliefs still see all but the most talented (and usually middle class) women as primarily wives and mothers, while at the same time acknowledging that today a large proportion of women are regularly employed. Changes in the nature of women's role are being recognized, discussed and acted upon to varying degrees all over the country. For some women greater economic independence has led to social and personal changes in their lives and a readjustment of their domestic role. For others more economically dependent, the construction of new towns and tower blocks has increased isolation, and the incidence of mental illness in housebound mothers has risen drastically. In this context the desirability of work, marriage and motherhood perceived by girls everywhere takes on new significance. The sorts of ideas expressed by the Ealing girls about their present and future lives will also be echoed by others, and while their own statements are personal and individual the subjects of which they speak are those faced by all girls.

The girls contributing to this book have had their ideas and hopes caught and held like stills from a film. They are suspended in time while real life moves on relentlessly, each day bringing more knowledge and experience to change or define their lives. They will all have left school by now; a few will have gone on to college or university, but most into a job. Some will probably be getting engaged or married and a few may already contemplate motherhood. Whatever they are doing I would like to think that if they read this book they would be pleased to recognize themselves in it. I would like to thank them for contributing so much. I am also grateful for the co-operation of the teachers in the schools involved. Many other people have given me help and support, in particular David Phillips, who gave me the confidence to write a book about the girls themselves when I was in despair at losing them in statistics, and then had to live with the consequences. Thanks also go to Sheila Rowbotham for reading it and making helpful comments and giving constant support, likewise Hermione Harris, Liz Waugh, Joanna Bock and all the members of Arsenal Women's Liberation Group.

Sue Sharpe, 1976

PREFACE AND ACKNOWLEDGEMENTS
TO THE SECOND EDITION

Nearly twenty years have now elapsed since the publication of *Just Like A Girl* in 1976, and several more since the original research was carried out. Much has changed to affect the lives of everyone, and not least those of young women growing up today. It is timely, therefore, to take a look at teenage girls at school in the 1990s, and their present and future perspectives on education, work, family life and other aspects of the 'feminine' role.

When I did the initial research in 1972, the Conservative government led by Edward Heath was in power. By the time the book was published, the Labour government had taken office under Harold Wilson. Labour stayed in power until Margaret Thatcher won the general election of 1979. At this time the girls in the second research study were two or three years old. Since this moment they have only known the socially devastating effects of a Conservative government, led by Margaret Thatcher until John Major took over in 1990. The immediate situation and future prospects for girls like themselves at school today have a rather different shape from those in the early 1970s. Many of their own families reflect the fragmentation of family life that has increasingly characterized the last two decades, with rising separation and divorce. Sexuality has come into greater focus, as young people's sexual activity is shown to start at ever earlier ages, in the context of the threatening spread of the AIDS virus. In the area of education, the school-leaving age was raised from fifteen to sixteen; GCSE was brought in to replace CSE and O level, and other vocational courses were created. There was a decline in single sex schools with the increase in comprehensive schooling; an expansion in separate sixth form colleges; and the 1988 Education Reform Act brought in the National Curriculum. Unemployment has risen dramatically; the government brought in the Youth Training Scheme (YTS) to absorb the high levels of unemployed school leavers; more women continued to move into the work-force at the same time as there was a decline in the power and militancy of the trade unions. Over this period Britain's manufacturing base has taken a severe battering as more and more companies have been forced to close.

The eighties have also seen a huge increase in privatization; the relentless dismantling of the welfare state; and a polarization of rich and poor – in effect, people with jobs have got richer, and those without work have become poorer. Although women's equality remains an issue and the principle of equal opportunities is endorsed, real advances in these are at a standstill, and in some cases moving backwards. The prevalent feeling in the 1970s that change was possible by and for women and men, both in the personal and the political sphere, has faded away to be replaced largely (though never totally) by a sense of powerless resignation. The women's movement of the seventies and early eighties no longer actively exists as such, yet plenty of women today hold what are essentially feminist views and principles. During and since the seventies racism as well as sexism has been put under scrutiny and social policies have had to take these into account, at least superficially, although there is no lack of evidence to show continuing racial discrimination. It is in the context of these and other changes over the past two decades that the Ealing girls in 1991 were expressing their own individual hopes and aspirations. Many changes have had significant implications for young women and the nature of their lives, as this new edition will show. Some have been more potent than others, and some have produced a greater change in attitude than in actual behaviour.

The way in which this book initially came into being and the ground it covers are already described in the Preface to the First Edition. The research for that first study was carried out in the summer of 1972. This second study took place in the summer of 1991. My aim was to return to the same four schools in the London borough of Ealing that I had visited for the initial research, to obtain a similar group of fourteen- to fifteen-year-old girls. Inevitably, there had been some changes during this time, and one of the schools no longer existed as such. I took up the offer of another school, which was in an area largely populated by the Asian community. In the end, 232 girls participated in the research, of whom a larger proportion were from Asian families than in the earlier study. As before, all girls filled in a questionnaire covering much the same ground as in 1972, and a proportion of the girls were interviewed in depth. All the schools were mixed comprehensives, and over two-thirds of the girls were working class.

The second edition has been updated with the ideas and expectations of these girls, placed in a contemporary social and economic context. Some parts have been expanded, such as the historical context of education and work described in chapter 1 which has been brought up to the present day, while the other chapters have been more comprehensively changed. The organization of the book has also been somewhat altered: a chapter on Reflections from the Media has been taken out, and this topic included within the second chapter, which explores the social construction of gender differences. For the first edition, published in the mid 1970s, I wrote a chapter about the position of the girls of West Indian* and Asian origin taking part in the study. Many had not lived in Britain for very long, and their situation at that time could be better understood by looking at their attitudes and expectations in the light of their family, religious and cultural context. For this second edition, I have incorporated their experiences and views on school, jobs, gender preferences, marriage and family life into each of the other chapters. At this time it is more appropriate to look at the similarities they face as girls growing up in Britain, while taking into account any pertinent cultural expectations, such as the prospect of arranged marriages in the lives of girls from Asian communities. They all face particular and shared experiences of discrimination by class, gender and race.

I would like to thank all the girls from the Ealing schools who contributed to this research for the 1990s. Their voices translate the written description and analysis into real feelings and experiences, hopes and expectations. As before, all names have been changed to

---

* As far as terminology is concerned, I have used 'black' as meaning those from both Afro-Caribbean and Asian origins. As the Afro-Caribbean girls participating in the book were almost all from the Caribbean, I have referred to them as 'West Indian', consistent with the first edition. I have referred to girls of Asian origin as 'Asian girls', while recognizing that some of their families came from Africa as well as the Asian subcontinent.

ensure anonymity. I am also very grateful to the teachers in the schools involved for their generous co-operation and administrative help. Many thanks go to Ann Phoenix for advice; to Sonia Lane for efficient tape transcription; to the friends who sustained me over the last condensed period of writing; and to Peter O'Shea for his help and warm support.

Sue Sharpe, 1994

A CENTURY OF CHANGES

The situation of girls growing up today can be understood better when it is seen as a part of a wider historical process. The popular view of a linear progression towards greater freedom for women is in fact an over-simplification. In Britain the story has been one of constant adaptation to changing circumstances. The education available to girls has, for instance, depended on social class and the demand for labour, and on the role of the state, as well as on the prevailing notions of feminine roles. The Industrial Revolution transformed women's working lives by changing their role in the labour force. It institutionalized the division of labour between the sexes by creating a formal division between work inside and work outside the home. For working class women, the growth of factories gave them a place of work outside the household, while the production of goods that had previously been made at home reduced the labour of the middle class woman. The Victorian middle class ideal of the wife and mother concealed the real helplessness of the married middle class woman and was irrelevant to the harsh conditions of most working class women. The middle class feminist movement which emerged in the 1860s put forward a cautious alternative to this idea of genteel leisure. But the main concerns of most feminists in the nineteenth century were the education and employment of middle class women; the narrow futures of working class women were not fundamentally questioned.

Working class girls' education in the nineteenth and twentieth centuries was to be affected not by the efforts of middle class women, but by the intervention of the state and by the growth of new types of work within capitalism. In the mid nineteenth century the job opportunities for the genteel and unsupported were limited in the extreme. But by the end of the century, young women from middle class families and from the respectable upper working class were entering jobs as typists – called 'typewriters' – or becoming teachers, telegraphists and telephonists. Mass education played an important part in this.

I am therefore concerned to look first at a brief history of the nature and provision of girls' education up to the present day, and to women's changing position in the labour force in order to shed light on the situation today.

EDUCATION

The 1870 Education Act made schooling available for all children up to ten years of age, and this became compulsory in 1880. Before this, education had been left on a voluntary basis, which meant that while middle class boys were sent to school, middle class girls were given sparse and irrelevant teaching at a few boarding schools, or at the hands of poorly taught governesses. Poor children, if they went to school at all, went to a dame school, or one founded by a charity or religious society, or perhaps a 'ragged school', a part-time factory school, or just Sunday school. Proposals for a system of state education had been unsuccessfully introduced in parliament in the early part of the nineteenth century, but it was not until 1870 that the effects of a combination of motives and forces brought it into being. As capitalism and industry had developed, so its technology and administration had become more complex, and it became increasingly important to have a working class with some minimum education and literacy. Even semi-skilled workers needed to read, write and obey written instructions. Social control was another requirement for an efficient mass labour force, which caused the ruling classes anxiety throughout the nineteenth century. It was thought that mass education would help socialize the working class by imbuing them with new attitudes to work, teaching them deference to the middle class, and raising the standard of living in their homes, and would thus allay the threat of their discontent. It was also seen as contributing to national power as strength in mind would make up for lack of strength in numbers.

The Newcastle Commission, inquiring into popular education in 1858, discovered that relatively few children went to school, few could do sums, read or write, and girls knew little of needlework or cookery. It pointed to the inadequacy of the voluntary system of education. If the standard of living of the working class was to be raised, then the education of girls in the area of domestic economy was essential. Emphasis had been placed on the 'three Rs' and since the children's results in these determined the financial position of many schools, domestic education for girls had been neglected and was taught much less than in the charity schools of the previous century. Lord Shaftesbury said in 1859, 'I would like to see every woman of the working classes have some knowledge of cookery, for ... I am certain that they are ten times more improvident and wasteful than the wealthiest in the land.' There was, therefore, a need to educate boys and girls of all classes. On this educational platform, campaigners with very different motives stood together. Socialists, trade unionists and radicals saw it as a way to raise working class consciousness, while feminists saw it as a way of helping women. The success of their campaign lay in its agreement with the state's need for a more literate, educated and disciplined work-force which would work skilfully and efficiently and thus result in increased production and profit. By making school compulsory for those between the ages of five to ten years, the state made its influence felt on the working class family, steering it towards the small unit of today. Children were taken out of the home, where they had previously contributed to family survival, and made dependent. Capitalism was helping in education as an investment in a more 'rational' exploitation of future workers.

The 1870 Act was really only a compromise, to fill the gaps where voluntary schools were inadequate to non-existent. In such places, school boards were elected to set up elementary board schools at public expense. These were attended by children of the very poor and working classes. Middle class girls made other private arrangements, or attended endowed secondary schools or public day schools. (Secondary education was assumed to be the prerogative of a minority, and for girls it was usually arranged privately.) But while the Act applied equally to girls and boys, in practice their attendance at school was not at all equal.[1] The working class family had been very dependent on the work and wages of its children, and schooling conflicted with this role. The consequent clash of demands caused frequent non-attendance at school, when children were required to earn essential money or look after younger brothers and sisters. Few schools provided crèches for infants, and since working class wives worked on and off for most of their lives, the only alternative was a paid childminder or nurse. Therefore girls were used for this instead because they did not need paying. The school board, through experience, turned a blind eye to these activities by girls – their being 'needed at home' was reasonable since schools could provide no alternative. The school board attitude to boys was different, and therefore a double standard came into being. Their non-attendance, for whatever reason, was viewed as truancy and was strictly followed up and dealt with.

In the previous collective working class family, there had been a tendency for boys to earn money or do work in kind, while girls were more involved in service roles, especially child-care. 'One effect of compulsory schooling was to emphasize this difference, bringing wage-earning under an increasing sustained attack, while extending a certain tolerance to unpaid domestic labour, especially child-care. Another effect was probably to strengthen the tendency for child-care and other domestic work to be seen as the province of girls.'[2] By the end of the nineteenth century, differences in boys' and girls' attendance had narrowed, but there were still more girls missing from school.

Teaching methods were mechanical, often just rote learning, and the books used were both sexist and moralistic. Discipline was strict and 'drills' were frequent. For girls, there was an emphasis on appearance: neatness and cleanliness were exaggerated as part of the concerted effort to raise working class standards of home life. A lesson in 'getting on in life' told girls, 'If you are a housemaid, it is "getting on" if your rooms look cleaner and fresher, your fire-irons brighter, your steps whiter, your whole house neater than other people's . . .'[3] Families were made to feel ashamed if they did not reach these standards, but many were too poor to fulfil any such demands.*

---

* The increasing awareness of 'respectability' among sections of the working class had other effects, one of which was to restrict girls' freedom as family status improved. It became necessary to show visible concern about girls' welfare and activities. In 'respectable families' mothers would ideally not have to work and could then more efficiently prevent daughters from roaming the streets. Girls with working mothers were able to snatch a little more autonomy.

Needlework was considered a subject of central importance for girls, and they spent about a fifth of their time on this while boys did other things usually more technical, scientific and arithmetical. It became compulsory to teach needlework to get a government grant, and in 1882 cookery also became grant-earning. Spending so much time on this made girls get behind in other subjects, but it was considered that they were being fitted for their present and future roles in life. The stipulations regarding girls' subjects severely limited any other opportunities as, for instance, in the 1876 Code, when every girl presented for examination in the higher standards of elementary school had to take domestic economy as one of her subjects. Since most schools only entered children for one subject, there was little choice for girls. They were completely excluded from science work when it was introduced, and few girls' schools took it when it was established. Where it was taught, scientific principles were often only applied to illustrate domestic contexts, like ventilation, and evaporation for use in drying and airing clothes.

Education for working class girls therefore concentrated on the domestic skills, a content that was determined by ruling class and educationalists' assumptions about limited ability and future role. For instance, the stringent needlework requirements would qualify any competent girl as a very skilled needlewoman. However, their training was less geared to either working, or making things for themselves, than towards family responsibilities, and being useful and thrifty wives. Similarly, cookery was seen as being of major importance, and investment in education in this and in needlework and domestic economy was an investment in social welfare for the people. 'In the rhetoric of the time, the family was in decay, and the state therefore threatened, but if women could be taught to be good cooks and housewives, all might yet be well: their men would be tempted home by the prospect of a tasty meal (concocted thriftily out of next to nothing) pleasingly served in a bright clean room, so they wouldn't retreat to the pub; family life would be saved, and the good of the country therefore secured.'[4]

In the eyes of the upper class, the education of working class girls was domestic in order to prepare them for every eventuality: either becoming wives and mothers, or taking the 'appropriate' job of domestic servant. Therefore, in the period up to the beginning of the twentieth century, when compulsory state education was founded, the roles of working class girls and women were already circumscribed. They entered the new century with inferior schooling due to absenteeism; and the low standards of teaching and limited content in girls' schools ensured that there was little opportunity for them to become proficient in any area other than housewifery and domestic service.

By this time it had been acknowledged that the education system was in a chaotic and inadequate condition. Elementary and secondary education had operated on parallel lines instead of providing continuity of schooling. Working class children who made up the bulk of pupils at elementary schools still had little chance of going further and class differentials were therefore being preserved and reinforced. The Education Act of 1902 was intended to remedy this situation by putting responsibility for all levels of education – elementary, secondary and technical – into the hands of local education authorities, who could then organize some continuity and attempt to increase opportunity. But secondary schooling was not free and this severely limited working class entry, although a small gesture was made in 1907 by the introduction of a certain number of free places – a so-called 'ladder of opportunity'. The class duality of this system was also perpetuated in other ways. For instance, secondary education became academic-oriented while elementary and technical had a more practical emphasis. This kind of division was to remain a pervasive one.

Following on the 1902 Act and the supposedly increased access to secondary education, the Elementary School Code of 1904 laid down that the curriculum should be widened to include (as well as the 'three Rs') instruction in English language and literature, history, geography, music, physical training and hygiene, etc., and for girls cookery, laundry work and housewifery. Critics of this expansion complained that girls' education should be linked more thoroughly with the 'chief business of their lives'. However, the curriculum in elementary girls' schools continued to be very concerned with domestic activities, while in high schools for middle or upper class girls, these were rarely emphasized and were even looked down on as something done by less intelligent girls – an attitude that is still found today. The curriculum for boys expanded to include science and mathematics at the end of the nineteenth century, but these subjects were minimized in the education of middle and upper class girls. Elementary school girls probably learnt most of their mathematics in lessons for increasing thrift in the home. 'Mathematics should be kept at a minimum for girls, it does not underlie their industries as it does so many of the activities of men,' said Sara A. Burstall, a distinguished high school headmistress in 1907.[5] It is easy to see how a basis was laid for girls to consider mathematics and science as beyond their capabilities. This attitude was reinforced by the poorly qualified science teachers that were the inevitable result of this circular process of education. At this time, adolescent girls were very susceptible to 'overpressure' of work. This condition of physical and mental strain was induced by the time spent on housewifery and other domestic activities at school, while the widened curriculum also demanded that they do more languages, music and art. This, on top of the duties they had to carry out at home, put tremendous stress on many girls. By 1913, 'over-pressure' in LEA-maintained schools was giving cause for concern and appropriate recommendations were made to ease the situation, although these were largely ignored. In 1923, it was reconsidered in a report on the 'Differentiation of Curricula between Sexes in Secondary Schools'. It was noted that similar stress and strain was seen in women teachers, which was affecting the quality of their teaching. Many sensible recommendations were again made but they inevitably had little effect.

The aims of education were made public in the official reports of this time. In 1906, the 'Report on Higher Elementary Schools' put great stress on character and subservience, noting the characteristics that employers said they would like to see in the 'products' of these schools. Overall the emphasis was on children being educated as efficient members of the class to which they belonged. Boys and girls should be fitted for their appropriate stations in life, which were determined by class and sex.[6] Feminists at this time were working ardently for the vote. Their ideas for obtaining increased educational opportunities for middle class girls were clear but they made no adequate analysis of the situation of working class girls, whose opportunities were limited to a few low level jobs and scarcely any apprenticeships. Some feminists thought that they were best taught to survive poverty as thrifty wives and conscientious mothers. They did not consider the situation in the light of changing the class inequalities. Meanwhile, more jobs were opening up for middle class women: in the Post Office or as typists and secretaries, as well as in the liberal professions like nursing and teaching. Middle class girls' education was now beginning to be recognized as having a possible occupational outcome, although this was seen as being of minimal importance in schools, and work was assumed to end with marriage.

After the First World War, the 1918 Education Act raised the school-leaving age and made recommendations for day-continuation schools in an attempt to check impending juvenile unemployment and as a compensatory gesture to counter the post-war inadequacies of the 'land fit for heroes'. Then came the economic slump and depression of the twenties and thirties. In 1926, the Hadow Report on 'The Education of the Adolescent' considered post-primary education in the light of the unemployment situation, and concentrated again on emphasizing women's place in the home. Once again the focus was on the teaching of housecraft to working class girls in order to help the national situation:

> They should also be shown that on efficient care and management of the home depend the health, happiness and prosperity of the nation. Distaste for the work of the home has arisen in great measure from the fact that housecraft has not been generally regarded as a skilled occupation for which definite training is essential, and it has too often been practised by those who, through lack of training or underdeveloped intelligence, have been incapable of performing it efficiently and of commanding the respect of their fellows . . . Greater efficiency in the housewife would go far to raise her status in the estimation of the community.

Class equality of education took yet another step backwards in the thirties when the cutback in education abolished the system of free places to secondary schools and for the first time the 'means test' was introduced into secondary education. Another significant development was the rise in educational psychology which began officially with the appointment of Cyril Burt on the London County Council. Intelligence tests were introduced and Cyril Burt and others claimed that it was possible to predict accurately at an early age the ultimate level of a child's intellectual powers. This was used to justify streaming, the eleven-plus, and the consequent segregation into different types of school according to ability, which laid the basis for the tripartite system of education brought in by the 1944 Education Act. This changed the elementary and secondary system into one of primary schooling to the age of eleven years and subsequent allocation to either grammar or secondary modern school on the basis of the eleven-plus examination. Technical colleges were also provided to supply specific technical knowledge and skills. This system made no progress towards equalizing educational opportunity for the working class, who tended to fail the examination for reasons that had more to do with social and economic deprivation than innate lack of intelligence. Once allocated, they absorbed the inbuilt status and assumptions of the school and it became very hard to break out of this channelling process. It was not until the 1970s that this system was largely replaced by comprehensive schooling.

At every stage in the development of state education, the question of the domestic training of girls had been considered. The importance attached to teaching girls, especially working class girls, to become efficient housewives and mothers appears ironic when it is compared with attitudes expressed outside the education system which define housewives as inferior and non-productive. While middle class girls' education became officially aimed towards some skill or profession in the labour market, that of working class girls, with their long history of necessary and exploited labour, has been viewed in the context of domestic life; either in order to improve working class home life, or because such girls were implicitly considered to be less able, and early leavers, who would not benefit from other kinds of education. In the late 1950s, the Crowther Report looked at education for fifteen- to eighteen-year-olds and recommended that for 'less able' girls, for whom marriage loomed nearer and nearer, the prospect of courtship and marriage should influence the course of their education, and the curriculum should be framed to respect the different roles of the sexes. 'It is plain, that

if it is sound educational policy to take account of natural interests
. . . [the direct interest of a girl] in dress, personal appearance and in
problems of human relations, [these] should be given a central part
in her education.' This report set alight many arguments in newspapers on the issue of similar education for girls and boys. Four years
later, in 1963, the Newsom Report ('Half Our Future') on thirteen-
to sixteen-year-old children 'of average or less than average ability',
expressed similar ideas for girls' education, suggesting that girls
unenthusiastic about housework 'may need all the more the education a good school course can give in the wider aspects of home-
making, and in the skills that will reduce the element of domestic
drudgery'.

Higher education had a relatively later expansion for girls. Although campaigners like Emily Davies were trying to get girls
admitted on an equal basis to Oxford and Cambridge as far back as
the 1860s, this did not happen until well into this century (1948 for
Cambridge University). Provincial universities were allowing
women in before the end of the last century, but it was not until
after the Second World War that the growth of universities and
some decline in sex discrimination combined to give many more
girls the opportunity for higher education. This progress was
interlinked with changes and demands in the economy and in
ideology. Developments in capitalism again created a need for more
educated workers, and could not officially deny 'equal opportunity'
for girls. The Robbins Report on Higher Education, 1961–3, emphasized the need for professional women to return to work, especially
in teaching, where there was a great shortage at that time. It noted
that a new career pattern for women had emerged which consisted
of a short period of work before marriage, and a second period
starting about fifteen years later and continuing for twenty years or
more. Details were given of the unequal ratio of women to men
entering university (one woman to every four men overall in 1963)
and the opposite trend in training college (two women to every
man), as girls channelled off into the lower levels of higher education. Robbins was very keen on higher education for girls, and
suggested that more girls would probably stay on at school in the
future, this being welcome 'if only from the national point of view
of making better use of what must be the greatest source of unused

talent at a time when there is an immediate shortage of teachers and many other types of qualified person'.

The Robbins Report also exposed the large class bias in higher education, showing, for instance, that only 25 per cent of undergraduates in 1961 came from families in which the father had a manual occupation. Educational sociologists in the fifties had already attacked this waste of ability, and had pointed out the low proportion of working class children who went to grammar schools. They suggested that it would be useful to look more closely at the relationship between home background and school. This was subsequently demonstrated by researchers such as J. W. B. Douglas[7] who found that the social conditions under which most working class children lived contributed greatly to class inequalities at primary school. These included the facilities at home and relative lack of parental interest and encouragement, which were themselves rooted in the conditions of the working class in society.[8] It was these aspects rather than ability that were non-conducive to educational performance and therefore the talents of huge numbers of working class children were being wasted. Similarly, he found that amongst secondary school children matched for academic ability, those from middle class backgrounds were twice as likely to stay on at school as working class children. This confirmed the decision to raise the school-leaving age to sixteen years implemented in 1972 (for pupils leaving in 1973).

This century has undoubtedly produced a great increase in girls' secondary and higher education, but this has still largely benefited the middle class, whose access to better education, and aspirant backgrounds have led them more easily into relatively higher status jobs and into the professions. Working class girls have been viewed, and tend to view themselves, in a different educational perspective. Historically, the concern given to domestic subjects has reinforced their traditional role, and up to relatively recent times the official reports on their schooling have concentrated on this aspect. By being defined as 'less able' they were excluded from any of society's so-called more 'useful' occupations. (As expressed, for example, in the Crowther and Newsom Reports discussed above.)

The publicly professed principle of equality of opportunity, and the switch from streamed to comprehensive schooling in the 1970s unsurprisingly made little impression on class or sex inequalities. It has a wider foundation since we live in a society whose efficient running is dependent on maintaining class and sex divisions. However, in such situations there are inevitably contradictions, and some of these have been felt strongly by many middle class girls, who have absorbed both the high aspirations of their class and the ideology of equality. They have found that despite higher education and raised expectations, their real position and opportunities are by no means equal. Although there is equal pay in more occupations at the top end of the job scale, they are expected to preserve most of the other aspects of their role and status which define their positions as lower than those of men. Women are still largely excluded from the top positions and when they have children they may still be expected to step down and slip quietly away. Women teachers became particularly conscious of this, and aware of their own roles in transmitting the basis of these inequalities in school. It is partly such conflict that raised feminist consciousness, and the Women's Liberation Movement in the seventies and eighties contained many women in these situations.

Extra resources were at that time allocated to educational priority areas. In the 1950s and 1960s, many individuals and families of Afro-Caribbean or Asian origin had come to work and settle in Britain. After years of discriminatory allocation of a significant number of their children to lower forms within schools or children being labelled as educationally subnormal, it was finally acknowledged that much of the apparent 'underachievement' of black children was not due to some inherent failing in them, but to the failure of the education system to recognize their culture and backgrounds. There was increasing focus on 'multicultural education'. At this time feminists were also revealing and criticizing the underlying and often overt stereotyping by sex, class and race in children's early reading books and primers. This led to the publication of less discriminatory texts. Feminist women involved in education formed a Women and Education group which published newsletters and usefully reviewed all new children's books. Gender and race became issues to be addressed within schools. In the attempt to provide more equal education, comprehensive schooling also brought a move towards coeducation. However, this did not have such egalitarian consequences for teachers in that the rearrangement of schools also removed women from senior teaching and management positions, and from headships. A typical arrangement that still exists in many schools today is to have a male headteacher and female deputy headteacher.

During the 1980s, the state education system was severely undermined by government cuts in educational spending. Schools were unable to expand or change the content of their curriculum by buying new textbooks due to the restraints on spending. Funds for Further and Adult education were also cut, which made it harder for women to retrain. The government's economic cuts halted any progress towards combating sexism as teachers and liberal educationalists found it hard to hold on to what facilities they had, let alone push for change. In the early 1980s, the ILEA (Inner London Education Authority) produced a working party report on equal opportunities for girls and boys, which contained lots of recommendations designed to promote equal opportunities in education and teacher training. An Equal Opportunities Unit was set up, and even a Girls' Education Fund. The 1985 Swann Report[9] revealed the way that many black children were underachieving because of the attitudes and expectations of their (mainly white) teachers. Anti-sexist and anti-racist policies were incorporated into school policy guidelines. Although it is difficult to know how far these have been effective, they represented a step forward in awareness. It obviously depends on teachers and the organization of the school as well as other factors. While it may be taboo to express any overtly racist or sexist attitudes or behaviour in school, there are plenty of covert ways by which these can enter the 'hidden curriculum'. However, the government of Margaret Thatcher helped to take these progressive policies a step backwards by abolishing the ILEA in April 1990.

The conditions of teachers themselves were eroded during the 1980s, and the 1986 Education Act began a process of removing control of the curriculum from the hands of the teaching profession. This took place at the same time as the government was placing increasing emphasis on linking the curriculum with the labour market. In 1985, the Certificate of Pre-Vocational Education (CPVE) was introduced, in which was included personal and career development and social skills, together with an introduction to the market economy and employers' needs by way of a short period of work experience.

In 1987, the Conservative government introduced the 'need' for, and then rapidly brought in, the National Curriculum within the 1988 Education Reform Act. This contained a notional assumption of equal opportunities, and presented a return to a more strictly controlled curriculum of subjects. It consisted of core and foundation subjects. The three 'core' subjects were English, maths and science, and the foundation subjects included these core subjects, plus history, geography, technology (with design), music, art and physical education. A modern foreign language was added to this at secondary school, and the basic curriculum also included religious education. Other subjects, including the more liberal humanitarian subjects that had expanded the curriculum during the 1970s and 1980s, such as sociology, would be fitted in around these if possible, together with the recognized needs of careers education, health education, aspects of personal and social education, and general coverage of gender and multicultural issues. The National Curriculum has been the subject of criticism and modification from its inception until well into the nineties. In 1994 the government accepted the recommendations made in a report by Sir Ron Dearing for trimming severely the complex curriculum, and ending the National Curriculum at the age of fourteen in England and Wales.

Once again an education system was being introduced that professed democratic, egalitarian principles while schooling children for a society that still depended on maintaining divisions by sex, class and race.[10] For instance, having a tier system for science (single or double science) creates an immediate division between those who are entitled to take A levels and thereby go on to higher education and those who are not. Evidence has suggested that it is inevitably girls and black students who suffer more as a result of this.[11] The National Curriculum received a controversial response to the idea of national testing of pupils in relation to specific attainment levels. This would serve to set artificial limits on children's learning and can thereby label children as failures from an early age, and further endorse any existing negative expectation on the part of teachers.

Debates about mixed and single sex schooling have remained unresolved. It seemed that the move to large, mixed comprehensive schools did more favours for boys' educational performance than for girls. In the early 1980s, it appeared that girls and boys had become even more stereotyped in their subject choices, and girls in mixed sex schools were gaining lower level results than those in single sex schools.[12] Heads of science subjects would invariably be male, whereas in single sex schools women took positions at every level. Mixed schools did help to make available to both sexes the opportunities of taking all subjects. Therefore, theoretically it was possible for girls to take things like woodwork or CDT (craft, design and technology), and for boys to take child development and food studies, without any clash in timetables through sexist assumptions. The extent to which girls and boys have taken up these options is small but increasing, as it is also closely related with other factors such as the appropriateness of these subjects in their perceived futures, and their current self concepts of 'femininity' or 'masculinity'.

Working class girls experience the most inequalities, both in education and later at work, but have experienced potentially less role contradiction because their expectations have been less often expressed through success in education. Historically, these expectations have been denied or channelled off into domestic subjects and concern with the primary role of wife and mother. The opportunities for unqualified girls are usually in semi-skilled and unskilled work, and in low level clerical work which are all jobs characterized by unequal pay and a low level of union organization. In the past, these conditions have been accepted as a result of women's need to work combined with their belief that their major role is in the home. Lack of knowledge about alternatives and ignorance about status, wages and position relative to other sorts of workers contributed to their acceptance of circumstances. School attempts to groom girls for its main goal of academic success but still neglects those for whom this has been made to appear meaningless or plainly out of reach. In the nineties, girls, like those participating in the research described in this book, take the desire and/or the necessity of a job or career for granted. This is in the context of a sexual division of labour that has become blurred through the coexistence of a range or ideologies and practices about how and when mothers should work, and how far domestic work and child-care should be shared with men; and a reality where economic needs dictate that women with families have to work, or become part of an 'underclass' dependent on derisory levels of state benefits.

The present education system can be viewed through its historical growth from the 1880s. But rather than being a straightforward and positive progression, the nature of girls' education at any particular time still reflects the outcome of a number of interrelated factors. These include the stated (official) aim of education, the prevailing idea of 'femininity', the sexual division of labour, and the demand for certain types of labour and levels of skill.

WORK

Middle and upper class girls in the last century looked forward to a womanhood of leisure and home management, and participated little in any outside work. Working class families, however, could ill-afford any idleness and both girls and women laboured in industry and domestic service. In 1861, about 2·7 million women over fifteen years old were gainfully employed – 26 per cent of the total female population (this proportion remained stable in later decades). Very nearly 2 million were in domestic service, while the rest were mainly in textile factories, millinery, 'sweated' and 'outwork' trades. Very few had any kind of skilled work. In the textile industry children were often taken on as 'pieceners', dealing with broken threads on spinning machines. One young girl of fourteen years, for example, worked on this from 6 a.m. to 5.30 p.m. with one and a half hours' break. She only moved on if someone left or died. She was earning two shillings and sixpence per week at fourteen, and by twenty-one years, when she left, she was getting nine shillings per week.[13] Women usually stopped this sort of work on getting married, and took on some work at home instead.

Many women worked in the sweated trades and did 'home-work' – trying to fit family needs around getting the essential few pence to survive. They worked as milliners and seamstresses, washerwomen, framework knitters, straw-plaiters, nail and chain makers, box makers – and at many other exploited homebased occupations.

There were apprenticeships for girls which were low paid or unpaid. A stonemason's daughter in 1891, who had been apprenticed to a dressmaker in Dalston, was lucky enough to earn a small wage – but never more than ten shillings a week – and she eventually left to go into domestic service.[14] For some sorts of home-work, the children would be drawn in to help. For instance, the stages of matchbox making would be divided up amongst everyone. At the beginning of the twentieth century, a number of inquiries had exposed the sweated trades and the situation of outworkers, and the government tried to regulate wages (through the Wage Boards Act, 1909). By 1915 the wages of about half these workers were regulated, though still relatively very low, and sweated exploitation on a major scale showed a decline. For many, however, their dependence on this sort of work guaranteed their continued exploitation.

Domestic service was the largest single employment for English women, and the second largest employment for all people in the nineteenth century up until the First World War. There was little else for an unskilled girl to do if she had to work, and living within another household also provided a relief for her own family, as it meant one less mouth to feed. Domestic service paralleled the growth of its employers, the middle classes, and reflected the development of their Victorian family pattern. It was a very acceptable occupation at first, because girls of twelve or thirteen with no experience or training would be taken on, but it suffered a decline in the 1870s, as it got more unpopular. It began to be avoided by young girls, partly due to developments in education, but partly also due to new employment opportunities. For those with some education, teaching, nursing and clerical work were becoming more acceptable and available, while for most working class girls, shop and factory work offered higher wages than domestic service, shorter and more regular hours, freedom from constant attendance and duty, and also provided more independence and sense of identity. The camaraderie found on the factory floor was far more enjoyable than the subordinate atmosphere of servant life.

By 1901 domestic service still accounted for 40 per cent of employed women, but its decline continued and was greatly accelerated by the 1914–18 war, when masses of kitchen maids, parlour maids and cooks moved into munitions factories, public services and subsidiary armed forces (400,000 of the girls and women in domestic service left it at this time). It had become regarded as low status by society in general, but out of all its disadvantages – like the long hours and the symbolic servility of their uniform – it was the social one, that of isolation and lack of freedom, that contributed the most to its downfall.

The First World War

In 1914 the outbreak of war greatly changed the position of women in the labour force. At first the general dislocation of industry caused unemployment, which affected women more severely than men. But soon an increasing number of women were entering the new openings in munitions factories and other industries that were being created as men went off to fight. In March 1915 there was still a surplus of unemployed women, and the government launched a scheme of national registration inviting women willing to do work of any kind to enter themselves on a Register of Women for War Service. This was aimed at finding out what sort of reserve women's labour force they had, and within two weeks 33,000 women had enrolled and a total of 87,000 registered in all.*

At first there was a transference from slack to busy trades, like women moving from dressmaking to grocery shops. Middle-aged professional women who could not do 'ordinary' occupations often took positions in banks, insurance and other forms of business, which were opened to women for the first time. Married women returned to work in industry, and soldiers' wives entered munitions in large numbers, probably motivated by rising prices and the inadequacy of their 'separation allowances'. As the war continued, there was a transference from 'women's occupations', to the more highly paid jobs like munitions. For instance, as skilled women left laundry work, their places would be filled by charwomen or girls

* Many workers' and women's organizations were very worried about the government's plans for introducing women workers without making certain guarantees both for women and for the men displaced. Resolutions and demands connected with this were made by, for example, the National Workers' Committee, the Women's Freedom League, and Sylvia Pankhurst.

fresh from school. Often skilled women moved into almost unskilled work in the munitions factories.

The proportion of previously unoccupied upper and middle class women going into war work was small. It was confined to some young girls who would not normally have worked, some older women who entered clerical work, and some educated women who were taken on as a weekend force for munitions known as the Weekend Munitions Relief Workers (WMRW). They were quite enthusiastic, although often their husbands were not so keen, being worried about the class of women with whom they would mix. Therefore, the new needs of industry were mainly filled by working women or wives of working class men. Former factory hands, charwomen and domestic servants were found on heavier work, while shopgirls, dressmakers and milliners undertook the lighter work. The increase in women workers can then be accounted for without saying that a great number of women new to work were employed, since lots of home-workers, half-employed charwomen, small shopkeepers, etc., suddenly became regular workers.

Women entered all kinds of work, previously the protected provinces of men. Although it was not possible to replace men in very heavy work processes, there was success in fairly heavy work, like rubber manufacture, paper mills, shipyards, iron and tube works, chemical and gasworks, stacking coal, brick-making, flour-milling and other trades. But this level of work was not really so new as Miss Anderson, the Principal Lady Inspector of Factories, pointed out: 'It is permissible to wonder whether some of the surprise and admiration freely expressed in many quarters over new proofs of women's physical capacity and endurance is not in part attributable to lack of knowledge and appreciation of the very heavy and strenuous nature of much of normal pre-war work for women, domestic and industrial.' Women were moving into lots of other areas. The pre-war expansion of clerical work opportunities for girls was speeded up by the war, and in shops the demand for assistants, doorkeepers and lift-attendants was great. Waitresses were replacing male workers in hotels and restaurants, and the Waiters' Union, in contrast to the attitudes of most other male unions, was actually training them for the work. Munitions work was very popular, and large numbers of girls were transported away from home to work in the big new factories. This work included some very dangerous processes, as the shells had to be filled with TNT. Many girls suffered from TNT poisoning which caused very unpleasant skin eruptions.

In the transport industry, women were taken on as carriage cleaners and ticket collectors. In the then new Maida Vale underground station, the staff were almost all women, but they were getting lower wages than men would receive for the same work. This often happened in other areas of work, and was usually further complicated by the male unions' reluctance to allow women to join. Many women who had previously been domestic servants became tram conductors. Entry into this work was successfully resisted by the unions at first, who said that it was 'most uncongenial and ill-fitted for women', but by 1917, there were 2,500 women tram conductors. In 1916 and 1917 the Women's National Land Service Corps and the Women's Land Army sent women to help on farms.

These women did a lot of tough outdoor work for relatively little pay, and usually proved to be excellent workers. Another profession that was opened up for women by the war was the police. The women's police force was first formed on a full- or part-time volunteer basis. Its main purpose was to protect women and girls who were living in hostels as a result of being brought together to work in munitions, or those who lived in towns near large military encampments. At the end of the war 100 policewomen were taken on into the Metropolitan Police Force, full-time and paid.

Many inquiries and committees looked into the effects of war work on women. In terms of health, conclusions were mixed, because many married women with children were unsurprisingly exhausted by working all day (or night) and dealing with the home as well. But on the other hand, many girls had benefited greatly from outdoor work, and from improved diets. Rationing, introduced in 1917, actually improved the standard of living for many working class families as their meat rations were more than they could ever have afforded before the war. In the munitions factories, girls also got regular meals. Reports by some women labour leaders on home life deplored the disintegration that resulted from long hours, hard work and bad accommodation, but they did not think of questioning either the social conditions or the organization of domestic work.

Other reports noted the change in personality and attitude of the women factory workers, and one writer in the *New Statesman* (23 June 1917) declared that they had developed a new independence: "They appear more alert, more critical of the conditions under which they work, more ready to make a stand against injustice than their pre-war selves or their prototypes."[15] Dr Marion Phillips held that the roots of change lay in the absence of millions of men from home, and in the fact that for the first time the demand for women workers exceeded the supply. Away from the influence of men, women had been able to form independent opinions, and had gained 'a new grasp of experience, a widened outlook and greater confidence in their own judgements'.[16]

When the war ended, unemployment hit women first because so many had been involved in war industries. The popular press exhorted women to go home after their war effort. Women were dismissed in their thousands, often with little or no notice. Twenty thousand women who had been made redundant by Woolwich Arsenal marched to Whitehall, and this demonstration effectively convinced Lloyd George of the need for some unemployment allowance. At this time, however, a system of 'out of work dona tions' was introduced instead of unemployment insurance benefit and in New Year 1919, 225,000 women were receiving this com- pared with 101,000 men. This reached a peak in March when 494,000 women and 234,000 men were receiving 'donations'. After thirteen weeks, donations were reduced, and they were finally discontinued in November 1919. The system was particularly unsatis- factory for women, because they were refusing to take the alternative employment offered to them, which was generally in sweated indus- tries, or in places either too skilled, or underpaid and unattractive. Eighty-one per cent of women were being refused donations because they would not accept 'suitable employment'.

The Ministry of Labour admitted that an unsatisfied demand existed for women in domestic service, laundries, needlework trades and textile industries, at the same time as half a million women were unemployed. But women did not want these jobs. At one point the Association of Laundrymen even appealed to the government to put pressure on women, but fortunately no action was taken. Women themselves said, very reasonably, that since the government had raised the rate of unemployment donations from twenty shillings to twenty-five shillings per week on the grounds that it was not possible for a single women to live on less, they could not be expected to enter laundries at eighteen shillings per week. There was a general unwillingness of women to move to work with lower wages, and also to places lacking the many conveniences of the new munitions factories. After much criticism of the donation system, a committee examined it but concluded that applicants should not expect the same sort of work or wages they had had during the war and that donations should be stopped if 'similar' work was refused.

Women were, however, staying on in certain jobs, such as at the lowest level of bank clerks and other clerical positions; also in shops, hotels and restaurants, in transport, and in some light unskilled work in the engineering industries. But it was clear that many processes, like flour-milling and sugar-refining, and other trades where women had worked satisfactorily in the war, were now closed to them. The protective legislation for women, which had been waived for the period of the war, now forbade them to work nights or on Sundays. The attitude towards women industrial workers as weaker and 'not quite adult', was reinforced by such legislation whose purpose was to protect jobs for men rather than to protect women. It was significant, as Winifred Holtby[17] noted, that this protection only applied to occupations that were quite well-paid and where women entered into competition with men. Others – like charwomen, domestic servants, nurses, etc., had no such prohibitions on nightwork, or Sunday working, and infringed the Factory Act conditions relating to lifting heavy weights and having statutory mealtimes. Similarly ironic was the difference between the capacity for work of the undernourished girl working in sweated trades, compared with that of a similar girl who had been well-fed in munitions factories during the war.

The middle classes were very concerned by the post-war unavailability of domestic servants, and set up committees to inquire into the problem. It seemed that nothing would tempt them back, and such committees were aware of the low status and contempt that being 'only a servant' had acquired, and were concerned to change this. For instance, amongst the training courses for unemployed women set up after the war, there was a special one in housekeeping.

The Ministry of Labour Committee investigating the problem again in 1923 suggested that training in domestic service should form part of the education of all elementary school girls between ages of twelve to fourteen years. As we have seen, this emphasis on domestic work was again expressed in the 1926 Hadow Report on elementary education.

The war had changed women's assumptions about work: upper and middle class women started assuming they had the right to work, and working class women who had done a man's job began to question their subordination. The number of women in trade unions rose at this time, and women contributed to the general labour unrest. They were especially concerned with issues of equal pay, together with various feminist and other women's organizations who were very anxious not to return to a pre-war situation. Women of different classes had also mixed and worked together during the war, and some of the rigidity of the class barriers had been broken down. In 1919, various working women's organizations arranged a meeting in the Albert Hall attended by women representing nearly every trade, at which speakers dwelt on the folly of unemployment at a time when the country was in need of all sorts of manufactured articles. Resolutions were passed giving three points of a 'Women's Charter': the right to work, the right to live, and the right to have leisure.

Post-war and the Depression

There was a short boom in industry after the war, and more jobs were opened for girls. Clerical work saw a great expansion demanding typists, secretaries, telephonists and post office clerks. Office work was considered a respectable job for middle class girls who took positions as secretaries, while the lower level work was taken by a new sector that was emerging – the lower middle class. The office girl had now really arrived, clutching on to her newly acquired but limited sexual and economic independence. There was a surplus of women over men, and many young single girls were willing and wanting to work. But unemployment was increasing all the time, and the economic slump followed a number of strikes which reflected the militancy and discontent of the working class.

After the defeat of the General Strike in 1926, both men and women were demoralized, and the gains previously made began to slip away.

There was antagonism between men and women workers, as men were afraid for their jobs, and accused women of causing unemployment. The majority of women were non-unionized (it was estimated that only one-sixth of working women were in unions in 1926), and men made little effort to change this situation, preferring to ignore it and concentrate on men at the expense of women. Women who needed work were getting desperate. They took work at appallingly low pay and, between 1921 and 1931 200,000 re-entered domestic service. In the 1930s typists sat with blank paper in their machines, trying to look busy. Office workers were rarely allowed to stay on after marriage, so they had the choice between spinsterhood or losing essential money. Some compromised by either not admitting their marriage, or settling for a 'common-law' arrangement. On 14 November 1933, Central Hall Westminster was packed by a mass meeting of women's organizations which proclaimed the right of married women to paid employment; and in March 1934, a similar rally was held over 'equal pay for equal work'.

At this time women often obtained jobs more easily than men since they were cheaper to employ, less well organized, and their numbers in industry and the professions were constantly being diminished by the drain of marriage and family obligations. Children were also more easily employed than men, as, like women, they were cheaper. As a result a new social phenomenon emerged: the earning woman supporting the unemployed man. Men found this very hard to come to terms with as it represented a denial of their masculinity: 'There are men who will not even kiss a girl in a taxi for which they have not paid'.[18] But taxis were not in the experience of most of the working class, and working class women employed in industry did not get much money. During the worst years of the Depression they were often lucky if they got a full week's work.

Unemployment hit its peak in 1933. Means testing was introduced, and a man often lost his unemployment benefit on the basis of the whole family's income. The early 1930s saw a general narrowing of ambition, ideas and opportunities, and a lapse into defeated resignation. Feminism was still voicing demands and mounting campaigns, but these were more in the context of seeking reforms from the state in the way of welfare* and family allowances, than demanding radical change in structure or organization, and woman's role was universally accepted as being in the family and domestic scene. The consequence for most working class women was that they had two heavy roles, at work and at home, and most were worn out by the time they were thirty.

The generation of girls growing up in the twenties and thirties had little of the feminist consciousness that had been so high before and during the war. Above the life-draining struggle of working class girls and women to keep their families going, the dizzy frivolity of the 'flappers' provided a public and superficial shield. The atmosphere of liberty, emancipation and sexual freedom† that had been around after the war was confined mainly to the middle class young. It was also reflected in women's fashions which showed a rejection of strait-laced Victoriana, and expressed itself in short skirts, cropped hair, flattened busts and no waists. The leisure industry was expanding to lap up the new earning power of the young working girl, and providing the beginnings of the mass market in clothes and cosmetics.

Towards the end of the twenties a wave of cultural anti-feminism began. New images of femininity were projected on a mass scale, both through fashions, which showed a swift and dramatic change in the thirties to deliberately ladylike styles – busts came out, waists went in, hair was long and hemlines dropped – and through the

---

* Some welfare reforms had been introduced around 1910–11, prompted by the concern expressed over the health of the working class, and over the declining birth rate and high infant mortality. Free milk, school meals, health visitors and midwives set off a glorification of motherhood which for the first time placed before the working class the opportunity of adopting some of the family patterns of the middle class, hitherto out of reach.

| The idea of sex for solely reproductive purposes was being eroded by such people as Marie Stopes, whose writings about the importance of sexual compatibility and pleasure were put into practice with her birth control clinics. The campaigns for contraception and abortion that were ultimately to have a great effect on women's lives, were fought at many informal and formal levels. The association of birth control with obscenity which made publishing information a risk, weakened in the twenties with the growing support of the labour movement. It remained a controversial subject, however, for many years.

expanding entertainment industry, which produced a spate of romantic films in which mean men heroically dominated soft helpless starlets, and popular songs echoed the joys of love and marriage. Women's status was seen as being at its highest in their 'natural' role and was supported by a false comparison with emancipation. This was paralleled by Fascist ideas and activities that were developing at this time. Reports of the position of women in Nazi Germany had filtered through, where the government had manipulated women using both psychological and direct measures to get them out of any employment and into the home.*

In Britain, it was implicit in middle class ideology that it was preferable for a wife not to work, and that any aspiring husband should be able to earn enough to keep his wife at home. This was the situation when the Second World War broke out in 1939.

The Second World War

Despite 10 per cent unemployment at the start of the war, mass mobilization soon absorbed this and by 1940 it was clear that the need for men in the services and the expanding war industries necessitated again calling on women to provide the extra workers. At first, this was dependent on women's voluntary entrance into such employment but in March 1941 it became necessary to register women of twenty and twenty-one years. By July, the situation was again desperate, as women had proved very reluctant to volunteer, especially for the services† which had gained some reputation for impropriety.

There was obviously a need for draconian measures and it was announced that all people, from eighteen-year-old girls to men and women of sixty, would be obliged to take some kind of war work. But the most striking development was that for the first time women were to be conscripted. No other country involved in the

* In his statement on Fascist policy (*The Greater Britain*, 1932) Sir Oswald Mosley declared the need for 'men who are men and women who are women'.
† Women's auxiliary services consisted of the WRNS (Women's Royal Naval Service), the WAAF (Women's Auxiliary Air Force), the ATS (Auxiliary Territorial Service) and various nursing services.

war went as far as this, and the War Cabinet were rather unhappy about it at first. It became law on 18 December 1941, but only applied to unmarried women between the ages of twenty and thirty (extended to nineteen-year-olds in 1942). They all had the choice between the auxiliary services and important jobs in industry. Entering the services meant the ATS, the WRNS, or the WAAF, where they were mainly employed doing the inevitable clerical or domestic work (in canteens, etc.). They would take no part in combat unless they expressly volunteered.

The reluctance of many women to volunteer for war work was in direct contrast to the First World War, when girls and women in jobs like domestic service and the sweated industries had eagerly exchanged these for the prospects offered by munitions and other essential war industries. In spite of active campaigns over the country, this time the response was very poor. Surveys conducted at the time[19] put forward several explanations for this reluctance. Women did not want to move, girls had been put off by stories from the First World War about the poisonous processes in munitions work, they were afraid of what industry was like, and seemed generally unaware of the urgency of the situation. Between the wars many other openings had expanded for working women (clerical, commerce, shops, etc.) and factory work had lost its advantages. A survey in Worcester gave the main objections to munitions work as follows: domestic problems (children, shopping, etc.), long hours, dirtiness of the work, monotony, impossibility of getting out of such work, and degradation of doing factory work. For married women with families, or young typists and shop assistants, the work had little appeal. Those who had already volunteered had done so through either patriotism or economic necessity, and in certain areas of depressed employment (like South Wales and the North-east) women were very glad of the opportunity for work.

Although the public attitude to conscription of women was favourable, and the result of one survey found that 97 per cent of women agreed 'emphatically' that women should undertake war work, many were in a state of confusion and consternation about the prospect. One typist wrote, 'I can lay my hand on my heart and say truthfully that I have not yet met a woman in the twenties who is not in an awful state about conscription'.[20] By 1943, it was almost impossible for women under forty to avoid war work unless they had heavy family responsibilities or they billeted war workers. In July of the same year, it was announced that all women up to fifty years of age had to register for employment, in an effort to release younger women for work in aircraft factories. There was an outcry against the 'direction of grandmothers' but it was passed. Most of the regulations, however, fell on the young unmarried women. Women were classified as 'mobile' or 'immobile', and girls could be 'exported' from their homes to work in war factories, a situation that was especially resented in Scotland when it was discovered that girls were to be sent south of the border.

The number of women new to work in this war did not show a vast increase, but again more an acceleration of peace-time trends. In 1943, the proportion of women aged from fifteen to sixty in the forces, munitions, and essential industries was about double what it had been in 1918.[21] Nearly 3 million married women and widows were employed compared with 1·25 million before the war. Of women aged from eighteen to forty, 90 per cent of single and 80 per cent of married women were in the forces or industries. The rest were looking after children or doing part-time or home jobs. It was estimated that without a war, there would have been about 6·75 million women working in 1943, and in fact there were about 7·5 million – representing an increase of only about 0·75 million. Women had worked in industries like the aircraft industry before the war, and within the engineering and metal industries; a quarter of working women had some pre-war experience, half came from different jobs, and the rest from school or from looking after the home.

As in the previous war, women entered many male-defined jobs, and usually proved to be as good as men. Their enthusiastic efficiency was again viewed with great suspicion by male workers. Although they did not go into mining, there were not many jobs below that requirement of physical ability in which some women could not be found. They worked on the railways as porters, in shipyards as welders, in the aircraft and other essential war industries. They produced work previously done by skilled men. Relations were not always easy between women and the men who trained them and with whom they worked. Men saw the threat contained in the 'dilution' of their jobs by women, and were often reluctant to give away all their knowledge. At the same time, many managements were loath to train women whom they considered to be a temporary labour force. Surprise was expressed at the ease with which the girls picked up skills – an ease which quickly reinforced male fears. When girls were first introduced into male-dominated factories, men often looked at them as if they were some new species. One girl, who proved to be a very competent worker, was described thus by her male workmates in an aircraft factory. 'We looked at her, nine of us, for days as though we had never seen a woman before. We watched the dainty way she picked up a file, with red-enamelled fingertip extended as though she were holding a cup of tea ... her concern for the cleanliness of her hands, her delicate unhandy way with the hammer.'[22] In a northern foundry an ex-waitress became the best machine operator in the shop, but an observer noted: 'This girl has so taken to machinery that she would like to become an apprentice and go right through the works. This, of course, is not possible on account of Union agreements. There is a feeling among men that at the moment women must be in the factory solely because of the war, but really women's place is in the home'.[23]

Women's real place at home was endorsed also at governmental level, and concern with the welfare of family life, particularly that of the working class, caused Beveridge to produce the basis of the welfare state in his report in 1942. He made these views very explicit, and they provide a complete contrast to the national situation of the time, in which women were being exhorted to leave their young children in nurseries and go to work, young girls were being conscripted, and other women being directed from less to more important occupations. It is obvious that in looking forward to the end of the war, the state was stepping in to ensure the maintenance of Britain as a nation. The position of women working was officially classified:

The attitude of the housewife to gainful employment outside the home is not and should not be the same as the single woman. She has other duties ... Taken as a whole, the plan for Social Security puts a premium on marriage in place of penalizing it ... In the next thirty years housewives as mothers have vital work to do in ensuring the adequate continuance of the British race and of British ideals in the world.[24]

The 'temporary' nature of women's work was reflected in the attitudes of men, management, and many women themselves. Trying to assess the potential state of women's demobilization, a special survey[25] found that most women were looking forward to going home when the war was over. It was the young unmarried women who were the most worried about their position and who welcomed the idea of staying on at work. This was also felt by elderly women who had been working for some time and were very financially dependent on their work. Married women, it was suggested, and those expecting to be married, saw their future goal as settling down to domestic life. This was unsurprising since much of the full-time factory work was very tiring and women with families became exhausted by their double job-load. For part-time workers, however, the situation was different. The war had made many employers offer part-time work to women for the first time, and those taking it on were often women of about forty or fifty years of age from quite comfortable backgrounds. They were delighted with the outside interest and freedom that this gave them, and were very keen to continue.

A different attitude was expressed by many girls, generally young and from families of high income levels, who had gone into the services. They were reluctant at the thought of settling down, and expressed a longing for travel and adventure. 'The wanderlust is very widespread in the women's services.'[26] They were anxious about their post-war destinies, especially as war had reduced the prospect of marriage, and yet their training in the anti-aircraft service had not trained them for any peace-time job. The survey suggested that these girls were having to think for themselves for the first time, and were beginning to exchange frank and political ideas. 'Women in uniform have become far more independent-minded, first because there is no male member of the family available from whom to take a ready-made opinion, and secondly because in this new communal life, private hopes and fears are being brought into the daylight and related to wider plans for reconstruction on a national and international scale.'[27] They were in favour of equal competition with men, while those working in industry were content to accept continuing inequalities.

Female inequality at work carried on in its historical tradition. Women in government training centres received just over half the pay of men, and sometimes this was even further reduced when they started full-time work! This happened particularly in the engineering industry. It was significant that although resistance to women working was not great, it was concentrated in the key places, and the AEU, for example, excluded women right up to 1943. The belief that things were going to be really tough for the working class after the war reinforced men's inclination to cling on to their present advantages. Very few women were to be found in the higher grades of industry, or on the Joint Production Committees formed during the war. Unequal pay was fairly universal, and when the railway companies were challenged to pay women clerks the same rates as men, they replied that 'Since the managers had been unable to find any industry where the principle of equal pay for equal work was applied, they did not see why they should apply it on the railways.' Despite agreements in the engineering industry to give women the full male rate after thirty-two weeks, this was easily and usually evaded. The unions did in fact recruit a lot of women – more in the general unions (TGWU and GMWU), although 140,000 women joined the AEU when it finally opened its doors to them. The number of women in all trade unions had nearly doubled by the end of the war, but inequality was taken for granted. Even a demand for equal pay for teachers, at first passed, was revoked by the House of Commons in 1944.

Women of different class backgrounds worked and mixed in the same jobs, although sometimes their status was reflected in the positions they took – for instance, women who had been teachers or had held other supervisory positions were often made supervisors in the factories, which was not always a successful arrangement. The influx of women into industry stimulated attention to working conditions, personal relationships, and welfare as related to industrial efficiency, and there was a significant increase in welfare provision and training of personnel managers.

The entry of girls from non-working class backgrounds shamed many firms into reconsidering the conditions under which women had to work. They were faced with the choice of either giving these girls clerical positions where conditions were better, or improving their facilities by providing better canteens and sanitary arrangements than those that 'the local factory-class girls had got used to'.

Married women had many problems with both shopping and child-care, as few firms gave regular time off for this purpose. The consequent absenteeism and bad time-keeping of many women reinforced management's already prejudiced views that married women were unsuitable employees. At first mothers had to leave children with relatives or neighbours, but the obvious unsuitability of many arrangements emphasized the need and demand for state-sponsored nurseries. This, in combination with Britain's overwhelming need to free women for essential work in industry, gave the final impetus to the delayed question of day nursery provision, which began a great expansion from mid 1941. Many mothers were reluctant to use these facilities at first, but attitudes did change.

Young working class girls leaving elementary school in the war years usually made their choice from factory, shop, domestic or office work. Office work was more often the preserve of girls with secondary school education and the 'snob' division between clerical and manual workers in the same factory was quite high. The most important aspect was the money, which made a much needed contribution to family income, as well as providing the important (though meagre) pocket money. Girls took on a multitude of different unskilled jobs both before and during the war. This often happened in very quick succession, and they slipped from one to the next with an easy and indifferent attitude reflecting the labour shortage. Here, for instance, is the career of a girl of sixteen and a half in 1942 who left school at fourteen and has never been without a job for more than two days, except during evacuation.[28]

> Job 1. Two months: Calendars. 'You shove a piece of paper over a machine that is printing calendars. It got on my nerves.'
> Job 2. Two months: Pipes. 'You just polish them.'
> Job 3. One week: Playing cards. 'You make up the pack.'
> Job 4. Three months: Darts and fishing-rods. 'You fit the flight into the base with two pairs of pincers. That was a nice job. Interesting.'

Job 5. Three days: Electric irons. 'You had to fit wire into an adaptor.'

Job 6. One month: Batteries.

Job 7. One year eight months (present job): Petrol tubes. 'You stick a little rod into the solution and seal the top of the tube. I might "stick up" or go on to the filling machine or do other jobs as I fancy. We can swap jobs amongst ourselves. It's all right.'

The same situation was found in clerical jobs, although this is more typical of London than the north, and one girl was known to have had twenty-four jobs by the time she was twenty-two. Such young girls were used as a very cheap source of labour, and were employed on the most tedious and insignificant of tasks.

Money and leisure became important to them, and they had more of both than their mothers had had in their youth. Much of their leisure time was spent at the pictures or dancing, and some enthusiasts saw films three to five times a week. It was often a relief to get out of the house, where lack of space gave little privacy. After the age of about seventeen most girls' dominant interest was marriage, and this crucial part of their future was discussed frequently with friends and mothers. The war speeded up the tendency towards early marriage, and the idea of women's domestic careers became strongly established.

Practically every girl says that she will want to give up her job when she gets married, and expects her career to continue for another five years at most. Even when the girl, like one very capable clerk who had risen from twenty-five shillings at fifteen to fifty shillings at eighteen, says that she herself would probably like to go on with her job after marriage if her husband were away, her boy does not favour the idea nor do the older people at her home.[29]

Those who considered continuing to go out to work did so only in the case of financial necessity. 'They see marriage as a full-time career, and want literally to make a job of it. It is a matter of principle ... that a woman's first duty is to look after her own home . . . Their boys take the same attitude . . . and what "my boy" says carries much weight.'[30]

After the war, women were called upon to go home again, and although many did, it was not without a change in attitude that would bring them back to work later on. The post-war withdrawal of nursery facilities made it harder for women who did want to carry on, but the relative independence that many women had experienced left them discontented with work solely at home. Some part-time workers were allowed to stay on, as employers had found them useful and another way of extorting cheap labour. It was, however, not totally an employer's market in labour terms. Unlike the First World War, there was very little unemployment after this war – in fact, there was a labour shortage in many areas. This meant, for instance, that part-timers who would have otherwise been forced to either leave work or continue full-time, were allowed to stay on. In some cases special shift systems were even worked out to best suit these women.[31] It is not absolutely clear how far women did follow the order to return home, or whether they were displaced out of men's jobs into perhaps more suitable 'women's work'. This is what appears to have occurred in America. Working class girls and women carried on working as they had always done, combining the belief that women's primary place is in the home with its economic contradiction. It was middle class women once more who saw the most change, clinging on to their part-time jobs, although certainly not denying their primary duties to the home.

Post-war and Beyond

The period after the war and in the fifties saw a general cultural reaction against the independent woman who had demonstrated her capabilities briefly in wartime. Fashion and the female image became restrictively feminine, and marriage was held out as the most normal and desirable state for women to be in. The implications of John Bowlby's* studies exaggerated the need for mothers always to be with their young children. The terrors of 'maternal deprivation'

---

* On the effects of 'maternal deprivation' on young children, and the importance of the mother–child tie, 1946. See also chapter 5.

laid the responsibility for children's future development at the mother's door. It served as a discouragement to would-be working mothers and placed most of the guilt on the working class since they were assumed to be the main perpetrators of this psychological offence. In spite of this, women (particularly married women) were still going out to work. Thus, they contributed to expanding industries and provided extra income for the family, giving everyone the illusion of being better off. The Tory government patted itself on the back for the affluence of the 1950s and said 'You've never had it so good.' But the credit was as much due to these women's labours as to government policy. It was the simultaneous expansion in the 'women's work' areas – the administrative, educational, welfare and service sectors, that created a demand for women and made it inevitable that they should be increasingly drawn into the labour force.

The 1950s saw more and more married women going out to work. Many factors had contributed to this situation: an earlier marriage age, falling birth-rates and shrinking families, reduction in time necessary for housework as a result of household gadgets and ready-to-cook foods, increasing demands for female labour, and the changing ideology of the modern world in which women were theoretically free to compete with men. Development of birth control, and changed attitudes to family size which emphasized the advantages of smaller families, meant that a smaller proportion of a woman's lifetime needed to be devoted to motherhood. In the period from 1881–1951, there was little significant change in the proportion of gainfully occupied women in the total female population: 25·5 per cent in 1881 and 27·4 per cent in 1951; although this obviously conceals the great changes in regions and types of occupation. But in the period 1951–61, this went up to 37·2 per cent, and this increase was almost totally through the employment of married women.[32] The public acceptance of the notion of women as an integral part of the labour force was hastened by the post-war situation of full employment, which meant that employers had to look to women as the only available source of reserve labour. The resulting opportunities for part-time work opened the door for many more married women. In the estimates made of women workers between 1951–61 through census figures, and by such studies as Dr Viola Klein's,[33] it appeared that over 80 per cent of part-time workers were married women. In 1957, almost half the population of married women were working, and half of these had children under fifteen years. The range of work, particularly for part-timers, was very limited, and reflected a high proportion of working class employment. In Klein's study, 45 per cent of working women were domestic workers, cleaners, canteen helpers and the like, then came clerical workers (15 per cent) and shop assistants (12 per cent). Altogether 67 per cent of part-time married women were in unskilled or semi-skilled work, endorsing the continuing predominance of working class women's employment.

These trends continued into the 1960s, when the expansion of higher education for girls reinforced the idea that women could make a meaningful contribution to the work-force, while also endorsing the class divisions in education and employment. Girls taking O and A levels in grammar schools were being groomed for work in the higher status jobs and professions (teaching and nursing being two areas currently having labour shortages), while in the lower forms of these schools and in the secondary moderns, girls left early for lower level jobs needing the minimum qualifications. The reasoning then seemed to be that if you had a good job, especially a higher status one with training, like teaching or medicine, it was a pity and a waste to give it up. It became acceptable for a girl in such work to carry on with it after both marriage and children. On the other hand, unless women were short of money there was little recognized reason for them to return to low status jobs like routine clerical and unskilled work. Even financial need was often lost in the myth that women only worked for 'pin money'. It was thought to be unacceptable for women to work because they wanted to get out of the home.

But as the sixties wore on, cultural changes occurred which questioned the strict gender definitions separating masculine and feminine. The expanding youth movement rejected the tradition of their elders. They were helped in self-definition by the need for new markets within capitalism, which exploited their earning power and manipulated their tastes. Teddyboys, beatniks and hippies demonstrated their ideas of alternative cultures. Boys and girls grew long hair and wore unisex clothes. The militancy that had started in the days of CND exploded on student campuses in the late sixties and challenged the system that had put them there. Women's liberation emerged as a movement partly out of this new radicalism and in 1970 the first organized conference was held in Oxford.

Working class girls who had been picking their way through school and adolescence in the 1970s, such as those who participated in the original research that formed the basis of this book, were relatively untouched by this upsurge of feminism although some may have encountered teachers in the women's movement. But their position was being changed and complicated by developments in women's role and attitudes. Like all girls, they confronted a situation that is the product of historical change – embracing economic, technological and ideological developments. For instance, middle class girls had now come to accept and expect their right to work. They took their choice from a better selection of jobs than working class girls, but were still barred from easy entry to men's jobs or high positions.

This may have provided conflict for some girls, but other contradictions particularly affected working class girls. The idea of job involvement, for example, which is so implicit in school careers teaching, clashed with the routine and monotony of most jobs open to them. It clashed too with the deep investment that many of their own mothers had made in family life. The resolution and outcome of contradictions like these in girls' lives depends not only on the nature of the economic and labour position but also on the active response and participation of girls themselves.

In the seventies the situation of women and work was brought to popular attention by the activities of the Women's Liberation Movement, who campaigned for equal pay and more accessible nursery provision, and tried to encourage women to join and become active in trade union activities. Nineteen seventy-five saw the implementation of the Sex Discrimination Act and the Equal Pay Act (which had been passed in 1970). Equal pay has always remained elusive, however, and the differentials between men's and women's earnings are still significant, mainly due to the persisting sex segregation in the work-force, and a practice of 'de-skilling' in which women's jobs tended to be defined as less skilled than similar work done by men. The 1980 Women and Employment Survey found that 63 per cent of women worked in jobs done only by women, and 80 per cent of men were in jobs done only by men. The continuing expansion of the service industries drew in increasing numbers of women, many of whom found part-time work to fit in with their family demands, in low level, low-paid, non-unionized ('women's') work like cleaning and catering. The proportion of women recorded as working part-time rose from 12 per cent in 1951 to 35 per cent in 1971, and had reached 42 per cent by 1981.

Throughout the eighties there was a continuing 'feminization' of the work-force, but in fact women were not moving into new jobs or into previously male occupational territory. More and more women were entering the same sort of low status service jobs as they had always done. An emphasis on careers for women and the successful entry of a few women into business gave an impression that more women were going into 'top jobs'. The rapid expansion of new technology in the form of computers and word processors transformed office and secretarial work. But far from benefiting women and making their work easier, the nature of this work often took on a more relentless pattern, and much worse, it brought a huge cut in jobs. A study published in 1984 by the office workers, union APEX showed that for every job created by new technology, fifty had been lost.[34] Furthermore, women's part-time work enabled employers to extend the length of the working day, and provided them with a flexible labour force, which was particularly appropriate in the service sector. The continuing lack of accessible child-care facilities helped to ensure a high supply of part-time workers. From the end of the 1970s, feminists attacked the principle of a family wage (by which men earned enough to keep their wife and children) which lay beneath many wage deals. This was eventually dropped but not before it had contributed considerably to preserving women's low pay levels: for instance, ten years after the Equal Pay Act, in the mid 1980s, the average pay for women was still about two thirds that of men.

The steady decline in the manufacturing sector through the eighties into the nineties has affected both sexes by increasing unemployment, but had a greater and more immediate effect on men than women. (Women made up 32 per cent of those unemployed in 1993.) The service sector also declined, and although it has been slower to do so, this has contributed to the increasing unemployment of women. It has been suggested that it is the high levels of sex segregation of the work-force that have contributed to women being less affected in times of recession. In the banking and financial sector, too, unprecedented cuts and redundancies have shaken up the lives of people who had happily assumed that they were in a job for life. It may have been thought that such universal economic contraction would propel women back to the home, but this has not happened – far from it. Their position has been cushioned by their predominance in the service sector more than industry; in still being a relatively cheap and flexible work-force; and also through being themselves unwilling to 'return to the home'. Beliefs that women working has contributed to family instability are countered by the fact that it is often women who are holding the family economy together.

Women are an integral part of the labour force. In 1993, women made up 44 per cent of the work-force (risen from 38 per cent in 1979), and a total of 65 per cent of all women of working age were in employment (compared with 59 per cent in 1979). Girls from all backgrounds now look forward to a life in which work plays a major part. Looking back to the beginning of the century, the gains made in this area for women have been large, but the disadvantages they still face as the end of the century approaches are both a reflection and an indictment of a society that endorses individualism as well as equality.

WOMEN AND THE FAMILY

Women's role in the home is of fundamental importance to the working of our society, in all its social, political and economic spheres. I have looked at how the role and expectations of girls and women in education and work have been transformed and developed through time, and it is now necessary to examine their present situation. Through such an analysis, it becomes clear that the attitudes and ideas of girls are not only formed through tradition, teaching and their own interaction with and interpretation of the world, but can and should be understood by examining the social conditions of their lives under the prevailing economic system. They have an integral part to play in the organization of work and of the economy, and therefore the way these operate will affect their position. At the same time it is possible for women by their own demands and actions to exert some influence on the economic organization of society. Women as mothers play an integral part in family life. Their role within the family changes with any alterations in its form and functions, subject to influences from outside. Conversely, as women have made modifications and extensions to their role, and marriage relationships have been broken, the family has had to adapt itself or be propped up with state aid.

There have been several important historical changes in the family which have affected women's situation. When most people lived on the land, the peasant family made up a production unit and the whole family was involved in working. Similarly in domestic industry men, women and children worked together. These economic functions of the family were gradually whittled away with the growth of the factory system. The movement towards towns and work in mass production and the emphasis on accumulating capital contributed towards reducing the extended agricultural family to the small nuclear unit recognized today, and reflected the effects of demands for different sorts of workers within capitalism. State intervention through education and social welfare has taken over and made public some of the private informal education which existed in the family, thus also altering women's role in the family. Every generation of girls grows up in a family situation which is trying to adapt and survive within present economic and social conditions, and eventually plays its own adult part in continuing this process.

The division of labour in society put production into the hands of men, leaving reproduction and child-care to women. Production was thus separated from both reproduction and consumption. From the time of the Industrial Revolution class divisions rigidified between the ruling class, who owned the factories and most of the other means of production, and the working class, who made up the mass labour working for them. The middle classes emerged in between, striving and aspiring towards the upper echelons of power and wealth.

Instead of working in family workshops and on smallholdings, men increasingly went *out* to work, and a consistent wage became the criterion for survival. A man's capacity for work, his labour, was exchanged or 'sold' in return for money with which he could then purchase back, at a higher price, the finished products of his or others' labour in order to maintain him and his family. Since the main emphasis in capitalism is on accumulation of capital, making profits is essential to success within this system. Therefore, a worker never receives back the real value of his or her labour. It is implicit that the relations of production – the relationship between worker and employer/capitalist – should be exploitative. The worker performs surplus labour producing surplus value which ends up as accumulated capital (profits). The aim of any capitalist is to compete successfully in the market place of commodities. The greater his profits the more capital he can accumulate, and the more he can expand his enterprise and keep up with competition. Within this process, workers have the dubious 'freedom' of selling their labour. They are 'free' to work their lives away and yet always remain powerless and subordinate to those who own capital and the means of production.

The relationship between men and capitalism, as described above, has been direct and exploitative. That between women and capitalism has been kept deceptively separate. The dominant set of beliefs and values of society which stressed women's place within the home contributed to this. As a result there was no official recognition of women as part of production despite centuries of their essential labour. This separation of work from home and family also led to neglect of any proper analysis of women's contribution through their husbands and children. In order to begin to rectify this, it is necessary to examine more closely the role of the family and the parts women play inside and outside the home.

The shrinking of family structure was accompanied by a corresponding erosion of functions. Children were taken out of the home for compulsory schooling, and other home duties, such as nursing, were eased by the provision of hospitals. The creation of the welfare state in this century made a great impact, giving aid to the sick, unemployed, elderly, pregnant and poverty-stricken. The changing image of women's role was intimately connected with these state interventions, which in turn were determined by the need for a more efficient society, a more rational capitalism.

To illustrate this point, we can look at the pattern of goods that have been produced since the beginning of the century. At that time, Britain was an important exporter of goods, but with increasing competition from abroad, was forced back on to the previously protected home market. The Depression in the thirties led to severe crises in some of Britain's older industries, such as steel, shipbuilding and textiles, which in turn led to mass unemployment. Simultaneously, newer home-based industries concerned with the manufacture of consumer durables were growing rapidly and helping to maintain a crippled economy. These products brought technology to the household and consisted of articles like washing machines and vacuum cleaners, which would eventually reduce the amount of labour necessary in the home. These domestic aids started being used in middle class homes, also helping to compensate for the declining number of domestic servants. This growth continued and was joined after the Second World War by the self-service catering development and the expansion of ready-prepared foods.

Therefore, during this period an increasing proportion of capital was indirectly being made by easing women's domestic work in the home. Combined with other factors – such as the tendency towards smaller families, the development and use of contraception, and increases in allowances and welfare – this facilitated the conditions for women to work outside the home. Thus, the changing pattern of economic production had its ultimate effects in the organization of domestic work.

Women's position at home and at work is also bound up with the variable demands of the labour market. In many areas of work, women need not be drawn into the labour force while there is a surplus of men, except into specifically female employment. But when this surplus decreases, or new sorts of employment open up, capital has to look towards other sources of labour power. This happened particularly in the post-war years with the increasing demand for white-collar office workers and secretarial staff, and the growth in computer work. From the fifties, capital was drawing on immigrant labour (predominantly for manual work) and female labour to fill the demand. The two World Wars had accelerated this labour market process for women, when they discovered for themselves that there was a far greater range of jobs within their capabilities than had previously been provided by domestic service. In the seventies this had increased to such an extent that the rate of acceleration in the growth in female labour was probably about four times that of the rate of increase in the population.

Despite the severe economic crises and large-scale unemployment in the seventies, there was no obvious redeployment of women back to the home. They had become an accepted and integral part of the labour force (although in some manufacturing areas they were still very much a source of cheap surplus labour and the first to be paid off in the event of cutbacks). At that time, women were becoming unionized and more militant about their rights, especially over the crucial issue of equal pay. The demand for women continued in the administrative, clerical and secretarial fields, in which there was no direct competition with men. Therefore, it seemed no longer so easy to manipulate a female labour force, and irrational to lay women off, since their contribution to the family income was becoming increasingly important within the economy. In all families, middle class as well as working class, it was women's wages that helped to ease the severe economic situation.

Under capitalism, the family lost a lot of its earlier functions in production, education and welfare, and women experienced corresponding effects. However, they still played the principal role in producing and maintaining the present and future elements of the work-force. This refers to the way that women are obviously the bearers of children, and they are still the major carers in the family, looking after husbands and children and bringing them up to the best of their ability. In this they are supplemented by, and contribute to, the welfare state, which gives token assistance to their work in the home by, for instance, provision of minimal child allowances. The traditional family has provided several other useful areas of indirect control: it provides the most socially recognized and approved place for sex and reproduction; and the cheapest place for the early care and socialization of children. It is significant that while the state has taken over so many other functions of the family, it has left parents responsible for the behaviour of their children. Therefore, they have to control their sons and daughters, making sure they keep within the rules and expectations of society. Any misdemeanours are first reflected back on the family, before other social conditions are considered. It is also a private sanctuary to accommodate the passions and emotions so inappropriate and disruptive if they occur in the outside world of business and production. This sanctuary has begun to fall apart, however, and part of the increase in domestic and inner city violence is one symptom of the social fragmentation and the meaninglessness of life for those who, under the Conservative economic strategies of the last decade, have no employment or financial prospects and feel powerless to change their situation.

Another major function of the family is to avidly buy and consume the products that are continuously made available. The economy gives the illusion that these are provided to fill a need, while manipulating the market to create this need. To provide the maximum consumption, the 'privatization' of the family is essential – an infinite duplication of needs. Every family buys individual foods, cooks on individual cookers, in individual pans. Each buys the products and gadgets that are supposed to make work and leisure more enjoyable. Each is encouraged to compare itself with others to assess relative affluence and status. A family may be judged by what it consumes. An immense consumer market is built up in which expensive luxury goods – cars, televisions, stereos, videos, freezers, washing machines, computers, etc. – take their place beside the basic needs for survival. Advertising has helped both to produce and maintain the demand, dwelling on a man's wish to compete and prove himself by encouraging him to buy certain large commodities, and on a woman's anxieties about being a 'good' wife and mother who has to buy the 'right' things for her family.

The economy rests on such individual consumption – collectivization would be disastrous for profits, although beneficial for people. But such a system is based on the needs of capital rather than those of people, and any slump, for whatever reason, is bounced back on to wages, which are then cut or frozen to preserve profits. Workers are persuaded of the importance of the 'national economy', and assume that its healthy growth is also theirs. To some extent this has seemed to be true because in a prosperous economy concessions can be made to the demands of the working class, but these are fragments compared with the corresponding profits. The more recent process of 'individualization' and people's belief in 'popular capitalism' has been promoted by the popular media (mainly in the form of the right-wing tabloid press) in the hands of a monopoly of newspaper owners, such as Rupert Murdoch.

For the family to efficiently carry out these social and economic roles, it is necessary to preserve the small autonomous family intact. But instead of helping in this, capitalism has shown one of many inherent contradictions and irrationalities. While expressing deep concern about the instability and fragmentation of contemporary family life, the government continues to implement a socially damaging economic system which has contributed to thousands being thrown out of employment on to state aid, and eroded these and other welfare systems that were keeping the family together. The result is helping to create the family disintegration that the government deplores.

The Parts Women Play

Women today still have two recognized roles: one at home, and the other in the work-force. But rather than these being alternatives, the domestic role has always been assumed to be a natural extension of being a woman. Any other activities like having a job are then performed as additional work. In the isolation of every home, women have performed never-ending tasks of cleaning, cooking, washing-up, washing clothes, and all the repetitive services that maintain the home. Mothers at home have the more exhausting demands of child-care as well. This work seems very far away from the production line or the office. It has not counted as 'real work' because it is unpaid and done in the privacy of the home. Here, women have the illusory freedom to organize these tasks. This has been an implicit part of being wife and mother, although the same things done for other people are counted as employment. The work itself is not light, and mothers may often work eighty or ninety hours a week in their homes. Housework has become easier and less time-consuming through domestic technology, but there are no consumer products to make children less demanding.

This unrecognized work is in effect the service and maintenance of the workers of today and tomorrow. It is related to the external world of production, but indirectly. A man relies on his wife's labour at home in order to be fit and able to earn a wage. Traditionally he was expected to provide for his wife and family without her going out to work. Their survival on this money is dependent on a wife's economical shopping, and the provision of her free services. Every day she reproduces labour power, her man's capacity for another working day. Her work produces things, not for exchange, but for immediate consumption. Meals are eaten, floors and clothes are made dirty over and over again. It is because she does not produce for exchange that a woman's labour has been deceptively unconnected with the 'real' economic markets. Therefore, it is seen as 'unreal', or 'invisible labour', but it is certainly real enough in that it greatly reduces the cost of maintaining and reproducing workers (and is, at least at present, cheaper than any other method), and therefore makes an important contribution to the efficient running of the economy and profit accumulation. If women accept this definition of themselves enough to say, 'I don't work. I'm only a housewife', it contributes to the persistence of the belief that housework and child-care are not 'proper' work.

Home-making and child-care are obviously real work in every physical sense, but as women's work and as so-called 'unproductive' work they are different because they operate on a social and personal level.[35] The power of labour lies usually in its capacity to be sold and withdrawn at will. If housework is 'real' work, then a woman should be able to withdraw her services. But the crucial difference here is that it is not alienated labour but 'love-labour'. The relationship between man and wife is not that between worker and employer. The emotional ties and responsibilities run very deep: 'love-labour' is capable of sustained production out of all proportion to that of wage-labour. It appears disguised as something that has escaped reduction to sordid economic terms, and yet without it the cost of reproducing and looking after the workers would have to be borne by the current economic system.

From childhood, girls grow up with a familiar and deeper investment in caring relationships. The reward held out for such caring is love and security, which are more highly valued by women in a society where love is a human feeling out of place and often distorted in the productive world, and where the development of capitalism forced women to become dependent on finding a husband for their support. Today, husbands are no longer a guarantee for support, but love and caring are still of great importance to women. But what are the consequences for a woman whose whole life is measured in terms of the love she gives and receives from her husband and children? Often her identity gets lost, submerged within her caring. Her success is the reflection of their success, their problems are treated as her problems, their happiness becomes her happiness. At first, her own self may hang suspended, sometimes returning for moments of expression, but when life gets filled with the immediate demands of child-care this becomes a luxury, drawing further and further back and finally forgotten. Her world is encapsulated within home and family.

Until relatively recently, a man's relationship to the home has been quite different. He had an independent role at work where he became someone in his own right, whatever his job and however well he did it. For him home was, and still is for many, a place to return to, to relax in and be recharged for the next day's work. It is the place where he is by tradition the head, however token this has become. Here he can dominate and satisfy expectations of masculinity denied to many workers who occupy a subordinate role in the workplace. The appropriate expression of such 'masculine' attributes as assertiveness, aggression, competitiveness and initiative are valued as necessary for success within a competitive economic system. However, the increase in male unemployment in all sectors, including manufacturing and historically more secure occupations like banking has undermined men's role inside and outside the home. 'Masculinity' used to be premised on maintaining the distinction between the two spheres of work and home, and male power rested at least partly on the hierarchy involved. Girls and women have not enforced such a clear distinction. Their domestic identity has rather been extended into the workplace, in many cases using domestic skills to earn an income. Their employment serves their domestic commitments at home rather than themselves. At the same time, women's recognition and acceptance of men's work–family split helps to maintain it, and the separation of these two aspects of their lives. Nowadays, boys and men can no longer look confidently towards a life of paid work. This has implications for the expression of masculinity that working satisfied, and points towards the contemporary violence and anti-social behaviour shown by many unemployed young men in inner cities.

Although 'masculinity', unlike 'femininity', does not generally involve an overt or generous expression of emotions, men need to express their feelings and share personal intimacies. These have traditionally been channelled into the narrow confines of home. Women are supposed to soothe away the stress and tension of the male working day. The same caring 'feminine' characteristics that have made women appear unsuitable as successful entrepreneurs are more appropriate to receive men's bursting emotions and unexpressed frustrations with work. In our society, it is sad that the family has been the only place where people are allowed to be themselves, safely prevented from disrupting the organized alienation that exists outside. There is now an alternative in the form of psychotherapy, which has an increasing market but mainly serves those who can afford to pay the fees.

Women isolated at home have adopted many strategies to cope with their situation, to refract its real causes and transfer them into some other form. Some have developed minor illnesses and nervous complaints; become neurotic and obsessional over trivial things, over-reacting to small crises.[36] To ease these symptoms, doctors prescribed tranquillizers or sleeping pills, which dull the senses enough to enable them to do the family duties. This was picked up and examined by feminists in the seventies, when the main criterion of women's 'normality' was how far they stayed within the domestic role. Rejecting this could cast doubts on their sanity.[37] Social workers were sometimes known to judge a woman according to her 'femininity' and domesticity, and saw increased neatness and cleanliness as an 'improvement' in her condition. But if there is no apparent alternative, investment in domestic tasks is a rational response, and many women have drawn much of their self-esteem from their indispensability to the family. To deny this is equivalent to removing the purpose of their existence.

Despite the fact that few women in the seventies were spending all their lives at home, and girls were growing up with firm vocational aspirations, women's dependence on home and family was slow to change. Their primary place was still believed to be at home with work running a closer second place than before, but only acceptable with convincing reasons and adequate provision at home. This masked the fact that many women, especially working class women, have been doing two jobs for many years, accepting their 'love-labour' and blaming themselves if they could not cope with the double work load. This belief served the interests of capitalism at that time, but we have seen how the state could also intervene in women's situation at times of critical labour need, as it had done in the Second World War. The same ideas that supported the oppression and exploitation of women at home also formed the basis of their conditions of work outside. The view that work was secondary was (and still is to some extent) held by both women and employers to justify giving them low level jobs at low wages. This was further reinforced by regarding women as a temporary, transient and unreliable work-force. They have been little helped in the past by male trade unions, who neglected them for similar reasons, even seeing them as a threat to their stability. Women themselves have been slow and difficult to unionize and organize, partly because they accepted their priorities at home. Many factors combined to give women little protection against exploitation, but the upsurge of industrial militancy in the seventies helped to convince some male unions and workers at that time of the need to support women's demands as strongly as their own.

For a social system to work people must believe in it, and for its survival it must have a convincing way of putting over its ideas. Political power is not only a matter of economic dominance, it requires an ideological hold over how the world is presented. It would be too simple to regard this as a plot or conspiracy. The existing values of dominant groups are reproduced through the structure of institutions like the family, schools and the media, and women play a crucial role in this process.

From many sources, and through many interactive processes, people pick up an apparent consensus of what has been, what is and what ought to be. People usually learn the nature of 'appropriate' behaviour, even if they do not conform to it themselves. It is through the dynamics of a combination of individual and social processes that girls and boys learn their appropriate gender roles, and absorb the class structure of society and their particular place in it. A dominant ideology is presented which has its own self-perpetuating and circular justification. It is put over as natural, and if it seems to fit in with the way things are organized and most efficiently run, it can accommodate conflicting ideologies and will not be seriously challenged.

At present, women are required to work and earn money not only to survive and support themselves and their families but also in order to consume. Yet they also have to look after husbands and children at home and keep domestic family life together to prevent society falling apart. At the same time the system looks to find scapegoats to detract from its own inadequacies, and ironically its most recent target has been lone mothers.* Ideas, beliefs and values help to validate the divisive social and economic conditions under which people live. It is through understanding and attacking ideology and the processes of 'socialization', as well as the material basis for class, race and gender exploitation that people can recognize and question the parts they play.

Twenty Years On

It has been over twenty years or since the first research was done for this book. Significant changes have occurred in the social and economic context of people's lives, and in the position and outlook of girls and women. There was, for instance, the liberalization of the laws on homosexuality and abortion in the sixties, while equality was brought into sharper focus in the seventies by the Sex Discrimination and Equal Pay Acts of 1975, and the Race Relations Act (1976). The Equal Opportunities Commission and the Commission for Racial Equality were created to implement and monitor the latter legislation. Such change reflected an increasing awareness and emphasis, however notional, on equality of opportunity regardless of sex, race and class. In 1979 the decade witnessed its third general election which returned the Conservative government to power, led by Margaret Thatcher. Throughout the subsequent years this government's policies have eroded many of the earlier steps forward made towards equality.

* For this purpose it seems to be forgotten that over a tenth of lone parents are fathers.

Thatcherism paved the way for a system of popular capitalism and individualism, by developing a programme of monetarism, large scale privatization and subsequent dismantling of the welfare state, reinforced with legislation which limited the power of the trade unions. The effects of government policies under Margaret Thatcher and subsequently John Major have been intimately linked with the lives of most women. For instance, taking apart the welfare state has severely undermined the health service, and facilities for child-care; and education, including nursery education, has suffered from severe cutbacks. Economic changes have also been reflected in education through the introduction of the National Curriculum, with its emphasis on linking education with work, and in the way further and higher education has been reconstructed with a greater emphasis on enterprise and profit making. There is little room for a principle of education for education's sake, but rather education for those who can afford it, the creation of courses for those who will pay highly for them, and a top-heavy management structure in these institutions consisting of highly paid business people (usually men).

The domestic division of labour has seen further change during this time as an increasing number of women have moved out of the home into the work-force, regardless of the age of their children. At the same time, the rising unemployment caused by a downturn in manufacturing took men out of the work-force. Some have been propelled into greater participation in child-care, but not to any significant extent. For many men any increase in their domestic role was precipitated by practical necessity, not volunteered by choice, and has not been taken on as a permanent change. Some deeper moves towards more egalitarian domestic arrangements have taken place within families, where change is driven by (often middle class) equality conscious women rapidly expanding their domestic expectations and demands of husbands and partners.

In parallel with a loosening of attitudes and behaviour around sexuality and religion, and a broadening of women's expectations from marriage, there has been a great increase in separation and divorce (and subsequent remarriage). This has radically affected the nature and structure of family life, reflected in the high proportion of lone parents in the population, the majority of whom are lone mothers. School classrooms today are filled with children for whom having a single parent or step-parent has become a 'normal' way of life. Having two original parents is just one possible option for the contemporary family. Marriage break-up is no respecter of class, and middle class and working class mothers alike have found themselves part of a kind of 'underclass' when they are trying to survive alone with their children, dependent on minimal state support. Many are caught in a poverty trap which is reinforced by the continuing lack of both the child-care facilities and well-paid work (part-time or full-time) that would enable them to combine earning money with providing good care for their children.

When writing this chapter in the 1970s I could describe the domestic division of labour as men taking the role of primary breadwinners for the family, while women had a secondary role in the work-force. In the 1990s, this no longer rings true, for women currently make up nearly half the work-force. Yet it cannot be said that the notion has disappeared, far from it. It lies on or just beneath the surface of many existing social attitudes and policies. In fact, a study of social attitudes in the 1980s showed that a majority of men and women considered married women's primary responsibility to be home and family and their wage-earning to be secondary to that of their husbands.[38]

The economic context within which I was writing in the seventies was one in which it was appropriate to talk about the relations of employers and employees under capitalism, about the oppression and exploitation of the working class to provide profits for a capitalist class. These terms now sound rather old-fashioned. People no longer talk about capitalism, what they refer to now is a 'market economy' in which market forces define the goods and the labour required. It sounds almost objective, almost fair, it suggests it means giving the people what they want. It is a popular capitalism. Yet the same characteristics still exist. Processes of discrimination and exploitation continue to operate, and employers are still applying the profit motive to running any business. What has changed is the economic language. Britain's dramatic decline as a large-scale manufacturer and the proliferation of small business enterprises and self-employment has made the relations of production less clear. The expansion of the service industries and the financial and banking sectors, including new technological industries hitherto unknown, have all helped to blur the appropriateness of the terms. Even talking about inequality sounds a bit out of date, as though it was something we were worried about yesterday but that has now been rectified. Women have made inroads into some areas of work, and some have succeeded in business and politics, but the real economic prospects for most women have not significantly improved. Their situation at work and at home remains unequal, whatever language you use to describe it.

Back in the 1970s there was an underlying and optimistic belief in the possibility of change, which could be brought about by the efforts of ordinary people. Contributing significantly to this at the time were the ideas and activities of the women's movement and the trade unions. In the 1990s both have become less active in an organized way, although there are many feminists, or women with feminist attitudes and beliefs, who apply these principles in their own lives, and many trade unionists who work hard on behalf of their members. But the traditional power of the unions has been greatly eroded by the Conservative government, and the increasingly conservative nature of popular attitudes has served to withdraw support and has classified unions as unnecessary or only concerned for themselves. The solidarity forged in the earlier part of the century, and taken well into the seventies, has been lost, or at least mislaid in the eighties and nineties. Within the growth of the women's movement, feminists helped to raise consciousness and change many things in the seventies: our campaigns had an impact on many areas such as contraception and abortion provision; equal pay; nursery provision; educational equality; and the representation of the sexes in reading primers and other literature. Today's consciousness and outlook appear extremely narrow in comparison. Change seems almost impossible to the ordinary person. There have been hardly any issues strong enough to create mass campaigns and mobilize people to action. The poll tax has been the only one to raise enough energy for this type of protest, and that has come and gone. The prospect of change is also only possible when you can visualize what sort of change you want, and although people can list many things lacking in society at present, there seems to be no consensus of a 'better' society, and no motivation to organize towards this if there was one. Individualization has fragmented any social sense of communality. It may not be dead, but it is certainly buried.

Teenage girls growing up today are aware of having missed some significant eras, particularly the swinging sixties, and the radical seventies. They are aware that important changes took place in the years just before they were born and when they were small, and whatever the state of the rest of society, they hold a general belief that things have improved for women. They hold a hazy and often inaccurate idea of how the world was for their mothers during this time, and many assume that inequalities have been largely resolved. But they are not totally wrong. They took on the society as it was when they entered it, within which things have since moved apace in all directions. They take the equalities women have fought for, and in some cases are still fighting for, as a right, and justifiably so. But to make these equalities a reality they will still have to grapple with many of the same processes and obstacles faced by the previous generation of girls growing up, whose ideas and experiences formed the basis of the earlier edition of this book.

NOTES

CHAPTER 1

1. Much of the information about working class girls given here is taken from work done by Anna Davin on children's conditions at the end of the nineteenth century, published in the History Workshop Series, *Childhood*, vol. 2.
2. Anna Davin, op. cit.
3. ibid.
4. ibid.
5. Josephine Kamm, *Hope Deferred*, Methuen, 1965.
6. These class-biased assumptions are expressed in education reports such as the Board of Education, 'Regulations for Secondary Schools' (1904) and 'Report upon Questions affecting Higher Elementary Schools' (1906).
7. J. W. B. Douglas, *The Home and the School*, Panther, 1967.
8. J. W. B. Douglas, *All Our Future*, Panther, 1968.
9. Swann Report, 'Education For All', HMSO, 1985.
10. A. M. Davies, J. Holland and R. Minhas, 'Equal Opportunities in the New Era', Hillcole Group, Paper 2, The Tufnell Press, 1990.
11. S. Miles and C. Middleton, 'Girls' Education in the Balance: The ERA and Inequality', in M. Flude and M. Hammer (eds.), *The Education Reform Act, 1988: Its Origins and Implications*, The Falmer Press, 1989.
12. J. Harding, 'Sex Differences in Performance in Science Examinations', in R. Deem (ed.) *Schooling For Women's Work*, Routledge & Kegan Paul, 1980; and A. Kelly (ed.), *The Missing Half: Girls and Science Education*, Manchester University Press, 1981.
13. Quoted in J. Burnett, *Useful Toil*, Allen Lane, 1974.
14. J. Burnett, op. cit.
15. Quoted in Irene Osgood Andrews and Margaret A. Hobbs, *Economic Effects of the World War upon Women and Children in Great Britain*, Carnegie Endowment for International Peace, Preliminary Economic Studies of the War, no. 4, New York, 1921.

16. Reviewing the effects of war on women at a conference of working class organizations in Bradford in March 1917. Also quoted in I. O. Andrews and M. A. Hobbs, op. cit.

17. Winifred Holtby, *Women and a Changing Civilization*, John Lane, 1934.

18. ibid.

19. Mass Observation, 'People and Production', in *Change*, no. 3, 1942.

20. Mass Observation, op. cit.

21. Figures quoted in Angus Calder, *The People's War*, Panther, 1971.

22. M. Benney, *Over to Bombers*, quoted in Angus Calder, op. cit.

23. Mass Observation, op. cit.

24. Beveridge Report, 1942.

25. Mass Observation, 'The Journey Home', *Change*, no. 5, 1944.

26. ibid.

27. ibid.

28. Quoted in Pearl Jephcott, *Girls Growing Up*, Faber & Faber, 1942.

29. Pearl Jephcott, *Rising Twenty*, Faber & Faber, 1945.

30. ibid.

31. This happened at the Peak Frean factory in Bermondsey which was the subject of an investigation by Pearl Jephcott *et al.*, *Married Women Working*, Allen & Unwin, 1962.

32. Table given in Edward James, 'Women at Work in Twentieth Century Britain', *The Manchester School*, vol. 30, no. 3, quoted in S. Yudkin and A. Holme, *Working Mothers and their Children*, Sphere, 1969.

33. Viola Klein, 'Working Wives', *Occasional Papers*, no. 15, Institute of Personnel Management, 1960.

34. 'The Impact of Office Technology in the Midlands Area', APEX, 1984.

35. Within the Women's Liberation Movement, Marxist feminists at this time were attempting to analyse this sort of work, see for instance: Mariarosa Della Costa and Selma James, *The Power of Women and the Subversion of the Community*, Falling Wall Press, 1972; Isabel Larguia and John Dumoulin, 'Towards a Science of Women's Liberation', *Red Rag Pamphlet*, no. I; Jean Gardiner's reply to Wally Secombe ('The Housewife and her Labour under Capitalism', *New Left Review*, no. 83, January–February 1973) in *New Left Review*, no. 89, January–February, 1975; also *Women and Socialism Conference Papers*, 3, 1974.

36. This was clearly shown in the research carried out by G. Brown and T. Harris, *The Origins of Social Depression: A Study of Psychiatric Disorder in Women*, Tavistock, 1978.

37. Phyllis Chesler noted that it was often when women stopped performing domestic tasks as part of their 'illness' that their husbands tended to have

them (re-)admitted to mental hospital. *Women and Madness*, Allen Lane, 1974.

38. S. Dex, *Women's Attitudes Towards Work*, Macmillan, 1988.

THE SOCIAL CONSTRUCTION OF
GENDER DIFFERENCES

As long as there are little girls
With ribbons in their hair
With bandaged knees and
  sunshine smiles
And cuddly teddy bears
As long as there are little girls
With all the joy they give
The world is sure to be
A brighter place to live.

A little boy means
Lots of mischief and noise
Energy, restlessness,
Banging on toys.
But a little boy also means
Sunshine and cheer
Hugs that delight you
Smiles that endear.

Birth congratulations messages

An understanding of how the position of girls and women is crucially affected by economic factors overlaid with ideology helps us to make sense of the nature, origins and perpetuation of existing sex and gender roles. So far, I have examined these from a historical perspective and through the demands of the present economic and social structure. Another dimension can be added by looking more closely at the ideas, beliefs and values about men and women which are embedded within biology and psychology, and some of the ways that these are passed on.

The economic requirements which demanded certain sorts of labour and technology and which developed efficient contraception, have combined with women's own demands and attitudes to transform the position of women throughout this century. It has been accompanied by an ideology of sexual equality, thought to be fitting in a modern civilized society. Officially, this gives the same opportunities to both sexes, and has meant that formal sanctions previously preventing women from straying too far from conventional gender roles have been lifted. Nowadays women are apparently 'free' to enter any area of education and occupation and are allowed to go into politics and other previously male-dominated spheres. The emphasis on people's rights and participation in a 'democratic' society makes it impossible formally to deny opportunity, although discrimination is still required by our social organization and division of labour.

The preservation of sexual divisions between and within certain types of work and other activities has therefore tended to rely on more 'informal' beliefs and sanctions. These are based on the biological and psychological differences thought to determine so-called masculine and feminine personality, often used to justify role and job segregation. Consequently, the 'socialization' of boys and girls, the ways they develop apparently contrasting personalities and roles, has had a more significant part to play in the perpetuation of the social structure. In a society in which obvious discrimination is condemned, 'natural' gender differences help to preserve the separation of roles and thus the inequalities upon which the economic system still depends.[1]

It is, therefore, not surprising that theories and empirical evidence that question the whole basis of innate and psychological differences between men and women have made little impact on popular social beliefs. For instance, the historic cross-cultural studies carried out by anthropologists such as Margaret Mead[2] have shown that there is no universal 'masculine' or 'feminine' personality. The tribes she describes either show characteristics that are undifferentiated by sex or they reverse the gender stereotypes found in modern industrialized society. The Arapesh, for example, are a passive, gentle and non-aggressive people, all of whom take responsibility for looking after the children. In contrast to this 'femininity', both sexes of the Mundagumor tribe demonstrate the characteristics that we understand as 'masculine', while the Tchambuli reverse many of our accepted differences. Other examples can be found in anthropology[3] to show further constellations of characteristics and behaviour.

The existence of so many differing types of masculinity and femininity contributes towards undermining the system of gender stereotypes. However, it is important to remember that gender differentiation and its surrounding values and attitudes does not develop in an arbitrary way. It is vitally influenced by the nature of the economic structure of a society and the division of labour that has been developed around it. Some cross-cultural studies have tried to show how a particular economy affects gender roles and the socialization of boys and girls and thus their resulting personality formation.[4] For instance, in examining the training of boys and girls in reports of 110 cultures, Barry, Bacon and Child[5] found that 'pressure towards nurturance, obedience and responsibility is most often stronger for girls whereas pressure towards achievement and self-reliance is most often stronger for boys', as in Western society. But they also noticed that where the economy depended on constant care of animals or regular tending of crops it was necessary that both sexes be similarly taught to be compliant, obedient and responsible (traditionally 'feminine'), because the economy needed these qualities. In cultures where the economy centred around hunting and fishing, however, children were encouraged in assertiveness, achievement and self-reliance (traditionally 'masculine'), although boys were still rather more assertive than girls. For both kinds of subsistence economies there was greater variation in the work of men and boys than there was in that of girls and women, whose reproductive role defined certain regularities and meant that they had to stay fairly near home.

Barry, Bacon and Child also concluded that the largest sexual differentiation and male superiority occur together in 'an economy that places a high premium on the superior strength and superior development of motor skills requiring strength, which characterize the male',[6] such as in a society where hunting, herding or warfare are important. This superiority has entered the value structure of most societies, related to other factors such as access to defined sources of power, and has pervaded many areas other than the original one based on primitive survival. Patriarchal values and superior male status have been preserved while the situation they accompany has changed many times. Applied to our society, it is clear that the division of labour and the separation of work from home and child-care are linked to personality, and that this is assumed to derive from innate male and female characteristics.

Anthropological evidence must not be used uncritically, however, as small societies are subject to many influences, such as the effects of colonization and the impact of Western culture. When these are taken into account, the dynamics of change become clearer, but it is still hard to dismiss the example of 'primitive' tribes as merely deviant and irrelevant. The argument put forward that every power-ful culture such as our own has similar gender differences and that therefore it may be the fact of not having these that contributes to the continuing insignificance of small societies, can be countered by understanding the demands of a specific economic system; we have seen how this evolved in our society by tracing the effects of industrialization and the development of capitalism on the roles of men and women.[7] Such cross-cultural studies showing the variety of roles that men and women can take and have taken in other societies are still relevant, even though some of them may now seem historic. They provide strong support for the social construc-tion of gender differences.

Another kind of evidence has questioned innate and predeter-mined explanations by focusing on the social influence of assigning a masculine or feminine personality to people at birth. This origin-ally developed out of research carried out mainly in America on patients with various kinds of endocrine disorders which cause them to develop ambiguous sexual characteristics. The researchers distinguish between 'sex', meaning the physical characteristics such as genitals, hormones, gonads, internal reproductive organs and chromosomes, and 'gender', meaning the amount of 'masculinity' or 'femininity' shown and felt by a person.[8] In most people, agreement exists between their sex, 'gender role', and 'gender identity', but there are some who are born with a discrepancy within their physical sexual characteristics. Such people are termed hermaphrod-ites or inter-sexuals. The contradiction usually occurs between the external genitalia and some internal feature, but this may not be discovered at birth. A baby with apparently normal male or female genitals will be seen, named and brought up in the appropriate way, and it may not be until the onset of puberty and physical maturity that an incongruity is revealed. By this time, the individual's as-signed gender identity is so well established that it is very difficult for them to adjust to the idea that some of their internal characteris-tics such as chromosomes or reproductive organs define them as being of the opposite sex.

Therefore, the sex label assigned at birth determines the way the baby is brought up and the appropriate gender role and identity development. The social factors of rearing override the biological structures. For instance, nineteen patients who had been brought up in a way that contradicted the sex of their chromatin pattern had all developed a satisfactory gender identity. Another thirty-one patients had gender identities in contrast to the sex of their hormones and also to their secondary sexual body development. It is found that the upbringing of a child as male or female can only be successfully changed before the age of eighteen months to two years. This coincides with the learning and growth of language which greatly expands the child's scope of social learning and cognitive understanding.

This sort of evidence has, however, been used to support both sides of the argument and other researchers have used it to draw the opposite conclusions.[9] For instance they point out those individuals who go for medical advice because they are unhappy about some aspect of their own masculinity or femininity and are then discovered to have been 'wrongly assigned'. However, this does not negate the weight of evidence that shows gender to be no simple biological heritage.[10] Genetics and biology do have a part to play in the process and should not be ignored for the sake of the argument. It is not necessary or reasonable to attempt to prove that men and women are exactly the same, but rather to show that there is great diversity and flexibility of gender, and that any differences are not important and do not warrant their exaggerated consequences in the social separation of male and female roles and personality. It seems more likely that the biological factors provide the individual variable basis on which is built the appropriate 'masculine' or 'feminine' personality and behaviour for a particular individual in a particular society. These factors in themselves do not appear to have a powerful predetermining role.

A basic biological difference exists in women's capacity to bear children and this has had crucial implications for their consequent role in production. Many 'feminine' characteristics are appropriately linked with the caring role of motherhood. But the reproductive role alone does not necessitate the assumptions of women's incapacity in other spheres of work, which are similarly questionable through cross-cultural and psychological evidence. Anthropology and psychosexual research have, therefore, both provided reasonable grounds for rejecting the 'natural' masculine and feminine roles that have grown into stereotypes. But no matter how many individuals are personally convinced, the many features of social and economic organization and functioning that use and exploit the popular notion of 'sex differences' will not radically change unless the social and economic system either no longer needs these divisions or is itself replaced.

IDEAL IMAGES AND UNEQUAL VALUES

I don't think it's fair on either sex really, because boys have just as hard a life as we do, I reckon, with the expectations of what a man is meant to be doing and stuff. No matter what you do, there's always going to be someone with a preconceived idea of what a woman is meant to be doing and what a man is meant to be doing ... And men have this preconceived idea that they're meant to be macho, and men aren't meant to cry, etc.

PAULINE

The wedge between male and female was driven deeper by the stereotyping which pretended to represent the typical or ideal characteristics of men and women. It can represent a prescription in which concepts of 'normal' behaviour are contained and where in the past, 'feminine' has been set as the opposite of 'masculine'. Through books and other literature, and the great expansion of mass media, ideal images have been created and reflected which force comparisons on their recipients. The extent to which these have effects must depend ultimately on the active interaction of the individual, but the barrage of images most people are subjected to, and especially children growing up, must carve out unconscious impressions about the nature of their world.

When I was first writing in the 1970s, conventional and exaggerated stereotypes were commonly found in the media, parodying the ways in which people are supposed to live. At that time, although it is to be expected that the 'heroes' and 'heroines' of any situation would possess many of the socially desirable attributes of a particular place and time, much of what was portrayed about women seemed to have its roots in an older tradition which reinforced the continuing gender differences and male superiority. The feminine ideal generally endorsed a gentle, demure, sensitive, submissive, noncompetitive, sweet-natured and dependent dream-girl who was not going to get very far with the 'equality' that modern civilized society appeared to be offering her. Her mid-Victorian virtues, although loosened here and there, were still more appropriate for the care of husband, home and children. In the nineties, such stereotyped images, which were never really so clear-cut, have become more diverse.

The media, in all their forms, cast an influence on the images and visions of 'femininity' and 'masculinity'. These obviously give children and young people information about the world as it 'normally' exists. In the previous edition, I devoted a whole chapter to looking at the images of girls and women presented at that time in reading primers, comics and magazines, advertising, music, and other media like television and film. This has not been included in this edition as these images change quite fast and need a more vigilant and long-term analysis. The media are subject to rapid change. Many of the comics and magazines I quoted then have disappeared in the intervening time. There has been progress in the publication of books (including reading primers) which have taken gender, race and class into account, and present both sexes in a less stereotyped way. However, there are still plenty of traditional images to be found. In love comics and magazines, girls have invariably played a secondary role in romantic interactions.[11] In the increasingly popular music papers, girls are predominantly presented with images of male singers and musicians. However, the cute and pretty image that Olivia Newton John was providing for girls in the 1970s has been replaced and confounded by the overt sexual assertiveness of Madonna. When asked what famous person they would most like to be, it was Madonna who was most frequently mentioned in 1991, for white and black girls alike. As well as provocative female sexuality, she has evoked an alternative image of femininity that girls themselves have responded to, fuelled by their own hopes and enthusiasm.

> I would like to be like Madonna. I always loved Madonna when I was small. I knew all her songs. I always envied her. She's a woman and look where she is!
>
> GEETA

The images of women presented in magazines over the last twenty years have become much more variable, as indeed have the lives of the girls and women making up their readership. In an analysis of women's magazines in the mid 1980s Janice Winship suggested that the images of women contained a new expression of greater assertiveness rather than passive sexuality. These were not necessarily freeing women from being seen as sexual commodities, but they were not simply reproducing this way of seeing them.[12] The impact made by aspects of the media on girls and their 'femininity' is an unstable one. At any point they may take it up differently (or not at all) depending on what else is happening in their lives, and the nature of their social group at the time. It is not a static or one-way process and girls are not simple consumers of media images, they are also helping to produce them. They are not such an easily manipulable market, they have to want what the image is offering. In their various forms, the media have achieved a level of intrusion in most people's lives. On the positive side, increase in media access has also illustrated more varied images of both women and men. How these are picked up and dropped in people's lives, and the relative influence they may exert, depends largely on the individual. But there is no doubt that the media are powerful, and if they appeal to people's current susceptibilities, then they can be a very persuasive force. They have an important place alongside all the other social influences and interactions experienced by girls growing up.

Of course, however they are presented, stereotypes can rarely be pinned down to real people, and the characteristics of what is 'feminine' or 'masculine' are elusive and resist being confined to one sex. They also resist being limited to one stereotype and change shape and form under the influence of other factors such as class, race and religion. They are not set, but flexible within whatever medium men and women are actively participating in.[13] There have been changes in the ideal images of both men and women as represented in the media in Western society. Although the traditional characteristics have been maintained to some extent, other characteristics have been added. For instance, although the ideal image for a (middle class) man is still quite 'macho', that he should be strong and assertive (in an achieving as much as a physical sort of way), he should now also be more sensitive, caring and sharing. Take for example several contemporary advertisements featuring strong muscular men (generally with bare torsos) cradling babies in their arms. They imply that men now have to put tenderness into their repertoire, but they still have to be strong and manly. Fathering has become more fashionable, at least in principle, even if our advertisement hero quickly relinquishes the baby to its mother after the photograph has been taken. This reflects a modified and fashionable view of modern man, and to some extent coincides with many contemporary girls' and women's hopes and expectations of how their ideal man might support their own working roles. Unfortunately it is often far from the nature of their male partners in real life.

For women, too, characteristics have been added to the 'ideal', but these do not seem very new. For instance, as well as being good wives and mothers, they should ideally have gained some qualifications and have a good job or career, be relatively but not too independent, and somehow successfully combine work with caring for a home and children, with the hoped-for help of their husband. Not only does she still have to be beautiful, the 'ideal woman' is also expected to be capable of holding an intelligent conversation, and do interesting things. The class basis of these ideals should not be forgotten, for inasmuch as it is the dominant class that defines these and other aspects of morality, so they also have the greater means to achieve them. For instance, the value of beauty for a woman is still high and is seriously pursued. But housework, childbearing and general worry soon take their toll on maintaining appearance. With money, however, the time and the means of preserving looks and a good shape can be bought, as can help with domestic work and child-care in the home.

Although, in recent years, the so-called ideals of masculinity and femininity have begun to overlap more than in the past, the essential 'masculine' ideals presented to boys and men are different from those of 'femininity'. These, too, vary according to social class. On the active side, opposing the alleged passivity of women, men are supposed to be more physically strong, aggressive, assertive and expected to take the initiative. They are supposed to be independent, competitive and ambitious. These characteristics coincide by no accident with those necessary for success within a competitive economic system. In comparison, feminine ideals have served to mainly exclude women from this. The success of working class men has traditionally been more confined to practical and technical skills. These are seen as more essentially masculine pursuits, while paradoxically the academic studies that take men to the top are perceived as more passive and 'feminine'. A 'swot' runs the risk of being labelled as a 'sissy'. Upper class boys at public schools are trained for leadership, business and the professions. At the other end of the scale, working class boys have been schooled for a mass labour force which constrains many of the 'ideal' characteristics such as aggression and dominance which in their work situation are potentially disruptive. These are then transferred out on to leisure activities like sport, and particularly into their relationships with girls and women.

Conforming to male or female 'ideals' may not be beneficial for either sex. For example, the expectations of full-time mothering applied to (middle class) women earlier in the century cultivated self-sacrifice and an implicit acceptance of inferiority in many areas of society, and still do today. For men, the active pursuit of ambition and an emphasis on work can consume their lives and destroy intimate relationships with other people, especially women and children. Whatever changes women look to make in their lives, these should never be equated with the self-destructive position in which traditional models of masculinity have placed men.

The active and passive dimensions of traditional male and female roles are visible in the way that a man's major activities are outward-directed and a woman's are inner-directed. In the past it has been his role to go out and confront and capture the outside world while she constructs a cosy inside shelter for them both. The masculine role has involved action and external achievement. It has no continuity and has to be 're-earned' every day. His success at any time can instantly be obliterated by failure. Yet a man's need always to be proving himself and his masculinity becomes more a reaction to insecurity than any form of independent creative activity, and a woman's acceptance of her position at home becomes more a resigned acceptance of inevitability than a positive choice from alternatives. Man is judged by his success and his position in the social structure. This is why unemployment often has devastating effects on male self esteem. Women, on the other hand, can be excused such failure because this is not their 'natural' sphere.

The absence of many women from the unemployment statistics is a reflection of this. Their position in the social structure has been traditionally defined by that of their father or husband. Theirs has been a role of 'being' while men always had the process of 'doing'. In the past the only thing that a girl had to 'do' was to find a husband to look after her. The end of the twentieth century sees this being modified, with the fragmentation of the family driving even more women with children out to work whether or not they want to, and the rise in lone parent families creating more women heads of households. In 1976, I saw most girls as having a 'preoccupation with men and marriage'. Today, girls like those in Ealing schools still have some level of preoccupation with boys and boyfriends, but many are aware of other issues and activities, and are less preoccupied with thoughts of marriage. This is not to say that they do not see finding a partner and having children as an extremely important thing at some time in their lives, but it is not such an immediate concern. This is the case for both working class and middle class girls, although their preoccupations may be tempered according to the nature of where they live and the extent of educational and work opportunities that are on offer.

I would like to be able to say that although quite different traits have traditionally been assigned to men and women, at least they have been equivalent in value and status. Unfortunately this is not so. In this respect it is still worth mentioning a study carried out in the United States in 1970,[14] which showed that the traits ascribed by a set of psychiatric clinicians to their male and female patients were very different in their social desirability, and those seen as 'mentally healthy' tended to be ascribed to men, while the 'feminine' characteristics they ascribed at this time to a 'healthy' woman (such as being more submissive, less independent, less adventurous, more easily influenced, less aggressive, less competitive, more excitable in minor crises, having their feelings more easily hurt, being more emotional) were seen as less socially desirable. Although a lot has happened in the years since then to show these characteristics clearly less universally applicable to women, there is still the sense in which what is feminine, or associated with women, is less relevant to getting on in life. For instance, it is good to be gentle, but where does it get you in terms of success in today's enterprise society?

Talking about ideals and stereotypes is not satisfactory because they represent intangible and abstract ideas that can be recognized but do not stand up to closer examination. Most of them are negated by the great variation that exists between and within people. Some researchers have pointed out that every characteristic that one can name as belonging to one sex can be found in some members of the opposite sex.[15] The concept of man and woman as extreme opposites, however, has no basis in physiology, nor in any other subject. It is the language that defines gender opposition, not people. Discussing gender in terms of stereotypes has been criticized, and it feels almost old-fashioned to talk about them, and yet opinions and behaviour based on their implicit assumption can be seen everywhere. The sweeping generalizations they embody obviously conceal the broad boundaries and overlap of characteristics and behaviours. It has been tempting, particularly within the social sciences, to over-simplify and use classifications that may be superficial and misleading. Sex and gender differences are frequently used as a major distinction, and similar assumptions are made about social class differences, when in fact many of the simple dichotomies that are drawn for both of these are not real. In the past two decades feminist researchers have done much to question the ways that such assumptions have been drawn. Exploring gender relations – relations between masculinity and femininity – is more useful than looking at sex role stereotypes. Gender relations can vary by history, society, class and ethnic group. Contradictions and conflicts between versions of masculinity and femininity provide the opportunity for individual resistance. For example deeper examination of masculinity, homosexuality and race can provide further insights into the nature of gender identity formation, make us more aware of the constraints and biases through which we see the world, and help to construct a more appropriate framework.

Teenage girls show a huge variety in dress, behaviour, language and so on, that represents their expressions of femininity, whatever class background they come from. In terms of their futures, however, there are some ways in which working class girls are likely to become more immediately aware of the different expectations and roles of men and women. Their parents are often working in sex-defined jobs and they see female friends and relatives leaving school, marrying and having children at a fairly early age. The differences in the educational and vocational opportunities for them compared to middle class children has helped to ensure this. Often bored and indifferent about school, the most obvious course is to concentrate on going to work (thus entering lower level and more gender-typed jobs), and having a good social life, which ultimately provides a husband/partner. Family attitudes and values have an enormous influence even if there is conflict between the generations at other levels. A mother's attitude to her own role will have some influence on her young daughter, and on the sort of person that she encourages her to be. There is no simple relationship with social class. A socially aspiring middle class mother may just as easily encourage her daughter to do well through marriage as to succeed academically and independently. And many working class mothers would not wish on their own daughters the feminine domestic and working roles that many of them have been prematurely thrust into. Differences in status and standard of living are deeply rooted in the social structure and the difficulty of finding alternative ways of living, but these cannot just be polarized by class.

There are, however, many more universal and fundamental ways in which the family plays an early and crucial part in how children become 'acceptable' people. Its influence on the development of gender roles at this time occurs regardless of class, and those parents who have begun to make conscious efforts to counter this have found it far from easy.[16]

INFLUENCES OF FAMILY LIFE

A child's early experiences are almost all contained within the family, and it is here that the direction of personality development is set. It is parents, and more specifically mothers, who have the closest interaction and relationship with children in our society. Their deliberate and incidental influence teaches children the intricacies of acceptable and appropriate behaviour. In the 1970s I could assert that 'they accept the existence and validity of sex differences and pass them on intact'. Today I do not think this is true. I think many women from all backgrounds have come to question the rigidity of at least some aspects of sex and gender differentiation, and even if it is only to expect their sons to do more domestic work, they are recognizing that these differences are neither right nor natural.

Socialization occurs in conscious and unconscious ways, and with the active interaction of the individual. In the light of the cross-cultural research and social-psychological studies mentioned above, its supposed influence in producing gender differences becomes exaggerated as theories based primarily around biological determinism become untenable. The child's social learning, which occurs initially in the family and is gradually extended outside, is then seen as being responsible for his or her behaviour and personality. But is this enough to account for the content and depth of emotion that is involved in being male or female? Can it explain the ways in which the differences are individually felt and enthusiastically defended, and the apparent need to pre-define sex roles and expectations in order to form and maintain self-identity? The mechanical nature of learning processes is rather unsatisfactory and lacking as a total explanation.

One approach which has attempted to fill this gap has examined the central importance of family structure and the nature of early child-care.[17] This explanation, by Nancy Chodorow, has a psychoanalytic orientation, and traces the development of masculine and feminine personality and the relative status of the sexes back to the universal mothering role of women. It focuses on the conscious and unconscious effects on boys and girls of their early involvement with women. Each sex experiences this differently, and it is such aspects of growing up that contribute initially to sex differences in personality. As a girl begins to form ideas about herself there is (universal) internalization of certain features of the mother–daughter relationship. Through this process the individual characteristics of society are reproduced, and this explains why although cultural differences in 'femininity' can and do exist, the majority of societies show similar female personalities and roles. According to psychoanalytic theory, personality develops not as a result of conscious or deliberate efforts by parents or other adults but out of a child's earliest social relationships, the nature and quality of which are appropriated, assimilated and organized by the child to form her or his individual personality. These aspects become internalized, and although they arise out of an ongoing relationship, they continue to exist independently and are organized to constitute a permanent personality. The unconscious operation of this process has a crucial influence on consequent behaviour, whether it be the 'normal' behaviour expected by society or that which is unique to the individual. The more conscious areas, like the way people see themselves (their self-concept), and the nature and extent of their feelings of femininity or masculinity (their gender identity), are thus dependent on the stability and consistency of the unconscious organization of personality. Therefore, the different experiences of girls and boys in their early relationships make an important contribution to their consequent development.

Children are normally very closely attached to a woman in their earliest years, usually their mother. During this time, they become involved in the issues of separation and individuation (developing some independent 'sense of self'). This involves weakening the primary identification* with their mother and becoming less orally dependent on her. Nancy Chodorow suggests that it is the experience of this process that differs importantly for girls and boys. For girls, early experience involves a 'double identification' in which not only do they (like boys at this age) identify with their mothers, but mothers themselves, as former daughters, identify strongly with their own daughters. This identification involves feelings of empathy towards the daughter's present and future, physical and emotional predicaments. A particular sense of attachment can develop from this which makes separation more difficult.

For boys, however, it is more usual for mothers to encourage a relationship that emphasizes their opposition and one which re-

---

* 'Identification' usually refers to the incorporation into oneself of a 'model' person with whom there is a strong emotional tie. As children grow older it refers to the tendency for them (or a person of any age) to take on and reproduce the attitudes, behaviour and aspects of personality and emotional response exhibited by real life or symbolic models (for example, characters in books, films, etc.).

inforces their son's self-awareness of the male role. Therefore, during the time covered by Freud's 'pre-Oedipal period',* the quality of relationship between mothers and their sons and mothers and their daughters is not the same.

After a child has reached about three years of age (the beginning of the 'Oedipal period'),† the different development of boys and girls is commonly acknowledged. During this period, a more specifically masculine identification must replace a boy's early identification with his mother and this coincides with the time when fathers usually appear more frequently in the child's world. However, it is harder for this to happen under the conditions of modern industrialized society. Here, men's work takes them away from home most of the time, or a significant number of children grow up without a father living at home, and therefore a boy's identification often has to be reinforced by his fantasies of the male role instead of through a consistent relationship. He may consequently resort to a more negative way of asserting his masculinity: by identifying with what is not feminine. This involves repression of things in himself that are seen as potentially feminine (thus rejecting and denying his attachment to his mother), and devaluation of whatever he sees to be feminine in the world outside the home. Thus the superiority of maleness is asserted against the inferiority of femaleness. Boys are perceived (and perceive themselves) as 'better' than girls, and this is reinforced through independent experiences outside the family.

For girls, the development of a feminine gender identity is more continuous. They do not have to reject early identification and attachment with mother since their final identification is with women, who are also the central characters of early dependence. Femininity and the female role are easily seen first-hand in daily life. There is no great need to reject mother-dependence, nor will a mother be very likely to encourage this, as she may still be identifying strongly with her daughter. Therefore, a girl's identification

* Freud sees the pre-Oedipal period as a time in which there is no differentiation between the sexes, both identifying equally with their mother.
† This period is interpreted by Freud in sexual terms: a boy represses his sexual attraction for his mother because of the (fantasized) power of his father as potential rival, to kill or castrate him. He therefore replaces mother-attachment by identifying with his father.

with her mother is not the rather distanced position of a boy trying to identify with a male role and its concomitant behaviours, which he has to 'take on', but is more a close personal identification with a mother's characteristic traits and values.*

Therefore boys' and girls' experiences of the inter-personal world in which they grow up may affect the different development of their 'masculinity' and 'femininity'. Thus Chodorow suggests that 'certain features of social structure, supported by cultural beliefs, values and perceptions, are internalized through the family and the child's early social object-relationships. This largely unconscious organization is the context in which role training and purposive socialization take place.'[18]

Girls' training in the traditional aspects of the female role can be viewed as fairly easy and continuous and involve many diffuse and affective relationships between women. They are drawn into helping their mothers, and practising this role as part of growing up. Pressure is put on them to become involved with others, and to be concerned with nurturance and responsibility. It is later that they find that the outside world, unlike the early home world of women, is dominated by men.

Boys do not practise their adult role in this way – this has to wait until they reach adulthood. Meanwhile, they are encouraged towards achievement and self-reliance, and away from dependent and close relationships. They tend to be freer to go off on their own or with a group of boys of a similar age. Girls participate more in the home, and are involved in an inter-generational world of women. They are less encouraged to go off and to develop individually and independently. In the relative violence of today's society, it is not seen to be safe for girls and women to go freely on the streets, especially at night, and this is a major factor in the constraint of girls. Their world is more concentrated around 'relational' activities, and in our

---

* According to Freud's theory the 'discontinuity for a girl comes when it is necessary to transfer the sex-object choice from mother to father and men, and the discovery that she has not got a penis, the shock of which results in her blaming and rejecting her mother, and turning to her father'. Freud suggested that girls' development of femininity via the 'Oedipal phase' is more difficult than that for boys because of this, but it seems more reasonable to view boys' development as more discontinuous and problematic.

society they are often defined in these terms, as someone's wife, mother or daughter, which reinforces their dependence on these relationships. This means that, unless she consciously counters this, a woman's individual sense of herself remains embedded within her relationships to others. She is less able to clearly differentiate herself from the rest of the world, and this may hinder the development of self-esteem* and self-confidence which would help her to change her position and status.

This unconscious process of internalization can reasonably help to explain how male and female personalities in different cultures occur and are reproduced through time. The material and economic basis of a society will be important in determining which characteristics are exaggerated, and which differentiate the sexes according to their roles in production. The fact that many societies are in approximate agreement about feminine personality and tend to see women as inferior can then be traced back to their common practice of holding women responsible for early child-care and socialization. This has important implications for sexual equality. Both boys and girls would benefit from having close relationships and identification with more than one adult of both sexes, from men's increased involvement in child-care, and from seeing women in a recognized and valued role and area of control inside and outside the home. Chodorow has suggested that men's equal participation in child-care could play an important part in breaking down the differentiated development of gender roles.

Identification is not a straightforward process, it may occur with a variety of people, in a variety of ways. Children may identify with one or both parents, and sometimes with adults outside the family. The person with whom a child 'chooses' to identify may be selected on several possible bases, such as their perceived power (usually in terms of control of economic resources), the type and extent of discipline they use, and the closeness and affectionate quality of their relationship with the child. On this basis, boys and

* However, after comparing different societies, Chodorow suggests that although men usually maintain their socio-cultural superiority over women, they always remain psychologically defensive and insecure, while women in certain circumstances can, in spite of their lesser status, feel a sense of security and self-worth.

girls may identify with their father on account of his economic power and status and this for girls will combine with their freedom to take on aspects of ('masculine') tomboyish behaviour. On the other hand, the warmest and closest relationship may be with the mother. However, models for behaviour are also chosen on the commonsense grounds of their similarity to the child, and therefore a girl will identify with her mother in recognition of her own future female role and will take on relevant behaviour, as Chodorow has described. Identification is greatest when the adult–child relationship is very warm and close, when the child wishes to be like a particular person, and adopts their values, attitudes and personality traits, and judges herself or himself through their eyes. But a girl, for instance, whose relationship with her mother is not close will still identify with aspects of the feminine role that are common to women as a whole and which exist independently in the culture outside the family, exemplified in other adults and passed on by other children and through the media.

In this context it would be interesting to know whether the movement of mothers out to work over the past few decades has made any impact on this process. Women who are earning money, especially those in well-paid jobs, will change the balance of economic power within the family. This would be complicated to untangle, however, because mothers who move from home to work change not only their economic status, but many other things, such as their relationship with their children and their conception of themselves. How far the father takes over or helps with the domestic work, and whether women work from necessity or choice may also affect these issues. When women's position at work, their economic independence and their consciousness of themselves begins to rise, and child-rearing and other roles are equally and co-operatively shared, this will help girls and boys to see a less rigid and value-laden range of gender possibilities.

The earlier unconscious process of differentiation is later overlaid with more explicit practices. In one early study[19] of children between one and five years of age, four such processes were observed in the family situation, and it is reasonable to assume that they still occur to some extent in most families. There was firstly an observed tendency for mothers to make more fuss over the appearance of their daughter. This involved fiddling with her hair, dressing her up, and frequently commenting on her looks. The emphasis on external features will consequently be absorbed and later reinforced by society's views on the importance of a woman's beauty. Secondly, parents inadvertently focus their children's attention on certain more 'appropriate' objects and activities. The most obvious example of this is with toys and games. In the past, toy-makers, sellers and buyers were all agreed in their assumptions of what is more suitable and enjoyable for boys or girls, reflecting children's supposed interests, skills and future roles. This has been questioned over the last couple of decades, and an attempt made to make the selection and purchase of toys more equal. The traditional assumptions, however, still exist, and agreement can still be found that boys' toys are more active and technical, and include cars, trains, planes, military (male) dolls, spacemen and cricket bats, chemistry sets and miniature microscopes. Girls still tend to be bought a selection of less active or exciting toys, many of which stimulate a rehearsal of women's traditional role. Traditionally they have dolls,* teddybears and other animals, doll's houses and prams, tea-sets, miniature ovens, pots and pans. There is usually some overlap, especially through sharing toys with brothers, but children soon become able to distinguish girls' toys from those of boys.

It is significant that many toys for boys have generally been not only more technical and scientific but have also involved the formation of plans, plots and strategies. Forts and toy soldiers provide plenty of scope for this. Piaget's work has shown that becoming familiar with an object can induce positive reactions towards this and similar objects or activities.[20] Therefore it is easy to see how a boy's apparently 'natural' leanings towards science can be elicited. His lack of mystification about these types of subjects compared to that of girls can be similarly accounted for, and is reinforced by the assumption that boys are better at them. Girls are often given toys which help them to practise playing 'mother', or

---

* We tend to assume that girls 'naturally' play with dolls but this is denied by some societies which do not have dolls. When for instance Margaret Mead presented dolls to Manu children, the boys ran off and played with them. This reflected the men's responsibility for children which was a characteristic of this tribe.

they have dolls and animals with which playing takes the form of developing relationships: this includes feeding, dressing and talking to them.

The content and style of language provides another process of differentiation. Parents and other adults distinguish between the words and phrases they use to praise or criticize children, and whether they do it intentionally or not, it helps to build up the child's self-concept. The answer given by a fourteen-year-old girl in a Social Studies lesson about gender roles gives a good example of this:

> Children learn how they are different from one another by the way the parents and their friends talk about them. Example – 'Oh what a sweet little girl you have and so pretty, does she help you around the house?' 'What a rascal of a son you have, always getting into mischief.' 'Oh, well I'd worry and think there was something wrong with him if he didn't.'

The fourth process is really an extension of the second, in which the sorts of activities that children are exposed to, and required to do at home, rehearse children for their future roles. Girls are expected to help with household domestic work, and look after younger children. Boys are shown how to do repairs and to construct things. They may give token help with domestic chores but it is not seen as a skill that they should acquire. One girl protested to me that whenever her brother did any housework he was paid for it as it was not 'boys' work', whereas when she or her sister did it, payment was out of the question!

Parents are usually quite unaware of a lot of their own efforts in the manipulation and production of sex differences. They believe themselves to be responding to innate differences that they presume to be present, and interpret similar behaviour differently for each sex. For instance, the way in which parents discipline their children may differ in that boys have more physical punishment and girls more often suffer the withdrawal of parental love and affection. Discipline may also be allocated more to fathers for boys, and to mothers for girls. The psychological effects of withdrawal of love are deep and long lasting (except where there has previously been little affection and therefore there is not much to lose). It is reasonable to assume that if girls do tend to be disciplined more like this, then this would increase the need for affectionate relationships, and dependency. It has been found that children disciplined in this way tend to be less aggressive than those who are punished physically. However, the process of individual development is complex and interactive and much use of the other physical forms of discipline can be destructive and equally constraining.

Girls generally receive more affection, more protectiveness, more controls and greater restrictions. They are not encouraged to be dependent but the relative lack of encouragement or opportunity for independence and autonomy has equivalent effects. 'Overprotection' has also been found to have a 'feminizing' influence on boys' personalities. It has been suggested that fathers distinguish more in their treatment of children, emphasizing the 'masculine' elements of achievement in boys while giving nurturance and protection to their daughters.[21] Whatever intricate operations are involved in the relationship between parent and child, there is much evidence that boys and girls are taught differently with different roles and goals in mind and that this has moulded the consequences, assisted by a combination of dependency, social pressure and expectations.

Aggression is sometimes seen as a characteristic which distinguishes the sexes more than almost any other. In tracing its biological origins to the endocrine system, people who hold this view often reinforce their argument that it is 'natural' for men to be more aggressive than women. However, in any situation an interaction occurs between a person's hormonal activity and their own interpretation and assessment of that situation. Individuals have a choice of action, which may or may not be aggressive, and this makes it untenable to suggest an explanation solely in terms of hormone levels. People are not at the mercy of their endocrine systems. Some research has suggested that it can be people's behaviour that activates the hormones, for instance in aggressive encounters, rather than it simply being hormones that produce aggressive behaviour.[22]

Therefore, although hormonal action can play some part in producing characteristics such as aggression, this will vary between individuals of either sex. Their expression of aggressiveness is influenced by past social experience and knowledge in which being male or female has played a major part. Differences in aggression between boys and girls appear substantial and are assumed to be 'natural' but these have been exaggerated out of all proportion by the process of social learning and identification. Physical aggression is more appropriately displayed by boys who more often (but not always) have a greater capacity to use it successfully and so to gain prestige and status. Aggression in girls is disapproved of and they often re-channel it into more acceptable verbal forms.[23] It is significant that it has been found possible to predict degrees of adult aggression from that displayed by boys, but not from that displayed by girls.[24] For women, something has happened along the way that has led to their more 'passive nature'.

But there is little point in demonstrating that girls have equivalent aggressiveness which is either displaced into another form or extinguished altogether. It seems more realistic to view most aggressive behaviour as misplaced in modern everyday life, and to see boys and men as demonstrating an exaggerated form of competitive behaviour that is in fact self-destructive and damaging to their relationships compared with the more 'civilized' ways of girls and women. Aggression is one example of characteristics used to stereotype and polarize the sexes that have become redundant in real life while their image and implications persist. While remaining as a distinguishing masculine trait, it is too disruptive to be useful to a society organized around maintaining a conforming labour force and is constantly being defused and diverted. Personal relationships are not facilitated or enhanced by the need for either exaggerated or repressed aggression, and its overt expression has to be suppressed at work. Therefore, although the capacity for aggressive behaviour may be distributed within both sexes it is no longer very useful unless displaced into some form like ambition. In a woman, however, ambition is seen as selfish rather than admirable. Similarly, women's assertiveness is often confused with aggressiveness, and translated into a negative (feminine) characteristic. Women asserting themselves at work may find themselves put down and labelled as aggressive and unfeminine.

Under the present economic conditions, many young men who would usually expect to be in some sort of paid work, are unemployed. It is possible that the increase in young men's violence and criminal behaviour today can be seen as a response to social and economic frustrations, which also serves to provide some compensation for the undermining of their 'masculinity' experienced in not being employed and therefore not possessing an important element of male status. However inappropriate, aggression still signifies male behaviour, and the power and dominance that resides in strength and force.

Tomboys and Sissies

I don't know why it's worse for a boy to be called a sissy, probably because boys have to have this image of being tough. I don't think girls are bothered about whether they're thought of as being like a boy or feminine. But boys think they've got to be hard.

TERESA

One feature that characterizes much of childhood is the mix-up of traits and behaviour which is allowed to occur. This is usually tolerated differently for each sex. Boys are monitored more closely than girls from about the age of four years for the development of appropriate personalities and interests. As children begin to take on their more recognizable individual characters, parents and other adults, and children themselves, start to judge them according to the stereotypes for either sex.

... my brother ... I used to say he was sissyish when he was little, I used to take him around with me ... even to parties for little girls, and he's a very feminine boy. He's gentle and good with children, and has ideas that are almost fatherly, he's not boisterously masculine or anything like that. He likes dressing nice and things you would associate with girls. And then there's my sister, who although she's a girl, she hates nice clothes, hates looking nice, can't stand her hair – she's got long beautiful hair. She's like a boy – it's got mixed up. I'm not sure how they'll land up. Now my little brother, he's a typical boy, he's only five and yet the other day he punched me and it nearly killed me.

ELLEN

The presence of 'sissy' characteristics in a boy has always been viewed much more seriously than the 'tomboy' activities of girls, and this is reflected in the difference in value of these labels. Being called a 'sissy', with its feminine connotations, has a negative value. It is an insult, laced with contempt and derision. Being a 'tomboy' is much more positive, and is a label that can be taken with pride. These differences mirror the wider values of society which devalue feminine against masculine activities. In their efforts to structure their world, boys are quick to grasp and exaggerate the perceived inferior quality and status of girls and women. This is reinforced by the action and excitement that seems to be embodied in the activities and toys deemed more suitable for boys. Girls carry on playing with a wide range of toys while boys soon leave more 'girlish' toys behind them. Boys express a far higher preference for 'masculine' activities than girls of the same age do for 'feminine' activities. Many girls also choose to take specifically boyish roles and interests as there is certainly no difference in their capacity to participate in and enjoy action and adventure.

Boys are constrained far more within the boundaries of accepted behaviour than girls, who are allowed access to many expressions that are not strictly 'feminine'. Some tomboy girls go as far as taking over the attitudes of boys towards girls, and reject other girls and the trappings of 'femininity' for some period of their young lives. Parents are not very concerned about their tomboy daughters who are after all indulging in the more prestigious activities of boys. They are considered to be going through a transient phase which will pass, to be replaced by one characterized by a heightened interest in clothes and boyfriends.

The exaggerated disapproval and parental anxiety attached to 'sissy' characteristics in boys should be considered more closely. I have already pointed out that many aspects of 'masculinity' are synonymous with the personal elements necessary to succeed within capitalism or any other economic system based on competition. If a boy is therefore lacking in these, or seems to move into areas of 'femininity', his future success is potentially jeopardized. So also is society, for the present system of production depends on the reproduction of appropriate characteristics in men and women.

Parents are unconsciously endorsing this when they become anxious for their sons to be accepted and successful. Fathers more than mothers are concerned that their sons grow up in a suitably 'masculine' way, and it has been noticed that fathers tend to differentiate more between their baby sons and daughters than mothers do, and endorse the more traditional gender characteristics.[25] They perhaps wish to identify with their son's emerging interests and activities and would have difficulty in relating to a 'feminine' boy who exhibited traits that they had been taught to despise in men. They want boys to avoid most of the characteristics assigned to women that are valued less. They reinforce their son's and society's devaluation of women by trying to steer his behaviour towards acceptable 'masculinity' using jeers and threats: 'Surely you don't want to grow up a sissy boy?' Some teachers have also used this as a technique of behaviour control in the classroom.

For a tomboy girl, it is of less consequence either to her future or to society that she is acting in an 'unfeminine' way. Providing she does not completely reject her reproductive and domestic role, she is allowed some eccentricity. Her apparent rejection of gender-appropriate appearance or behaviour is not a threat to society. Again the 'doing' and 'being' aspects are relevant, because it is far more straightforward for a girl to give up tomboy behaviour and settle down than it is for a 'feminine' boy to suddenly take on the active components of the male role. The resultant insecurity involved with perpetually proving 'masculinity' is expressed in childhood through the often cruel treatment of boys by other boys who have labelled them as 'sissy' and use them as scapegoats.

It is also related to an underlying fear of homosexuality, which is experienced much more by men than by women. Sex has had a long history of repression and 'normal' sexual behaviour has been narrowly and rigidly defined. It is only relatively recently that sex without reproduction has been officially accepted. Through repression and ignorance, people developed an irrational horror or contempt for homosexuality. Parents saw the development of this in their children as a stigma that reflected on them. Despite the loosening of attitudes since the 1960s, many people still view it as illness or perversion. Homosexuality questions the divisions between men and women that are believed to be 'natural' and right. It implicitly suggests a form of relationship which runs counter to male supremacy, the family, and the fundamental values of capitalism.

The fact that male homosexuality is more likely to be feared as a consequence of effeminacy in boys than lesbianism is for a tomboyish adolescent girl, again reflects the values placed on traditional characteristics of the masculine role in this society. It is also supported by a belief that women cannot have a sexuality independent from men.

In the 1980s and 1990s, the language of insults in this respect has changed slightly, in that instead of boys (or girls) accusing a boy of being a sissy as a form of insult or put-down, this is often replaced by 'poof', or 'poofta'. The higher profile that homosexuality has taken in our society has brought with it the greater use of this label as derogatory.

> Boys don't get called sissies. They'd have to go out in a skirt or something to be called that now. If a boy walks along funny, it's 'poof' now, not sissy.
>
> FIONA

They are equivalent insults, but different in implication in that 'poof' implies a particular sexual orientation that 'sissy' does not. The increase in the use of the label 'lezzie' (lesbian) for girls parallels this, but it is used less often and is not perhaps as potentially threatening to girls' sexuality as the implication of being homosexual appears for most boys.

It is potentially worse for girls to be labelled a slag. Sue Lees[26] carried out research into the way such terms are used as a means of controlling girls, which carries a wider implication than sexual behaviour. Girls are often placed in a no-win situation in which if they risk their reputation they are labelled a 'slag', but if they refuse to have sex they may be denounced as frigid or a 'tight bitch'. These constraints do not apply to boys. A double standard defines boys' sexual exploits as a positive gain in their reputation, a confirmation of 'masculinity' and status, mainly in the context of their male peers. It gains them less admiration from girls, but that takes a less important place. Although this gives boys more potential power, resistance is possible for girls, and with enough confidence they can quite effectively deny or otherwise undermine a boy's reputed sexual prowess.

Processes of 'Socialization'

Many of the basic distinctions between male and female are laid down within the family, and children learn these in a variety of ways, some of which have been described above. Unconscious processes of identification and assimilation are built on by other processes, including the more mechanical operation of social learning or conditioning, in which the 'right' behaviour is reinforced through a system of rewards and (appropriate) punishments and becomes generalized out on to many other situations. This may be done consciously or unconsciously by parents and other adults and children. As soon as children begin to recognize themselves as boys or girls they take a more active part in the process, seeking to discover what boys and girls do and what they are like. This forms the basis of the cognitive learning theory described by Kohlberg.[27] Out of this, they observe, imitate and identify with people, often parents, and usually those of the same sex as themselves.

Another approach has looked at the way children learn about maleness and femaleness, masculinity and femininity through language, which provides the means by which the social structure is created and maintained. Bronwyn Davies[28] studied four- and five-year-old children in Australia, and in particular their reactions to feminist stories that often challenged traditional concepts and behaviour of men and women. Children take in the implicit constraints of language. They learn they must be socially identifiable as male or female, and this is signified in the nature of their dress, hairstyle, choice of activity, speech patterns and content. All these can contribute to them successfully positioning themselves as girls or boys. For instance, skirts and trousers not only constrict and sexualize girls, but they act as powerful signifiers of masculine and feminine ways of being.

Sex and gender tend to be seen as fixed entities but they are not. People can be 'masculine' or 'feminine' in different ways with different people and at different times. Anyone, child or adult, can be positioned in many ways during any one day, in some they are powerful and in others they may be powerless. Davies uses poststructuralist theory to 'recognize that what children learn through the process of interacting in the everyday world is not a unitary, non-contradictory language and practice – and it is not a unitary identity that is created through these practices.' That is to say, our identities are not set, they are made up of lots of different moving parts. Masculinity and femininity are not inherent properties of individuals, but are inherent and structural properties of our society, which both condition and arise from social action. Through this social interaction children learn the meanings of sex and gender in their particular society at any time. They learn to position themselves correctly as male or female, since that is what is required of them, to have a recognizable identity within the existing social order.

This analysis is critical of the way sex role socialization theory has tended to assume a biological base of sexual difference over which a child's feminine or masculine role is laid through the influence and teaching of others. Davies says this does not recognize the child as an active agent, who works out for herself or himself the way the social world is organized. This is not totally true as Kohlberg's theory of cognitive learning does suggest that children recognize whether they are boys or girls and actively seek out what they see as the appropriate behaviour, but it does not go quite far enough.[29] Socialization theory's concepts of roles and stereotypes are not adequate to acknowledge the complex and contradictory ways in which people constantly constitute and reconstitute themselves and the social world through their participation in various discourses such as reading, talking and other activities. Women may at times be economically dependent, powerless or physically weak, but this does not render us as permanently passive, weak and dependent individuals. The socialization model tends to present an oversimplistic causal model which shows the ways adults create narrow stereotypical behaviours in children. It does not take account of the simultaneous accommodations and resistances that may occur in every social interaction.

'Maleness' presents the idea of power as male power, with female 'power' confined mainly to the domestic sphere or assisting men in the male sphere. Knowledge of this is embedded in narrative structures of books and of play, which formulate and sustain a child's identity. Positioning themselves as male and female is not just a conceptual process but a physical process by which maleness and femaleness also becomes intricately taken into the bodies of the children, and how they sit and move and play, as well as in identifiable practices such as hairstyle and dress.

The assumption of maleness and femaleness as opposite concepts is contained in allour social texts and communications, and therefore in the interactions a child has with others. Simply referring to boys and girls reinforces the way they are always set as contrasts, as separate. That power resides in the male lies at the heart of the male–female splt. This power imbalance will remain as long as we seperate male and female as we do. Davies queries why children are so concerned th get their gender right and why current programms for change have such little effect. She suggests that in the social and narrative interactions that children have, the only comprehensible identity available to them is as 'boy' or 'girl', 'male' or 'female'. These are exclusive categories which take their meaning in relation to each other. They are seen as natural and almost morally applicable. Perhaps we should also ask why we seem to need to create opposites in this way, and also take into account the historic and economic contexts in which we take our gender positions.

Traditional sex role socialization theory can thus be criticized in that it seems to take a unidimensional approach. It looks for social influences on the individual, and minimizes the importance of conflict and resistance, and the impact that individuals themselves have on the social structures and individuals around them. Cultural theories have also been developed to look more deeply into gender differences. While each influence may be valid and interesting to explore, there is no linear process operating, and nor is there a uniform 'role' although we can usually define some level of stereotype. We must also consider the interrelationships of social divisions such as class and race. 'Socialization' is not a mechanical one way process, but a tangled web of social interactions that continue throughout life. Women can be positioned as more or less 'feminine' at different moments in their lives. Gender differences and inequalities cannot be reduced to a series of attitudes that can simply be modified. They also have a material and a historical basis; they are not universal nor static, but vary according to time, class, race and so on. All in all, a pluralistic approach to sex and gender roles would appear to be the most fruitful.

The years since 1972 have seen changes in men's and women's

roles at home and work, and enough talk about equality to allow us to hope that boys and girls may encounter more egalitarian beginnings in the world. Books have been published which draw together some of the extensive contributing to each side of the nature-nurture debate.[30] They demostrate that although gender development starts very early in life it is certainly not predetermined and unchangeable. At present, however, the validity of gender differences is protected in many ways as we have seen, and not least through a continuing patriarchal system backed up by a social and economic structure that still largely depends on sex segregation inside and outside the workplace, and implicitly reinforces an unofficial ideology based on sex differences. Changing this system goes far in the right direction, but even in this event, ways of changing gender roles and personal relatioships must be consciously sought by both sexes. It is not an automatic process. In many areas of their lives girls and boys (like 'femininity' and 'masculinity') have been seen and treated in a contrasting relation to one another. In education, training and work, girls encounter a system that is still premised on such gender differences, which not only denies opportunities, but also assigns a lower value to much of what is seen as 'feminine'.

NOTES

CHAPTER 2

1. See H. Holter, 'Sex Roles and Social Change', *Acta Sociologica*, 1971, 14, reprinted in H. P. Dreitzel, 'Family, Marriage and the Struggle of the Sexes', *Recent Sociology*, no. 4, Macmillan & Co., New York, 1972.
2. M. Mead, *Sex and Temperament in Three Primitive Societies*, William Morrow, 1935; and M. Mead, *Male and Female*, Penguin, 1950.
3. See Ann Oakley, *Sex, Gender and Society*, Temple Smith, 1973.
4. See B. B. Whiting (ed.), *Six Cultures: Studies of Childrearing*, John Wiley, 1963. Also H. Barry, M. K. Bacon and I. L. Child, 'Relation of Child Training to Subsistence Economy', *American Anthropologist*, 61, 1959.
5. H. Barry, M. K. Bacon and I. L. Child, 'A Cross-Cultural Survey of Some Sex Differences in Socialisation', *Journal of Abnormal and Social Psychology*, no. 55, 1957, p. 330.
6. ibid.
7. Discussed in the previous chapter and also in greater detail in Sheila Rowbotham, *Woman's Consciousness, Man's World*, part 2, Penguin, 1973.
8. See J. and J. Hampson, 'Determinants of Psychosexual Orientation', in F. Beach (ed.), *Sex and Behaviour*, John Wiley, 1965; and J. Money, *Sex Research: New Developments*, Holt, Rinehart & Winston, 1965.
9. See for instance M. Diamond, 'A Critical Evaluation of the Ontogeny of Human Sexual Behaviour', *Quarterly Review of Biology*, 40, 1965, pp. 147–75; and C. Hutt, *Males and Females*, Penguin, 1972.
10. Other psychosexual research has been described by researchers such as R. J. Stoller, *Presentations of Gender*, Yale University Press, 1985.
11. A. McRobbie, *Jackie: An Ideology of Adolescent Femininity*, University of Birmingham, Centre for Contemporary Cultural Studies, 1978.
12. J. Winship, 'A Girl Needs to Get Street-wise: Magazines for the 1980s', *Feminist Review*, no. 21, winter 1985, and *Inside Women's Magazines*, Pandora, 1987.
13. See for instance, Dorothy E. Smith, 'Femininity as Discourse', in *Becoming Feminine: the Politics of Popular Culture*, Leslie G. Roman and Linda K. Christian-Smith (eds.), The Falmer Press, 1988.

14. I. K. Broverman *et al.*, 'Sex Role Stereotypes and Clinical Judgements of Mental Health', *Journal of Consulting and Clinical Psychology*, no. 34, 1970.

15. S. J. Kessler and W. Mckenna, *Gender: An Ethnomethodological Approach*, Wiley, 1978.

16. June Statham, *Daughters and Sons, Experiences of Non-Sexist Childraising*, Blackwell, 1986.

17. Nancy Chodorow, 'Family Structure and Feminine Personality', in M. Z. Rosaldo and L. Lamphere, *Women, Culture and Society*, Stanford University Press, 1974.

18. Nancy Chodorow, *The Reproduction of Mothering: Psychoanalysis and the Sociology of Gender*, University of California Press, 1978.

19. Ruth Hartley labelled these four processes 'manipulation', 'canalization', 'verbal appellation', and 'activity exposure', respectively. R. Hartley, 'A Developmental View of Female Sex-Role Identification', in J. Biddle and E. J. Thomas (eds.), *Role Theory*, John Wiley, 1966.

20. J. Piaget, *The Construction of Reality in the Child*, Basic Books, 1954.

21. U. Brofenbrenner, 'Some Familial Antecedents of Responsibility and Leadership in Adolescents', in L. Petrullo and B. M. Bass (eds.), *Leadership and Interpersonal Behavior*, Holt, Rinehart & Winston, New York, 1961.

22. S. J. Kessler and W. Mckenna, op. cit.

23. For more discussion about aggression and sex differences see Ann Oakley, 'Sex, Gender and Society', and J. Archer and B. Lloyd, *Sex and Gender*, Penguin, 1982.

24. J. Kagan and H. A. Moss, *Birth to Maturity: A Study in Psychological Development*, Yale University Press, 1983.

25. Brian Jackson, *Fatherhood*, Allen & Unwin, 1984.

26. Sue Lees, *Sugar and Spice*, Penguin, 1993.

27. L. Kohlberg, in E. Maccoby (ed.), *The Development of Sex Differences*, Tavistock, 1966.

28. Bronwyn Davies, *Frogs and Snails and Feminist Tales*, Allen & Unwin, 1989.

29. L. Kohlberg, op. cit.

30. J. Chetwynd and O. Hartnett (eds.) *The Sex Role System*, Routledge and Kegan Paul, 1978; J. Archer and B. Lloyd, *Sex and Gender*, op. cit.; Janet Sayers, *Biological Politics: Feminist and Anti-Feminist Perspectives*, Tavistock, 1982.

CONTRADICTIONS IN FEMALE EDUCATION

Domestic science is another popular lesson. The girls regard it as a serious business and are prepared to work hard at it. This attitude appears to be fairly general. An older girl who said that she did as little work as possible when she was at school . . . still thinks of 'cooking and laundry' as lessons which did not turn out to be a waste of time. Senior girls, who perhaps spend one whole day a week, for six months, in the school kitchen, set about their work in a business-like manner, are not afraid to handle ovens, and have a confidence in their own abilities that is in marked contrast to their hesitating approach to such subjects as letter-writing or history . . . A good many girls indicate that they do not really think schoolwork has any bearing on their future . . . 'When I was in the senior school . . . I didn't really bother. They don't teach you no more than last year and I was bored stiff. I used to give out the tea and the milk. I wish they taught you something a bit useful.'

GIRLS GROWING UP, 1942[1]

The domestic crafts start with an inbuilt advantage. They are recognizably part of adult living. Girls know that, whether they marry early or not, they are likely to find themselves making and running a home; moreover some quite young schoolgirls, with mothers out at work, are already shouldering considerable responsibility, a fact which needs to be taken into account in school house-craft programmes. There may also be some girls who are far from enthusiastic, because they have had their fill of scrubbing and washing-up and getting meals for the family at home; and yet they may need all the more the education a good school can give in the wider aspects of homemaking and in the skills which will reduce the element of domestic drudgery.

NEWSOM REPORT, 1963[2]

We did a load of cookery and needlework at school . . . I used to hate it. We did biology and chemistry, but all we had for equipment was a couple of old bunsen burners and you got five bad marks for turning them on. Only a couple of people did physics – I don't remember ever having the chance. You hardly ever found anyone doing it for O level. We never had the chance of doing technical drawing or anything. We really hated needle-work and cookery – we would've jumped at the chance to do anything different. I used to rip my needlework up every week so that I wouldn't have to finish it the following week.

JANE, 1972

. . . successive Secretaries of State have aimed to achieve agreement with their partners in the education service on policies for the school curriculum which will develop the potential of all pupils and equip them for the responsibilities of citizenship and for the challenges of employment in tomorrow's world.

THE DES ON THE NATIONAL CURRICULUM, 1987[3]

More girls should do more science subjects. They don't do it because maybe they feel there won't be many girls. You don't get many boys doing child development and cooking and things. I think more boys should get the guts to take it. I think some of them won't take it because they're afraid they'll get the mick taken out of them by their mates, that they're sissies. I took technology because I liked it. If I was the only one and they did tease me, I wouldn't get that bothered about it.

HARRIET, 1991

The advent of mass education in the last century broadened the educational opportunities of both girls and boys. But as we have seen there was widespread discrimination by sex and class. The separation of girls' future roles in life from those of boys greatly influenced the content and form of teaching and girls' own self-expectations. In the 1970s these were still with us, although many were concealed beneath an umbrella of professed equality. Women were taking and assuming an increasing role as workers while their responsibilities at home remained almost intact. This had many implications, as girls at school tried to balance out the academic demands of school and the changing image of working women on the one hand, and the traditional role of wife and mother on the other.

Girls' attitudes to school are affected by their social backgrounds, personality and ability, and the sheer implications of being female. These influence their views on the value of education, how long to stay in it, and the sorts of jobs they want to enter. It is well known that many children obtain little satisfaction or enjoyment out of school. Working class children in particular, whose social position has always influenced the kind of schooling they received, have in the past seen education as of relatively low value or relevance to the opportunities that were open to them. Their position in schools has traditionally been at the lower levels, where they have been categorized as 'less able'.

For girls, there has been no clear relationship between academic and technical schooling and being a 'good' wife and mother. This point has been consistently emphasized throughout their history and has only changed with the development of a need for certain sorts of workers and with the demands made by an increasing number of educated women. But the contradiction still exists for girls for whom school represents a compulsory and boring prelude to the time when they are allowed more independence and freedom and given adult status. Their most popular job choices in the past have generally been those demanding minimal qualifications and which made it meaningless to extend schooldays much longer than necessary. Earlier physical maturity and sexual awareness emphasize the discrepancy between adolescent girls as developing women, and the child status and prolonged lack of responsibility accorded them by the school. Many girls have consciously objected to the way that school treats them like children until perhaps the magic status of the sixth form, if they stay that long. They are often very mature by the age of fifteen or sixteen and may be already taking responsibility for certain jobs inside and outside home. They wear adult clothes, most are already physically capable of bearing children, yet the rules and discipline demanded by the school institution allows no exceptions to its rules. Adolescence is a very 'marginal' time, when girls and boys can gain adult status through going to work, while others of the same age suffer the non-status of schoolchildren.

LEAVING SCHOOL IN 1972

> I would stay on but I want to be a receptionist, so if I stay on
> when I do not need qualifications for the job I want to do, it will
> be a whole year wasted.

In 1972, the girls in Ealing schools who participated in the first
study were vociferous about the boredom and dissatisfaction of
school. Most looked forward to leaving, whether or not they were
discontented with school life. A third of them wanted to leave at
the first opportunity, at fifteen, a third at sixteen, and the rest at
seventeen or eighteen. They felt 'shut in and bored', and wanted to
'work independently to a certain extent without staff, etc., breathing
down my neck'. Some wanted to 'get a good job and get married',
wanted to 'earn my own money and not have to depend on my
parents to give me pocket money'. Others felt they were wasting
their time because 'I don't really have a set ambition', or thought
'you can get good jobs whether you leave school later or not'.

> Might as well leave really, 'cause I'm not really doing anything.
> It's all right up until the third year, but once you get into the
> fourth year you don't do hardly anything ... We don't learn
> anything. We might as well be doing something useful, some-
> thing worthwhile.

Doing 'something worthwhile' seemed to have little connection
with being at school every day, being treated like children, and
being taught many things that apparently bore no useful relation to
their situations in the present or the future. Yet this girl would
probably have disagreed with the one in 1942 who saw things like
cooking and laundry as useful school subjects. She was aware that
there is more to life than household skills, although exactly how
this related to the rest of the school curriculum may not be clear.

For some girls the boredom and irrelevance of school had led to
continual truanting until such time as they could legally leave. It is
interesting that girls truant as frequently if not more so than boys,
but whereas boys often move into delinquency, girls' truancy is not
particularly associated with delinquent behaviour. Their rejection of
the monotony of school and its imposed rules and constraints is less

frequently rechannelled into anything very anti-social. There were, however, certain days when the frequent truants I spoke to in the seventies did like to attend school. These were the occasions of community activities like Task Force and organizing playgroups. They seemed more 'worthwhile'.

But in 1972, not everyone was keen to leave school. Some girls wanted to stay on for several years to obtain qualifications and emphasized 'the importance of a good education'. Others were nervous and frightened of leaving the familiarity and protection of school life. Those who wanted more education did not necessarily enjoy school, but those who doubted their ability to cope with independence emphasized the enjoyment of school and the importance of their friends. The social life of school is very important for girls, possibly more so than for boys.

> All my friends are at school. I am shy and don't make friends easily.

> I enjoy school. School sort of protects me. I don't like being out there in the world, trying to find your own way.

At this time, the Ealing girls from West Indian families wanted to stay on at school somewhat longer than their white class-mates, most of whom wanted to leave at fifteen or sixteen. About an equal number of the Ealing West Indian girls wished to leave school at sixteen, seventeen or eighteen years of age, and relatively few at fifteen years:

> If I stay on a little longer I would be able to know and understand the work better and to leave school well-educated hoping to get a good and well-paid job.

These hopes often reflected those of their parents many of whom had come to Britain during the previous two decades. For them, education was often seen as a particularly important issue because of the relatively good opportunities offered by the education system in Britain.

> They [parents] all want to see us brought up the right way not the wrong. They want us to get as much education as we can because back in the West Indies, y'know, some parents didn't

really get a lot of education. So when they come over here, they want their children to get as much as they can. They go on 'Oh yes, my daughter is this, my daughter is that,' that's what my dad says. He's sort of pushing us to be something. What he says, he goes – 'I want you to be a lawyer, I want you to be doing medicine, I want you to be a professor.'

FLORETTA, 1972

Similar observations were made nearly twenty years later:

My parents think education is important. They prefer us to stay on and take A levels because they had to come over from Jamaica, they missed out, so they like us to do it. When my dad came over he had to finish schooling, then he had to start at the bottom of his job. He's been there for over twenty years now and he's worked his way up. He wishes he had got his education and got in higher up.

LORRAINE, 1991

The hopes impressed on them by their parents at that time were often higher than the performances they could achieve in school, to which the implicit discrimination experienced by black children and their position in the school hierarchy contributed. The opportunities for black children at that time were limited by the social and material deprivations that also faced the indigenous white working class community – by poverty, by overcrowded homes and schools, and by the lack of the influence and knowledge that benefits middle class children at school. For them, this was also aggravated by prejudice and discrimination within schools, by the language problems, at first undetected, and by the culture-biased intelligence tests that put many black children into ESN (Educationally Sub-Normal) schools.[4]

Teaching is dominated by middle class values and language and the progress of schoolchildren is judged by the same standards. This has always militated against working class children of any colour. But black children suffered even more from the hierarchical rigidity of the streaming system and, as a result, from the bad behavioural problems inherent in the classes in the bottom streams taught by constantly changing teachers. At the time of my first research many black parents in Britain were very distressed to find that their children were being allocated to the worst schools and placed in the lowest forms. The implicit assumption of lower ability compared with white children in the same forms was often reinforced in school organization.

Like their white classmates, however, many of these Ealing West Indian girls keenly looked forward to leaving, whether sooner or later, seeing this as their opportunity for independence, freedom and money to spend as they liked. But whenever they expected to leave, there was an overall emphasis on the importance of doing well at school, gaining an education and making a career. Research on black and white school leavers in the early 1980s, however, was to suggest that although young black women increased their level of education and married later, this only improved their occupational position relative to other black women, rather than white, through continuing discrimination in the job market.[5]

The response of the West Indian girls to education at that time expressed an ambivalence. They felt the boredom and irrelevance of school as much as their white contemporaries, but at the same time they stressed the importance of qualifications and of education itself. By endorsing education they were trying to work within the system – but this is not the only response they might have made. Among black teenagers in the 1970s there was already evidence of a growing alienation from and resistance to striving within the educational structure, and black experience had begun to change the will to perform in some areas.[6] They were recognizing that they are schooled for low level employment and were rejecting what was offered to them. This had begun to happen mainly in areas of high unemployment and probably more in male than female youth, since girls were able to get 'better' work more easily, like clerical work (although this was limitedly available to them) and nursing. They were refusing the work that society was allocating them. 'their rejection of work is a rejection of the level to which schools have skilled them as labour power, and when the community feeds that rejection back into the school system, it becomes a rejection of the functions of schooling.'[7]

The situation for the Asian girls in the earlier research was somewhat different from either their white or West Indian contemporaries. At that time many of them had not been in Britain for any significant length of time, some were still wrestling with a new language, and their home and social lives, as well as their futures, were far more circumscribed. Girls from the Asian communities do not represent a homogeneous group. Their families have varying origins in India, Pakistan, Bangladesh, Uganda and Tanzania, and differing religions, such as Sikh, Hindu and Muslim. Within this the caste system effects further divisions. Therefore, although their position in Britain shares many cultural similarities, the nature of families and individuals can be quite diverse.

Asian parents' attitudes to their daughters' education can vary greatly according to their religion and backgrounds. Many have expressed a great concern and enthusiasm for education in Britain. It is often seen as a way of acquiring social standing and breaking through the confines of the caste system. Sikh parents for instance are as concerned for their daughters' education as they are for their sons'. This interest is not new in India, as there were schools for girls in the Punjab in the early nineteenth century. But for girls particularly, education can also provide a route round the dowry system, and a way of bypassing the caste system. This is a response partly produced by the material circumstances forced on them in Britain. With the difficulties and cost of marriage, if girls' education helps towards getting them a better match it is a material investment.

But the ambitions of parents and daughters can create problems. On the one hand the parents' demands may place great responsibility and strain on their children who are expected to stay in night after night to study. For girls in particular, going out is rarely allowed in any case. On the other hand, the girls' own ambitions may begin to take off on their own. They start to view the traditional prospect of early betrothal with reluctance, and many want to delay this, preferably until they have qualifications and an established job. It is ironic, however, that the more time girls spend at school or college, and thus the more education they receive, the more opportunity they have for meeting boys and damaging their reputation. And consequently in some ways they are becoming less eligible for a 'good' marriage. If continuation of education is in conflict with the time for marriage, girls may be given more say in their marriage arrangements. Many can now postpone marriage by choosing to carry on with their studies. Although for some girls the initial aim of their education is to make them more marriageable, at the same time it is also constantly teaching them about other ways of life, and to examine the organization of their own lives. In direct contrast to their white classmates, the Ealing Asian girls in 1972 described their lives as being confined to coming directly home from school, helping with the housework, doing their homework and then reading a book or watching television. Sometimes there were strict ideas about what television programmes were suitable for them to watch.

In 1972, the Asian girls, like the West Indian girls, wanted to stay on longer at school but they also expressed more enjoyment and enthusiasm for school than did either the English or West Indian girls. They did not find it boring and irrelevant, and the majority wanted to stay on into the sixth form, to the age of eighteen. There was a greater proportion of Asian girls in the higher forms compared with the West Indian girls, but many of them still clustered in the lowest forms and in special classes for those with language difficulties. Those who had come to Britain most recently had a slow and incomplete articulation and understanding of English. They all laid great emphasis on doing well, and systematically confirmed the importance of education. This can be seen partly as a product of the high value placed on education by their parents and their community in general, and partly as a result of its being linked to the prospect of a better marriage. But most girls also expressed the wish actually to use their future qualifications to make something of their own lives, commenting for instance 'I like to study hard and become something really great,' and 'I want to get more education and live a better life.' Almost all had some idea of the job they might take up.

But their enthusiasm may have served little practical purpose then for those girls who were to be married soon after leaving school and who would perhaps not work at all, or who would work until marriage and then have to stay at home. Others, especially girls from Pakistan, could be sent back there, where they might do some work but probably nothing very interesting or important. Almost all the girls expressed career hopes but these may have turned out to be wishful thoughts. Those who came from middle class backgrounds and whose parents were in good jobs, especially professions like law and teaching, were more likely to make these hopes a reality. They were also more frequently in the higher forms, and their home and family life provided more help and support for studying.

LEAVING SCHOOL IN 1991

I like school. I've got a chance to meet all my friends, talk to them. I was doing a survey about school and it said 'Do you like school?' I thought they'd all say 'no' but most of them said 'yes'. They all said 'We need education', things like that.

NASHEEN

There have been significant changes in the educational and occupational structure over the past two decades and in the prospects facing girls and boys, as described in an earlier chapter. These have modified their enthusiasm about leaving school. The school-leaving age was raised in 1972, so that in 1973, the year after the Ealing girls were first interviewed, all pupils had to stay on until they were sixteen. In the years that have followed, there has been a continuing emphasis on the importance of equal education by sex, race and class. Girls have consistently shown themselves to be more than capable in academic achievements, and, for example, often gain better A level exam results than boys. Yet girls still tend to aim lower than they should, and fewer than should go into higher education, and into types of work and higher positions where they would be equally as capable as men.

Important changes have also occurred in women's position at work and at home of which girls at school are aware. Increasing levels of unemployment since the mid 1970s put pressure on women's already existing desires to work outside the home, whether or not they had children. Although money was obviously an important factor for working women with children, many had other essential reasons why they preferred to go out to work rather than be full-time mothers at home. They looked to working to provide, for instance, a separate identity outside the home, and an often crucial sense of independence. Therefore, girls have been increasingly looking towards a working future, and one which encompasses the possibility of a career rather than just a job. The Ealing girls in 1991 were more or less unanimous in endorsing the importance for a girl of making a career for herself. Although progress has been slow, women have become more visible in the public sphere, whether it be in professions like law and medicine, or in the more serious areas of the media, in journalism and television newsreading and current affairs programmes. However, the current paucity of work opportunities and the sight of homeless young people living on the streets of the inner cities, makes young people today conscious of the relative advantages, whether they enjoy it or not, of continuing education beyond the age of sixteen. One girl expressed her views:

> I'll probably finish my education at eighteen. They say school's the best time of your life, enjoy it while you can. But I mean, with the recession, nobody knows how long it will be for. Nobody gets jobs at the moment. One of my dad's friends, he's really well-educated, he's got so many qualifications but he just can't find a job. He's just too over-qualified. I don't want to do that, and I don't want to be under-qualified either.

LOUISE

The school structure in Britain has also changed considerably since the 1970s. Whereas it was usual at that time for schools to have a sixth form into which students moved to take A levels, or some to retake their O levels, now only a certain number of schools have preserved their own sixth forms. (Only two of the Ealing schools had a sixth form.) There has been a welcome expansion in options for further educational opportunities to the extent that sixth form colleges were set up which have a less school-like organization and atmosphere. There is more of a sense that these are places for young adults rather than children, since everyone is over the age of sixteen. They offer a variety of vocational and non-vocational courses.

Girls leaving school in the 1990s therefore look out on a very different occupational landscape from those in the early 1970s. Their experiences and feelings about school itself, however, were remarkably similar. Like those in the earlier study, many of the Ealing girls in the 1990s looked forward to leaving school whatever background they came from. This was much more pronounced, however, for the white and West Indian girls (of whom two-thirds liked the idea and a fifth did not mind) than Asian girls, almost 40 per cent of whom liked the idea of leaving school, and a similar proportion disliked the idea. Those who looked forward to leaving school generally expressed similar dissatisfactions to their counterparts of twenty years before. Many asserted that school was boring, they wanted to be independent and in particular, they yearned to be treated as more adult.

> I just don't enjoy school much as we are treated like young children instead of young adults.

> Because I would like to be independent and get out. It's like a prison leaving each class waiting for the bell to go, at work you just get treated like an adult and you more or less do the same things.

> School's boring, well it's not boring but everyone's distracting you and you sometimes join in, which you shouldn't but you get encouraged to. The classes are so overcrowded, there's too many children for one teacher to handle.

For the relatively few who did not mind or did not like the idea of leaving school, the reasons given were again similar to the earlier study, and for many this involved the attraction of being with friends in school. For many, being at home would be more boring than being in school:

> I like coming to school. I like getting up in the morning. It's good. We have a laugh, with your friends and that. If you're just at home it's boring, at school it's all right.

> When it comes down to the subjects, they're boring. Coming to school I can meet people of my own age and talk to them and have fun. Normally I wouldn't get a chance to go out a lot, so school is another way out. If I was at home right now I'd be tidying up all the time. School is OK. I don't like the work, I like the playtimes and lunchtimes, and the debates in class, like in sociology. I enjoy those because you can express your views.

INDERJIT

For the Asian girls in particular, like Inderjit, coming to school was less boring than being at home, where they would have to help in the home rather than go out, although a few did talk about their truanting. For all of them school was a chance to meet and talk to other girls, and boys. Rajwinder mentioned how school especially contributed to the development of self-confidence:

> I think it makes a lot of difference when you're not allowed to go out of the house that much. You don't build that much confidence in yourself. Coming to school is the only place where you can really learn confidence. You learn everything here. It's really important that the school makes sure they're doing the right thing. I know my confidence and everything I've learnt is from school. When you're with the family it's a different thing. If you don't learn confidence you just get walked over. You've got to stand up and show the teachers what you're worth. If you show them you are hardworking then they'll make the effort as well to talk to you and make sure you're doing well. If you sit down and don't do anything they will think 'I won't bother helping you'. And some of the boys in this school are so rude. They think just because you're a girl they can say what they like to you. When you turn round and say a few words back they get quite a shock.

The recognition that work was scarce and many young men and women left school to become unemployment statistics was reflected in girls' expectations about when they would actually leave school. Overall, many of those in the later study – and especially the white girls – thought they would leave school at an older age than had the majority of their earlier counterparts, a change that stands over and above the fact that the school-leaving age had risen by a year. Whereas in 1972 Asian and West Indian girls had shown a significantly higher investment in remaining in school, there was now no difference between these white and black girls in that most aspired to stay in education until at least eighteen. Their responses reflect the shared reality of young people in today's economic recession and high unemployment.

For parents too, there was a heightened awareness that there may not be much going for their children in the world of work unless (and even if) they have qualifications. Some of the Asian girls also described the specific relationship that still exists between education and marriage and the negotiations this involved.

In our religion [Sikh] it was always the boys who would be allowed to go to university. We know someone she wasn't allowed to go to university, her grandmother wouldn't allow it so they stopped her and now she's getting married. Two boys came to see her – because it's arranged marriages – and they turned her down because she wasn't educated enough. So she was very angry at that. She said it was all their fault that they didn't let her have her education. Some people aren't so bothered if they get an education or not, especially Muslim girls, they just know they'll end up getting married so it's not worth it to get an education. I myself want to get an education and my parents push me. They really want me to get somewhere.

KULJIT

My mum wants me to become a doctor. My dad doesn't mind. They think education is very important. I tell my mum if I pass my O levels and A levels and go to university, I'm not going to get married. And if I do bad in them, I'll get married. So it's marriage or university!

AYESHA

Today, the purpose of staying to gain qualifications has even more of an edge than it did in the seventies. Young people in the nineties are well aware that there is not much work for those who leave school early. There may be little available, either, for those who stay on, but at least they may have slightly more chance now or in the future if they obtain some qualifications, and attending school or college may be seen as better than doing nothing at home. Therefore, many more in the nineties than the seventies said they expected to stay on at the same school or go on to college in another place, either to take A levels or to retake or take more GCSEs, or perhaps do a BTec course.

I'm not in a hurry to leave school as I would like to get a good job and not be left at the bottom of the pile.

I don't particularly like school but I want to get my qualifications.

Going to a sixth form college has the added attraction of providing a place of study where they may be treated as young adults rather than children, and have a more mature relationship with teachers.

I'll go to that new sixth form college. I just think the sixth form here – well, I just think you get treated with more respect in a college. You get treated much older and you get more work done, so I'm hoping.

HEATHER

I don't mind school, the lessons are OK, and I've got lots of friends. It's OK. I will go to college. I've got lots of friends who are older and go to college and they say it's good. I don't like being treated like a child. I hate being patronized.

LYN

At the time of my first study, the ambitions of many, especially working class girls, were more immediate and practical. They almost certainly hoped to be wives and mothers at quite a young age, and were expecting to work predominantly in offices, shops and factories, and some in teaching, nursing and similar work. The paradox of trying to make school seem less irrelevant then was that this seemed to involve doing things that related more obviously to their lives, like perhaps cookery, needlework and child-care, as advocated by so many social reports since girls' education began. Yet it was this aspect of their futures that also needed to change. The association of girls' education with their domestic roles had been consistently voiced in official reports, while being simultaneously modified by the accompanying decrease in household skills brought about by the development of time-saving products and cheaper mass-produced clothing. In a similar way, the teaching of typing and shorthand in school had led several girls to express their opinion on the usefulness of these classes, but it also meant that they were already conceptually confined within the four walls of an office.

It seemed then that domestic science had lost much of its intrinsic appeal for girls in school, while academic studies still appeared too abstract and arduous. Their experience of doing community work and helping with children and playgroups through school was enjoyable and rewarding, but still confirmed them in the traditional servicing and maternal roles. The inclusion of more social and community studies in the curriculum, and humanitarian subjects like sociology helped to widen horizons by at least giving girls the concepts and context in which to examine their own position, even if this was not seriously criticized. In the past, school had been a rather artificial world which often assumed a predominantly middle class belief in education for its own sake. In the 1990s, the aim of the 1988 Education Reform Act, and the National Curriculum it brought in, has been to link education more closely with the labour market. The earlier emphasis on a domestic education for girls has gone, submerged in a deceptive pool of equal opportunities, but inside and outside the school women still occupy the domestic role in the family.

GIRLS AND HOUSEWORK

Girls' home situation often made it harder for them to study seriously. Neither working class white nor black parents have much time or the means to stimulate and encourage their children's schoolwork. Cramped housing, absence of helpful books and materials and the domestic duties imposed on them can make it even harder. Although parents may be willing to work hard and sacrifice a lot for the sake of education, it can be difficult to translate this into meaningful help for their children. As well as this, it is daughters within the family who have traditionally been expected to help at home with the domestic work, despite whatever schoolwork they may also be required to do. In the mid 1980s, Alison Kelly looked at the extent to which girls and boys were expected to help in the home, and predictably found girls doing the major share, and that they were often expected to do different tasks around the home: girls did more washing-up, cleaning, cooking and tidying, while boys tended to clean windows, take out the rubbish, wash the car, help with minor repairs, etc.[8] Other research has also documented this.[9] Girls, rather than their brothers of whatever age, are given housework to do as well as having to look after their younger brothers and sisters, especially while their mothers are out at work.

A significant number of girls in both my earlier and later studies spoke about the amount of help they had to give with housework or care of younger brothers and sisters. They were vocal in their complaints about the way their brothers were not expected to help either as much, or in some cases, at all, even if this was going to conflict with doing their schoolwork:

> I was willing to stay on at school – but I wanted to get out and earn money, but the main reason that I wanted to leave was because every night I go home and do me mum's housework and I hate doing that, so the only way I can get out of doing that is to go to work. Me little sister does it too. My mum goes out to work to earn more money for clothes and things like that for us, and she's always gone out to work, and she went on condition that I took charge of the house, and got meals for the evening and things like that, so I took over the housework when she went out to work . . .
>
> MICHELLE, 1972

> At the moment, because I am still going to school, my parents want me to only think of my lessons and nothing else which I find rather difficult at my age and when I leave school at least I won't be tied down with looking after younger brothers and sisters as they will be somewhat older.
>
> VERA, 1972

> When my brother was doing his GCSEs it was 'Terence can't wash the dishes, his GCSEs are important.' So I had to wash the dishes and all that. Now he's doing his A levels and I'm doing my GCSEs and now they say 'Oh, Terence has so much A level course work to do', they don't say the same things about me doing my GCSEs. That's not fair, I think that's a bit sexist. Well, my mum expects me to cook and do the ironing and wash dishes, despite what homework I get. They automatically assume I can do it, they don't bother asking me if I've got homework that night.
>
> CATHERINE, 1991

Although girls resented doing housework, Christine Griffin noted how they also used it as an excuse for taking time off school.[10] The greater numbers of mothers working today will be reflected in increased pressures on girls to do or share the domestic labour at home. Many of the Ealing Asian girls, many of whose parents did long hours, and occasionally two jobs, were also frequently expected to do a major share of the housework, unlike their brothers.

> I get back from school, I wash the dishes, feed my little sister while my other sister is getting ready for work and when she goes I do the ironing and then I start my homework.
>
> REHANA

> At home it's all a rush because our parents are always at work so we have to do all the work and everything. I do mainly all the housework so I feel pretty tired. I have a hard time with my sister, she doesn't like any of my cooking. I cook for my parents, but my mum's started eating at work so it's only my dad. My mum tells my brother to do chores but he won't even pick his own dishes up. He won't do anything. He says, 'No. My dad doesn't do anything, so why should I?'
>
> HARWINDER

FRAGMENTED OPTIONS

In the 1970s, the alternatives faced by girls at school appeared fairly straightforward, and predominantly based on their measured performance there. If they did well they stayed on for the qualifications that would provide a better job or entrance to college or university. If they didn't do well, they began to think about leaving, getting a job, earning money and developing more socially. If on the other hand they were not very good at school but they and their parents had high aspirations, they would struggle on to get through the necessary examinations. Twenty years later things are not so straightforward, and while girls and boys may go for and succeed in whatever qualifications they may choose, these do not always guarantee either a job, or a place in further education at college or university. Even Youth Training has shown itself inadequate in offering either the appropriate quantity or content of courses.

Nevertheless, the way that girls see themselves and their abilities still contributes to structuring their range of job opportunities and also combines to temper many of their views on, for instance, the substance and value of working and having careers, getting married and setting up a home. Their future intentions build on these sorts of foundations, interacting with what they have learnt and feel about femininity and female roles. Even in the 1970s, different kinds of ideas about women's position were beginning to be presented and schools could not be accused of putting forward a totally biased picture. Successful women were in evidence and equality was becoming a commonplace word, endorsed in 1975 with the Sex Discrimination and the Equal Pay Acts. But it takes more than passive and legal demonstrations of this to counter the strength of traditional beliefs which are more acceptably reinforced. Adoption of self appropriate ideology rests on deeper sources, and unless girls belonged to the minority (mainly middle class) that moved upwards into higher education, they tended to fall back on the familiar expectations of feminine roles.

Every girl (or boy) has a unique view of the world and life, and usually shares common goals and values with friends. The importance of friends for many teenagers at this time in life cannot be underestimated. Their individual views and their unique positioning in relation to aspects of 'femininity', for instance, are continually changing. These are formed out of experiences of 'informal' education: for instance through their own experiences, family, friends, the media, and the teachings of the law and the church; and the 'formal' education of school. They are interactive with all these elements, and not mere consumers of received knowledge. As Chanan and Gilchrist put it:

> From these elements each individual fashions the store of behaviour models, moral and aesthetic touchstones, criteria of action and reference points of meaning that he carries round in his head. These are not passively ingested, and are not fixed once and for all, but are creatively synthesized, and the synthesis is either recharged or revised at each encounter with new works of art or entertainment, other people's values, public customs, laws and institutions.[11]

Most girls still retain a strong hold on many of the traditional ideas about womanhood and this is not surprising. It reflects a depth of internalization of femininity, lack of confidence about change, un-critical acceptance of the ways things are, and a lack of viable alternatives. Even where girls recognize and understand their position and its limitations and discriminations, it is often hard to conceive of realistic ways to change this. At this age girls have not usually had a wide experience outside home and school, and have read relatively little that deals comprehensively with aspects of their own lives. They may have seen many of their relatives and friends doing jobs from which they seemed to gain minimal enjoyment. In the early 1970s, it made a lot of sense to make their priorities love, marriage, husbands, children, jobs and careers, more or less in that order.

Their feelings and views affect areas of decision in their lives already circumscribed by factors like sex, class and race. They consider and arrange opinions subjectively and objectively, in ways which do not necessarily coincide. These are weighed up with personal needs, self-image and actual school performance to set in motion the motivations that can have consequences in their lives that are hard to reverse.

Girls in the early seventies were aware of the value of academic achievement but saw this still as more to do with boys and men, whose relative nonconformity and irresponsibility did not seem to prevent them from gaining the higher positions. It had become easy for girls to acknowledge the objective worth of scholarship while excusing themselves for not being 'that sort of person'.

Many of their lives followed a similar pattern – boredom with school, early leaving into a local job that had marginal interest, finding a steady boyfriend, saving up to marry, settling down and having a family. Marriage and home-making appeared as a meaningful distraction or welcome release for those with boring jobs or those who had no intention of making work a central part of their lives. For a significant number of girls at school in the 1990s, this still rings true as a description of their lives. Others have placed a stronger investment in education and training and pursuing a career. Their needs and feelings form part of an evolving self-identity. This is very malleable and open to change, but once the options of technical or academic courses have been rejected it may be hard to pick them up again. Women who left education a long way behind them while pursuing family roles have often realized the vacuum when their children are grown up, when their lack of qualifications and training makes only mundane work available. Retraining schemes for women have more generally offered access to a narrow range of (usually women's) work, which leave most with only the choice of lower level employment.

School has never given equal opportunities to girls and boys whatever (formal) egalitarian ideology it may seem to represent. Twenty years ago the way forward was far more clear-cut for boys who, unlike in the nineties, could still assume a life of continuous working. Whatever level of job they were steered towards, they looked unambivalently towards a working future. Girls, however, were (and still are to some extent) schooled with the marriage market in mind, although this may not be acknowledged consciously. This inevitability in their lives provided as much excuse within the school, as for girls themselves, for underachievement or lowered aspirations. The belief that a girl finds her deepest and truest satisfaction in a husband and children was very prevalent (and many of the Ealing girls endorsed this in 1972), despite talk of sexual equality and women's increasingly visible presence in the work-force. It is not necessary that any direct or conscious conflict should have been felt by girls between the idea of marriage and its accompaniments, and that of achieving a qualified position or career. It is more reasonable to suppose that the expectations of marriage served to cast an intrusive shadow over the continuity of their views of the future and make long-term planning a more difficult commitment to make.

Historically, many of the advantages that school has to offer have been largely denied to working class girls. Social and domestic roles have consequently overshadowed the possibility of other interests and occupations and have increasingly narrowed their lives. Being a housewife and mother does not demand the passing of examinations. It has not been considered failure but success in the terms of our traditional ideas of the feminine role, and bringing up children involves skills in its own right. There has generally seemed no need to risk a venture into higher or more unusual aspirations unless you are obviously bright at school or you and your parents are intent on your reaching a certain career or level of education. In the nineties, girls' attitudes have changed, and being a full-time housewife, and to some extent a mother too, is seen as simply not being enough, and to some extent a failing. Being a housewife at home is now viewed by many girls at school as boring and a waste of time (and of qualifications). Being a mother is viewed positively, but the most acceptable idea is to get back to work or a career sooner or later. The real opportunities for doing all this, however, have become even more of a hit and miss affair. With many more young people electing for some form of continued education or training there has to be a fall-out. Working class girls without courses or jobs may elect for a more meaningful road of marriage (or cohabitation), and early motherhood. Some will combine whatever work they can get with family demands. Some may return to education, as the figures on mature students, especially in the 'new' universities, have shown. But the financial costs are high and the odds are once again stacked against working class and less well-off families, of whatever ethnic origin. Yet it would be wrong to be too pessimistic, for such shifting patterns can also create pockets for resistance and change.

'CAREER GIRLS'

By the early 1970s, marrying and having children and leading a working life were no longer assumed to be incompatible, although in practical terms the facilities for combining these were sparse and this shown little change since then. At that time, girls no longer chose one of these apparent alternatives or the other, but many had decided to add a career to their domestic role in life. Where marriage was accepted very much as the primary aim, girls still needed to work for the money necessary to support themselves; and where a career was confidently chosen, marriage was usually also a definite part of the future although it might seem vague and further away. The experiences of those for whom marriage had always loomed like a large heart on the horizon, and especially those who had not progressed at school, included no real clash of interests. Their way forward was self-apparent, and the prospect of investing time and effort in a specific vocation could be implicitly dismissed.

It was commonly accepted then that everyone had to get a job when they left school, and unlike many of those from generations before them, most of the Ealing girls in the first study saw work as something more than a time-filler before marriage. They recognized the need to work after getting married, and when their children were old enough to be left, and not necessarily just for the money. Most stopped short, however, at wanting to do anything carrying the deep commitment they saw as characterizing a 'full-time career'. This appeared to require a special type of woman, with attributes that they saw lacking in themselves. They erected a barrier between the capabilities of this imaginary person and themselves, despite the relatively interchangeable use of the terms 'job' and 'career' in schools. Girls acknowledged the traditional dichotomy between marriage and home-making, and a 'full-time career' which has always had its roots buried in prejudiced attitudes and the very real lack of facilities for women to work successfully outside the home. Many girls at this time effected a solution in which they expressed their intention to take their chosen job more seriously.

Some of the Ealing girls in 1972 had definite ideas on girls who committed themselves to a career:

> A person who does do full-time and doesn't have any breaks at all I don't think should have any children anyway as it would interfere with her career. I think people who do go in for full-time like that don't stop for anybody. The whole of their life is round their job.

> I think men should [have careers]. If they [girls] want to they can, but I think it suits men really. Once men start out on something, I suppose they go ahead, but women they always change their minds, and never do good in full-time careers really.

But not all girls at this time accepted this kind of thinking so easily:

> Well, [women's] brains are just as good as a fella's. They're just as intelligent and that. Just because they're supposed to be weaker than men doesn't mean that they are. Not every girl will get married, and even if she does get married, she'll have something to fall back on, and if she takes a career for a few years she can do it after she's had her children. When she's about thirty-five to forty she's got nothing. She can always take a refresher course and go back to work . . .

Although a few of the girls in the earlier study were hoping to go into some sort of profession, such as law or medicine, they did not readily identify themselves with being 'career women'. By the 1990s, this concept is no longer so alien and many girls believe that they would like to be women with careers, even if they do not aim to be as 'high-powered' as the previous image had implied. Many more than in 1972 were looking at jobs or careers that required some full-time further or higher education, and most wanted and expected to work in these whether or not they married or had children. In general, girls no longer see there being such a need to make this choice.

> I think it's important to have a career, rather than just wait to get married, although I love children. I don't think women still have to choose [between a career and a family]. I think if they really want a family they can work round it. It might be a bit of a struggle at first but I think they can do it. My mum did it. A lot of my friends want a career, they're set on careers. I think more girls now want careers, and families later, which I think is good.
>
> MELANIE

The formal concept of marriage is no longer such an attraction for girls, they express a high level of unsureness about the prospect and anticipate that this will happen at a later age, if it happens at all. The idea of cohabitation, which many endorse, does not seem to plant a full stop in front of a career structure in the same way as marriage has done. In spite of, or because of, the knowledge that jobs are scarce, the importance of having a 'career' is automatically endorsed. Thus, all the Ealing girls strongly disagree in 1991 that 'it is more important for boys to get good jobs than it is for girls', and they strongly agree that 'girls should be able to go for the same jobs as boys'. They also understandably disagree strongly with the now old-fashioned-sounding idea that 'it's not worth a girl getting qualifications because she'll only get married'; or that 'getting a job just fills the gap between leaving school and getting married'.

The 1991 Ealing girls recognized that combining a career with a partner and children was not always easy, but there was no clear-cut separation for either working class or middle class girls between themselves and someone who was 'going for' a career. The concept of a career has been made available to everyone. Not everyone wants one, or will get one, but it no longer applies only to a special sort of girl. Whether you will get and keep a job within it is another question. These days, nothing's guaranteed: a girl's got to look out for herself.

> I want to work and get some money. It takes two to bring in all the money. I think it's a good thing that women have full-time careers. I don't think staying in the house, looking after the children is right. You should earn your own money, not wait for someone else to tell you how much you can have. I'd like the person I marry to have a good job too, bring in enough money. I wouldn't want to struggle. It's too stressful and depressing.
>
> EILEEN

Whether consciously or not, girls and women have found themselves embracing a fundamentally ambivalent position. Many have drawn a lot of satisfaction and enjoyment out of activities specific to their 'domestic' role as women, while these are generally assumed by society to be inferior to the activities of men. They have been attracted to a role that, in a patriarchal and capitalist society, has always taken second place. For girls in 1972, it was still such a double-bind situation: if they went after what society deems most important, succeeding financially and academically in a career, then they might lose in 'femininity'; while if they concentrated on their 'proper' role, it was inherently of lower economic and ideological status. However fervently women's role in motherhood may be extolled, especially at times when the quality and future of the nation has seemed to be threatened, this has never been reflected in their treatment and position (especially as mothers) in the rest of society.

In the 1970s, I suggested that jobs and careers came last in the perceived priorities of many girls. Twenty years later, these priorities have become a little blurred, in that love and relationships are still extremely important, but jobs and careers run in parallel as necessary to a woman's life these days. Marriage and husbands have faded in priority, although still significant, and while children are important, for many girls the idea of having them is preferably postponed until a little later in their lives. In 1991, the Ealing girls did not identify their deepest satisfaction with having a husband and children. In addition, it is no surprise to find that all profoundly disagreed that a woman's place is in the home.

At the beginning of the 1970s, marriage was something that most girls included somewhere in their future regardless of their opinions about the appropriateness of jobs and careers for women. Mother-hood was assumed to go with marriage and added to the reluctance that many had felt towards the commitment they saw involved in pursuing a career. Most of the white Ealing girls in the first study hoped to marry, many before they were twenty years of age, and almost all by the age of twenty-five. They probably did not differ significantly in these hopes from an equivalent group of girls drawn from more middle class backgrounds, but as they grew older and their opportunities grew narrower, early marriage and having chil-dren would likely appear increasingly more meaningful than further study or work. At this time the black girls showed a different pattern, and were comparatively less enthusiastic about marriage. In the nineties, things have changed: marriage is seen as an optional choice compared to cohabitation and having children is still impor-tant but can be left to a slightly later age. Relationships are still forged at an early age, but marriage may be delayed or abandoned altogether. Around half of all the girls participating in the 1991 study said they wanted to marry; a significant number said they were not sure; and the rest (about 10 per cent) said they did not wish to marry (see chapter 6). The economic depression and high unemployment make it very hard for families to survive, financially and emotionally. The current situation of the rising numbers of lone parent families are testimony to this.

In this context, girls will eventually find that the economic and personal commitment involved in further study and/or the reality of unemployment may lead to them making many compromises in their career aspirations. Although positive relationships and children provide meaning in life and more especially if girls' career aspirations are dashed, the primary role they come to assume may be through necessity rather than choice.

Nevertheless, girls of all backgrounds are putting more value on academic achievements than ever before. When increasing numbers of women added working to their role as wives and mothers after the Second World War, this gave them a double identity. Now girls have added the need to gain some qualifications for a more significant job or career, in the contradictory context of a declining job market. Contributing to this are not only the changes that women have been making in their own personal and working lives but also the recognition that family life can be unstable, and men in Britain can no longer look forward to a continuous working life. It is now almost taken for granted that both working class and middle class women will be required to work for at least some if not all of their lives.

SCHOOL PERFORMANCE

In spite of so many girls' enthusiasm to get out of school, evidence has shown that in fact they have been consistently more successful than boys at primary school and through much of secondary school.[12] At pre-primary ages, tests of general intelligence have generally shown girls scoring higher than boys; and in reading, writing, English and spelling at primary school, the average eleven-year-old girl beats the equivalent boy.[13] She excels in the whole area of verbal ability, speaking and reading earlier, and with greater articulation. Although she does retain some measure of superiority over boys in these skills at secondary school, she does tend to fall behind in areas needing arithmetical or numerical reasoning, in which boys have already moved ahead, and have usually attained a better level of analytical ability. They have a greater interest and apparent capacity for areas needing an objective approach, such as maths, geography and science. But in considering these apparent differences in ability, it should be remembered that there is always a considerable overlap between boys and girls and the range of differences within a sex can easily be as great as the differences between them. Girls do well later in their school life, they attain better results than boys in GCSEs, more girls than boys tend to enter sixth form and do A levels, in which they perform better. In the subjects they choose, girls no longer 'underachieve' in performance, but these subjects are not equally distributed between the sexes. Girls are very much more represented in modern languages, social science and biology, while boys still predominate in the physical sciences and various technologies.

Girls achieve better results and do better in examinations than boys throughout much of their school life. However, there is an inconsistent relationship between their actual intellectual abilities and performance before leaving school, and their subsequent employment. This means that while girls of poorer intelligence go on to achieve accordingly, this is not necessarily the case for girls of higher intelligence. At the time of the earlier research in the early 1970s, whatever their abilities, girls were to be found in general office work, shop work and other occupations with few prospects, as well as being full-time housewives and mothers. Therefore, at some point during their adolescence, girls had begun to under-achieve in relation to their real capacities in the occupational world. This often occurred around the onset of puberty, coinciding with the time when both boys and girls are becoming increasingly aware of their sexuality and their future adult roles. For boys, this period in their lives involves an emphasis on intellectual and practical achievements, and on various strengths of physique and character. For girls, conformity has been more appropriate, and achievement may be translated into the context of appearance, social life and popularity. At this time school pressures increasingly conflict with social and other pressures.[14] Some teenage girls experience a clash between studying and having a good time and do not want to regulate their social lives according to homework. Boys, love and romance and sex have been part of their thoughts and conversations, if not their activities, for several years already. Meeting and keeping boyfriends is an important and time-consuming business, and it takes a strong commitment to studying, or very strict parents, to keep a socially active girl's mind on schoolwork.

Girls are in an ambivalent and contradictory position. On one level there is pressure to succeed academically, which is rewarded by school, parents and the self-satisfaction of doing this. At this level, boys and girls alike may be hindered by a fear of failing, which can undermine self-confidence and produce a reluctance even to try for success. For girls the situation is more complex, and girls have often been omitted from achievement motivation studies because they did not yield consistent and meaningful results and therefore 'mess up the model'! Traditional interpretations of femininity fostered the belief that it was not desirable that girls should be as clever as boys. This implied that high achievement involves losing an important ingredient of 'femininity'. In relation to this the majority of the Ealing girls in 1972 agreed that boys do not like girls to do better than them in schoolwork. This was similarly endorsed in the 1991 study. It also shows that, as usual, boys' attitudes have changed less than girls, and therefore the implication still holds – if you really want to attract boys, don't start by showing how clever you are.

This is not to suggest that a girl's role demands that she be stupid, but she must modify or disguise her success in relation to that of the boys (and sometimes girls) with whom she wishes to be popular. She should ideally confine her 'success' to acceptable 'feminine' pursuits which don't involve male competition. In American society, Margaret Mead noted that: '. . . throughout her education and her development of vocational expectance, the girl is faced with the dilemma that she must display enough of her abilities to be considered successful, but not too successful . . .'[15] It is an interesting contradiction that using your brain, getting on and working hard in school, and achieving well has a more 'feminine' connotation, while rejecting school, being deviant or delinquent, and doing very manual physical jobs or activities have a more 'masculine' association. Yet in the 'developed' world, physical strength wins little power and status (apart from in sport) and the men who hold the most powerful and well-paid jobs have generally applied themselves and their brains to get where they are.

Competition is the important underlying factor. Many men still do not like to compete with, or be beaten by a woman. This is as true in the nineties as it was in the seventies. Research has shown that teachers at school use comparisons with girls as a way of getting boys to behave better or work harder.[16] Since women's status is inferior, losing reflects badly on the men concerned. There are areas in which girls and women can succeed, indeed excel, but these have traditionally been the ones in which few men even bother to compete – or if they do it is for the top positions, such as men learning cookery and catering to become chefs, and male hairdressers quickly moving upwards to become salon managers. It is in such areas related to cookery, needlework and child-care that female success can be ultimately put to male advantage at home. Competition is a disguised form of aggression, and society disapproves of aggressive women. (Even where a film features an aggressive heroine, she must ideally also be beautiful, glamorous, and have a tender heart underneath.) Although both men and women are encouraged to compete equally within our democratic society, it is still the case that a girl who both competes and succeeds in a male-dominated area is often regarded with suspicion, and not as a 'normal' woman.[17] Both girls and boys hold their own profiles of the successful 'career woman'. The characteristics that are associated with success in business, for instance, include those of being decisive, ruthless, powerful and assertive, which are far from the traditional characteristics associated with 'femininity'. They may be charismatic in a man, but can be seen as unattractive in a woman, especially by any man working under her authority. At other levels of achievement, a working class girl who does very well academically may find it hard to draw her male friends from the boys that she intellectually left behind. (The film *Educating Rita* effectively illustrated this process.)

In real life there is less antagonism between men and women at work than may be actually anticipated, but this is often because the competition is made less direct by some means, or because a woman loses her female identity in the eyes of her male companions and becomes 'one of the lads'. But this still remains a concern, especially among those girls and women who have succeeded against men and are concerned not to appear 'unfeminine'.[18] It is significant that men denigrate the sexuality of women who are above them; if they can seduce them, this is one way of stripping their power, and finding that they are 'only women after all'. Since girls are brought up to be less competitive, their attitudes towards success are more likely to be mixed with doubts and lack of confidence. The girls in my 1970s research were very willing to accept responsibility for intellectual failure, while success was seen to depend more on chance or the whims of others.

It is an advantage to be supported and encouraged by family and friends. Working class girls have felt pressures to conform to the traditional feminine role earlier because they and their families were usually less orientated towards achieving high academic goals. Their 'underachievement' was consistent too with the nature of the most popular and available jobs which frequently require minimal qualifications and made it appear unnecessary to linger on at school. In the 1990s, school success is no longer seen as so 'unfeminine'. Attractive and intelligent female role models now feature in the media and the general acceptance of an aim of sexual equality have helped to make it somewhat easier for girls to unreservedly pursue academic achievements. The lack of immediate employment prospects has also made many follow an apparently more sensible course of continuing with education rather than leaving at the earliest opportunity. However, in the fight for education and jobs, being male or middle class still has some advantages over being female or working class, and although women have sometimes found it easier than men to get work during these years of rising unemployment, this has been in the lower status, lower paid, often part-time areas of (women's) work. Working class girls' lower level of schooling and gender role learning interact with this to place them in the ranks of the less skilled workers. Middle class girls who continue their education do not escape these pressures, but they may be postponed until they reach the apparent equality of the lower levels of middle class occupations. Moving out of these positions may then prove more difficult.

Upbringing and Ability

It is necessary to look at the relationship between upbringing and personality in order to discover more about the origins of 'underachievement' in girls. It has already been noted that the characteristics that have been pinned on to the traditional 'feminine' personality are ill-suited to making progress in a world where competitiveness, assertiveness and independence are the axioms of success. The early experiences of the majority of girls hinder the development of such qualities and add a psychological dimension to the existing social and practical obstacles. The upbringing of boys and girls has traditionally reflected the different goals that have been assumed for them. A son is brought up to make some impact on his environment, while a daughter is protected from her environment. He is implicitly being encouraged to control and direct, while she is steered towards becoming more malleable and dependent. While there is no advantage in advocating that girls develop the more destructive and emotionally inhibiting aspects associated with masculinity, or that they should emulate and compete with men, they should receive encouragement and the appropriate conditions to develop the autonomy, confidence, independence and assertiveness that would increase the quality and equality of their lives, and give them the understanding and power to change their own position.

A lot of differentiation by sex has already occurred within the family long before children begin to demonstrate their different abilities at school. Boys, for instance, are already more independent and adventurous, while girls are more restricted, protected and given less chance to 'stand on their own feet'. A mother's behaviour is very important here – whether or not she closely supervises her daughter, what expectations she expresses for her, and how much she criticizes or praises her successes and failures. A girl is seldom given as much opportunity to develop, test and assess her abilities for herself, and consequently she often underestimates herself and is less confident of doing things alone. She obtains her sense of identity through relationships rather than actions and becomes dependent on the approval of other people for her self-esteem. If she has been mainly disciplined by withdrawal of love as girls often are, she may become even more dependent on gaining affection, an attitude of mind which promotes passivity and conformity.

This treatment of girls is very important since a relationship is thought to exist between intellectual ability and independence. A key part of this ability concerns analytic thinking: the capacity to perceive problems in more global terms, to apply general principles to them, and to use analysis and reasoning to solve them. This is particularly relevant in science and related fields. Several psychologists suggested that early independence and mastery training are important characteristics in the development of this ability: which refers to whether and when children are encouraged to use initiative, take responsibility and solve problems for themselves instead of relying on others. The upbringing of many girls obviously militates against this and since independence and mastery training also seem to have some influence on children's orientation towards achievement, girls are once again at a disadvantage.[19] Researching pre-school children in the United States, Serbin[20] observed how boys' toys and activities were more concerned with spatial reasoning, which was related to a general problem solving ability. It was noted that although not all the children divided their activities in this way, the teachers reinforced this differentiation both verbally and in other ways. Boys also got more teacher interaction, a greater amount of both praise and telling off, and a more detailed type of instruction.

The effects of parental support and encouragement also play their part. Boys have been shown to do better when their father encour-ages them, and their mother gives them emotional support (although this need not be the only model). Girls too, need encouragement and support, and research on fathers and daughters has suggested that there may be a relationship between high achieving daughters and the quality of their father–daughter relationship.[21] It has also been shown that primary school children's attitudes to schoolwork and their performance improved when parents showed a high degree of interest and encouragement. Working class children were more positively affected by encouragement, while parents' 'interest in schoolwork' benefited children of all social classes and especially girls.[22] Therefore, girls may be held back by the affectionate protec-tion of their parents if it is given in the absence of any serious inspiration to do things for themselves. In 1972, most of the Ealing girls said their parents wanted for their daughters whatever the girls wanted for themselves. In several cases where parents gave more explicit encouragement, girls did have significantly higher job aspira-tions. In 1991, the Ealing girls' parents were similarly supportive of most work or careers their daughters wanted to do, and almost all said their parents wanted them to go on to further or higher education. Although dependent on the nature of the relationship between children and parents, parents play a significant role in encouraging and supporting their children in education and job choice. In the Ealing study, many girls, and black girls in particular described the emphasis their parents placed on education. It has been argued that parental disposition towards education and the labour market are signif-icant factors in educational success for young Afro-Caribbean women.[23] The girls from Asian families in Ealing also described how their parents strongly endorsed their daughters' education, although, as some girls described, this might interact with the timing and nature of their marriage.[24] There were only a few instances of opposition, and these appeared to come more from mothers than from fathers.

In the context of subject choice in schools, some research revealed that working class parents showed greater sex-typing of school subjects like cookery and needlework, which they saw as more important for girls; while middle class parents tended to apply more sex-typing to academic subjects like languages and science, which they saw as more important for boys. Using a scale of general statements about men and women, and girls and boys that related to this issue, Alison Kelly found that parents with only girls scored lower on this scale than those with only boys; and those from families with working mothers also scored lower than those where mother was full-time at home.[25]

Other factors contribute to prejudice girls' ultimate success from the start. One of these is the implicit conflict mentioned earlier between academic and social demands. The subculture of being a girl leads to a multitude of distractions, such as fashion and style, music, boyfriends and romance. Academic pursuits allow relatively little time for these preoccupations which promote increasing lack of interest in studying and school which can in turn radically influence the subsequent course of girls' personal and working lives.

SCHOOL AND THE HIDDEN CURRICULUM

School reinforces what children have learnt about sex roles in the family, through the media, and in everyday experiences outside the home. Children find, for instance, that boys and girls are treated differently: boys' activities have higher status than girls' and boisterous aggressive behaviour is less tolerated for girls. Inside school these sorts of sex inequalities and differences have been perpetuated, together with those of class and race. Like a self-fulfilling prophecy, the various labels that children may fall under, like female, working class and black, the particular schools they attend, and the subjects and classes to which they are directed all channel them in certain directions, often downwards towards low level jobs. School represents home and work and the relationship between them differently for girls and boys, and it prepares them differently for each of these. For instance, boys have little training for fatherhood although a few are beginning to take child development, sometimes seen as a soft option.

The main function of school is ostensibly to educate and pass on knowledge, but it has other important social functions which include the suppression of unacceptable social behaviour, and an emphasis on the social importance of control and subordination, and the acceptance of discipline. The exaggeration of this aspect of school can extinguish autonomy, confidence and curiosity in its pupils of both sexes, many of whom become skilled at negotiating or flouting the authority structures. Other pupils may react by tolerating discipline as a necessary evil or accepting it as correct and desirable.

Schools are fairly effective in 'domesticating' and pacifying the 'masses', but it is over-simplistic to assume that the dominant values of society are passed on through teachers in a straightforward fashion. It would be hard to find consistency in values either between individuals or contained in how and what they teach. The need for acceptance of authority, discipline and subordination is certainly demonstrated if not learnt, but adoption of social values is not a straightforward process. It comes through family and individual experience, and values may coincide with and be influenced by those emerging from particular teachers and the content of their subjects. But there is often a gap between public acceptance of attitudes and values perceived to be desirable and 'right', such as the importance of education, and the consequences in terms of behaviour, which in this case would mean working hard and remaining at school or college to get the maximum education.

There is an implicit contradiction between institutional conformity and the idea of 'free' intellectual creativity. The 'right' answer and good behaviour become the important criteria for success. Form rather than content becomes the primary consideration. Illich[26] emphasized this in his theory of the hidden curriculum and has shown how the structure of schools can have as much influence as the knowledge taught in them. The early social experiences and training of girls predisposes them to accept the school's demands for conformity. Their increasing awareness that feminine status is lower may add to this process.

Equal opportunities may be a commonly professed aim in education but there are many factors that still more or less subtly discriminate by class and race. There are many ways in which it is easier for girls from middle class white families to concentrate on studying and achievements at school (although similar conflicts between work and 'femininity' may be faced later if they move on into the predominantly male arena of further and higher education). Social and educational aspirations are very much part of middle class life. The continuing inequalities of the education system mean that although all parents want 'the best' for their daughters, some 'bests' will be better and more accessible than others, and it is more likely to be the middle class (and well-off) who can provide most for their children. They have often benefited from education themselves, and give help in the form of interest and support, as well as better and quieter facilities for studying.

Many parents from the working class communities have seldom had the time or the energy to involve themselves deeply in their daughters' work and progress, often because they work in time-consuming jobs. Some have less faith in the usefulness of a long academic training. They often adopt the verbally supportive but passive attitude of 'it's up to you what you do, as long as you end up in something respectable'. Also they may combine a relatively limited knowledge of available jobs and careers with a narrow view of what is more suitable. It is notable that the class system of our society allocates more worth to those with academic qualifications and high salaries, whatever socially 'useless' work they do, and implicitly undervalues and downgrades less 'brainy' manual work, even though the latter is seen as more positively masculine (macho). With the current high levels of unemployment, more fathers are finding themselves at home with time available to devote to their children. Whether or not they do so is speculative, as helping with homework may not be how they wish to spend their time, and their own knowledge may be lacking, or superseded on subjects like technology.

How girls see themselves in relation to school will affect their attitudes to it. Doing reasonably well at school is obviously an important factor in generating interest and enthusiasm in subjects, as well as increasing expectations that affect performance and attitudes towards studying. If in the early years of school a girl does not do well, she defines and labels herself as not being intelligent, and absorbs and reflects her teachers' limited expectations of her. Girls and boys from working class or black backgrounds are often placed in this position, and become well aware of their status in the school. The apathy and lack of interest characterizing many third and fourth form girls in school at the time of the first Ealing study showed that they had understood only too well that academic interests were not for them and often directly clashed with social pursuits, forcing them to do work for which they could see little relevance.

Looking around her, a working class girl in the early 1970s saw a tradition of early marriage and early child-bearing. Men were involved mainly in some type of skilled work, while women worked in offices, shops and factories, or full-time at home. The pattern in the 1990s is similar, except that the decline in Britain's manufacturing industries has eroded many sources of male employment. It is still easy to fall in with this tradition. The schools themselves may help to perpetuate the pattern. They increase the alienation felt by their pupils by upholding middle class values and couching ideas in middle class language, and until recently gave little attention to the diverse cultural backgrounds from which many pupils came.

The gulf between middle class and working class children at school is linked to the difference between education inside and outside school, i.e. 'formal' and 'informal' education. School institutionalism tends to ignore the autonomous thinking and tastes of its pupils, suppressing their interests and current images of the world and attempting to impose another approved model. Connections are rarely made between the formal areas of culture that have to be learnt and the informal knowledge about life that is built up and reassimilated every day.[27] Language emphasizes this separation, and has also served to reinforce stereotyped ideas about working class intellectual inferiority. Although this has been questioned[28] and, for instance, many different accents and styles of speaking are now acceptable on radio and television, middle class language and culture are still regarded as superior. Working class language and social background are seen as culturally deprived – as needing compensation and change. This attitude rejects working class language and expression merely because they do not meet the stringent requirements of neatness, grammatical correctness and clarity with which most teachers, examiners and other judges of ability have been preoccupied.

Schools respond more positively to certain acceptable attitudes and to pupils who are thought to be suitable for formal education. They are seldom concerned to establish common reference points with pupils who do not so conform and therefore a large number of children fail to relate their own everyday preoccupations to the relevant areas of formal knowledge. School then seems to have nothing to offer them and although the capacity for interest and the ability are often present, the incentive to use any part of this education may be absent. In the early 1970s, girls, and more especially those from working class backgrounds, were seen and saw themselves primarily as aspiring girlfriends, wives and mothers, and then as aspiring typists, secretaries, nurses, teachers and so on. In the early 1990s, their priorities were less clear and their intention was to try and combine whatever occupation they chose with a partner and children.

There are many facets to the hidden curriculum within school. There is the organization practised in some schools, for instance, of having separate playgrounds, cloakrooms and toilets for boys and girls, and separate sports activities. Strategies for teaching contain implicit differentiation and discrimination, and include teachers' methods of motivating pupils through setting girls and boys against each other. This is applied as another form of control for behaviour, as well as in lesson content and in the teasing, telling off and banter that occurs between teacher and pupils in the classroom situation. Another form of behaviour control which goes on inside and outside school is the sexual labelling of girls by boys, and by other girls, through giving them a sexual reputation, as described in the previous chapter.[29] All these processes interact with the gender-typed assumptions and views that pupils themselves bring into school.

The 'Femininity' of Primary School

Due to their close associations with caring for children most primary school teachers are women. Their job usually involves controlling and teaching a large number of children because of overcrowding and understaffing. Inevitably they demand obedience, silence, passivity and conformity from their pupils: all features of traditional female behaviour. For boys and girls alike, their primary school thus confronts them with an almost totally 'feminine' environment – not only through the teachers, but also through the type of behaviour that is being enforced.[30] Differentiation within the family contributes to the different reactions of boys and girls to this situation. Girls find that the school's demands coincide with the way they are expected to behave at home, while boys experience a conflict between the two environments. In fact, the primary school values directly contradict the independent assertiveness that parents usually try to encourage in their sons. Although teachers may obtain some obedience and conformity from boys, it is likely that they see primary school as being a more appropriate environment for girls. As a result boys have less incentive to work hard, and become more difficult to control. This may partly explain why girls do better at primary school than boys.

Evidence has suggested that primary school teachers tend to expect boys to be more difficult and unresponsive than girls. They see them as less hard-working, less able to concentrate and less amenable to discipline.[31] Boys often rebel against the enforced 'passivity' of school but this need not put them at a disadvantage, on the contrary, it has been suggested that teachers spend more time interacting with troublesome boys, giving them both disapproval and encouragement.[32] It is claimed that this helps boys in their approach to learning, but cannot be uniformly true or else a lot more working class boys in lower forms would succeed than do at present. It is more likely that the advantages of such pupil–teacher interaction work in a more complicated conjunction with other forces, such as class and race.

It has long been suggested that the situation could be improved if there were more men teachers in primary schools. This would be a positive step in providing more equality in role models but it still would not alter the 'feminine' characteristics that are deemed necessary to maintain school discipline. Delamont points to the contradictions inherent in men's role as teachers because this involves aspects of 'femininity' such as working with children, using the mind rather than the hands, and not swearing.[33] It would not necessarily make boys behave better in the classroom. Girls and boys alike also absorb the idea of a hierarchy that places men in the top positions from which they issue directives and make important decisions. Men are already identified as figures of authority, much like fathers in the home, and this image maybe endorsed by the figure of the headmaster who rules over a primary school largely staffed by women. And there are many other models that have already shown children their appropriate roles and behaviour. At home, for instance, the noisy aggression and naughtiness of boys is more often overlooked as part of their 'nature'. This is often reinforced by literature such as children's reading primers and stories in which this sort of behaviour in girls is absent or discouraged. The process of differentiating between girls and boys begins early and most children will already have started conforming to its tenets before they enter primary school.

For girls, there is less conflict at primary school. The characteristics which have led to reward at home gain even more implicit approval in the classroom. In fact the relative quietness, obedience and greater passivity shown by girls is often held up as a mark of their greater maturity and responsibility. It is ironic that these same attributes are later used to demonstrate inferiority! Nor are these characteristics likely to encourage the independence associated with intellectual curiosity or analytical problem-solving. Teachers have their own conscious or unconscious hidden curriculum about gender differences which is reflected in their treatment of boys and girls in primary school. It is reinforced through interaction with the related attitudes and behaviour that their pupils bring with them into the classroom.[34] Girls get on well at primary school. They rate high according to its 'feminine' values and rules, and achieve well. But they are already beginning to realize more about their present and future roles through its teaching.

A Secondary Education

The span of years at secondary school covers a time of important events and crucial decisions. The advent of puberty and increasing maturity begin to emphasize the distractions of sexuality. The adult world holds out a wealth of temptations but reproves those who respond to them too quickly. As adolescents, girls and boys at school are in a situation characterized by an uncertain and ambivalent status. Friends and interests are quickly made and lost. Some school subjects are selected and others dropped, and the choice of alternatives becomes narrower. Decisions are made about further education and jobs, and working futures come into clearer focus. Social activities start to proliferate and boyfriends occupy a large space in the minds and often in the activities of many girls. Attitudes, beliefs and values begin to settle into an appropriate pattern, not fixed but constantly re-forming, out of which emerge the contours of a life-style. School and family life do not tell the whole story and the literature published about youth cultures in the seventies and eighties began to fill in the gaps about other important aspects of young people's lives. Cultural studies looked at subcultures and their shared meanings, values and beliefs, and in the case of youth, the challenge and resistance they presented to the dominant culture. The initial emphasis was on male youth culture,[35] but this imbalance was retrieved by the Cultural Studies Department in Birmingham who put a special focus on the lives of girls and young women.[36]

Boys' and Girls' Subjects

One way that the secondary school plays a part in instilling meanings and values is through nudging pupils' choices in different directions. This has been clearly illustrated by the range of subjects available to, and taken up by, boys and girls. Although efforts have been made towards equal choice, there may already have been some subject divergence at primary school, and in secondary school the differences may become more entrenched. In the mid 1970s, a study carried out in secondary schools in Britain illustrated the strongly gendered nature of school subjects. So-called 'male' subjects were chemistry, physics, geography, maths, handicraft and technical crafts; while 'female' subjects were art, language, biology, history, music and housecrafts.[37] Since this time, efforts have been made to encourage more equal participation in every subject, and the National Curriculum has made many of these compulsory for both sexes in the early years of secondary school. Nevertheless, there are certain subjects that can still be broadly classified into 'girls' subjects' and 'boys' subjects' by virtue of the continuing predominance of girls or boys respectively in these.

Traditionally, 'girls' subjects' have included the 'arts', and, more exclusively, cookery, needlework, typing and commerce. 'Boys' subjects' are scientific and technical, involving mathematical problem-solving and analysis, as well as the practical skills of woodwork and metalwork. Both boys and girls tend to avoid those subjects which are the more exclusive domain of the other sex, but while girls often reject maths and science because they see them as being too difficult and technical for them to understand, boys reject domestic subjects as simply irrelevant for them. Being seen as 'female subjects', they have little or negative status for a boy. Whereas some boys do take and succeed in arts subjects when they choose to do so, girls are viewed as being relatively incapable of succeeding in 'boys' subjects', especially the exclusive ones like metalwork and engineering. Their relative success at science, although high according to the figures of passes at GCSE and A level, impinges little on either the sexual division of scientific labour or the conventional stereotype. Research by Waldon and Walkerdine[38] into the area of girls and maths showed that even if girls were performing adequately in maths, they were less likely to be entered for examination. This suggests assumptions made on the part of teachers in their assessments of girls and boys were implicitly discriminating against the girls.

Girls Into Science and Technology (GIST),[39] was a four year action research project carried out with the aim of exploring the reasons that girls do not take science subjects and careers, and incorporating various strategies whereby girls were positively encouraged to do so. Although there was some success in reducing pupils' general gender-stereotyped attitudes, gender differences in attitudes to particular subjects were preserved, and girls showed no

significant take-up of science and crafts subjects. Although awareness was clearly raised, it suggests the need to try different kinds of
intervention. One problem is that the school is only one area in
girls' lives, and there are a multitude of other important influences
constantly interacting with their own immediate gender concepts. It
would be interesting to set up a comparative action research project
on boys taking languages, which has been a relatively neglected area.
Britain as a nation is notoriously arrogant about assuming that
everyone should understand English, and this is reflected in the small
numbers of boys who choose to do modern languages at school.[40]

It is not surprising that many girls have relatively little interest in
or understanding of scientific or technical subjects. Their lack of
experience of these at home, the restrictions on developing the
independence associated with analytical abilities, and the apparent
non-scientific nature of women's adult role has contributed to this.
Technical toys have always been reserved for boys, and when
something is constructed or repaired at home, it is usually boys who
are taken aside to be taught, rather than girls. This exclusive
knowledge has made women dependent on men inside as well as
outside the home. Most of the gadgets that women use in everyday
domestic life are put together and break down on fairly elementary
scientific principles. Yet few women know what these are, or how
to use them to repair or improve things. For most, science remains
an abstract mystery, full of apparatus and experiments peculiar to a
school laboratory, and apparently meaningless to girls' future lives
at work or at home. In the intervening time since I wrote about the
first Ealing girls, some changes in educational organization, increasing awareness through the efforts of feminists, and changes in the
ideas and aspirations of girls themselves have resulted in more girls
going into areas of science and technology.

The computer and computer games have revolutionized aspects
of children's play. This has been taken on by both girls and boys,
although it is boys who are most commonly seen obsessively
playing on a Nintendo. Word processing has taken over from
typewriting for girls, and as such has brought women closer to the
world of computing skills, although without the appropriate training
a girl may easily feel intimidated by what she sees as the scientific
or mathematical demands of computer use. In many ways word

processing has de-skilled secretarial work. Learning computing and its related analysis needs keyboard skills and to some extent has brought boys and men closer to the world of the typist, although few would consider extending this skill to obtaining a typing job.

To effect any change it is also necessary to challenge the discrimination and segregation in the occupational structure. Making it possible for girls and boys to study all subjects is of no use unless the jobs that the subjects relate to are seen to be accessible, suitable and acceptable for both. If this condition is not fulfilled the exclusion and inequalities will continue but with curriculum restrictions removed, and the reasons for boys' and girls' continuing rejection of the other sex's more exclusive subjects will provide even more justification for the assumption of 'natural' aptitudes and abilities.

When I was writing in the 1970s, the school curriculum was often organized on the basis of sexist assumptions about subject suitability. This deprived many girls and boys of their freedom of choice by assuming that they would not want to study certain subjects, and by arranging the timetable on the basis of those assumptions.[41] For example, some girls described how they could do either art or technical drawing, but not both. Subjects like woodwork and metalwork were similarly set against subjects like cookery and needlework. Today, school timetables are less rigidly organized and, in theory at least, there are more opportunities, for instance, for girls to take craft and technical subjects, and boys to take subjects associated with domestic science and office skills. One girl commented in 1991: 'It's more acceptable for women to work now and for girls to take subjects that were thought to be boys' subjects, and the other way round.' However, the numbers of boys or girls who take subjects more usually associated with the opposite sex are as yet fairly low. This was even more apparent in the largely Asian school I visited:

This is a school for equal opportunity. I think they should encourage more girls to do double science. There's so many boys, hardly no girls. I couldn't believe it, only four girls in science. It's ridiculous! And the girls are quiet and won't put their hands up if they don't know the boys.

SOPHIA

But as girls move into technical subjects, care has still to be taken to ensure that they are given the same opportunity as boys to develop skills. For example, in subjects demanding manual dexterity boys tend to be given access to the more complex tools and are consequently enabled to produce more advanced pieces of work than girls in the same class. A double standard is then created whereby girls are praised for the obviously less sophisticated objects they manage to produce. It is therefore also necessary to ensure that teachers are not unconsciously applying a different standard to girls and boys in any of the more sex-typed subjects, and to provide opportunities for both girls and boys to use common skills in the occupational world. Segregation of education has channelled girls of all backgrounds into courses leading to devalued and underpaid jobs. False beliefs in ability differences based on sex have blocked many avenues for girls, and in so doing have justified and perpetuated the subsequent economic discrimination. In opening up new areas of work care must be taken that women are not once again used to fill up the lowest levels. It can be argued that computing has been an innovatory new area which is open to both sexes, yet it is still men who occupy the higher or more responsible positions.

Over the last twenty years or so since the first Ealing study, there have been changes and improvements in the range of subjects available for both sexes. For instance, it is not so outrageous for girls to do woodwork and metalwork, and a significant number now take CDT (craft, design and technology). But they may be well in the minority, or not there at all:

> For CDT – most say it doesn't matter what sex you are, if you've got the ability. But two or three boys say we can't do it. They say they can do it because they're boys, and they mean it. You get annoyed sometimes. It's not all the boys, most of them are all right, but one or two are really arrogant. I took media but I wanted to do CDT. I held back because I thought all boys would be in there, but it turns out there are some girls in it as well.

SALLY

My friend wanted to be a graphic designer, and is really good at art and she did CDT. But she moved out after a few weeks because she was the only girl there. She got on with the boys but she felt that when they sat in groups she would be by herself. She just felt odd being the only girl, so she moved. It's all boys now.

HARPINDER

On the boys' side, they can now take subjects previously seen as the sole preserve of girls. Home economics, which incorporated cookery and needlework, is now divided into food technology and textiles, (or similar names) and child development is taught in many schools. Boys do take these but whether they will see them as a career option is another question. On the other hand it can be argued that many domestic aspects of these subjects are very relevant to men's future lives as husbands/partners, and if girls' expectations of them are also taken into account, then they should be made compulsory. Unlike some boys' attitudes to girls in predominantly 'boys' subjects', girls are far more accommodating to boys:

A lot of the boys take child development, and a lot of them get a lot of stick for it, but I think it's good that they take it. And the ones that took it didn't seem to care what the other boys said. I thought that was good. It was mainly the boys that did that, all the girls were saying it was really good. They gave them more encouragement than the boys did. And a lot of the boys went to work in nurseries as well, and they loved it. I think it is changing. I think boys are more open-minded about their subjects.

TERESA

Some girls suggested that boys choose 'girls' subjects' because they think they are a 'soft option', although work experience may change their ideas on this:

I don't think there are really girls' and boys' subjects, because in child development you might think just girls would go into it but we've got boys as well. We had a lot of boys working in a school for work experience. I think they were interested but some of them said they didn't want to work with kids after they found out what it was like. They found it hard work! To them it was a bit harder maybe because girls spend more time with babies and they're more used to it.

DENISE

Laura was attending a school where the majority of pupils are Asian. Although gender roles within the Asian community in Britain have changed slightly, many boys and men still endorse traditional domestic activities. The ones that she describes certainly appear to do so:

> More girls go into the boys' subjects. Boys think they're too mature or macho to go into girls' things like cooking and stuff. It's silly. When I came here there was just one boy in my textiles group and then after a few months he just left it because he thought it was too girlish. In food nutrition there's only four boys. They don't like cooking when we have a practical, they don't want to cook. They won't put on an apron or anything like that. Stupid. I think they just think it's for women to cook. They have to keep up a certain kind of image. But girls can do anything, they don't care what other people think.

Greater resistance by Asian boys was confirmed by Harpinder, but she found that her own assumptions were revealed:

> Boys don't take food studies or textiles, you never see them do that. They feel that someone will tease them if they do, that's why. But a boy from this school is doing his work experience in a school with little kids. I thought that was nice but I was really shocked. No boy has done that. All the boys apply to go into mechanics and things.

Sport is a subject within which the 'gender' labels have changed and it is now seen as much a girls' subject as a boys'. Football is played by both sexes in many schools, and in the Ealing schools, girls had formed their own teams. However, I heard no reports of boys playing netball or hockey.

> The first school I went to, I was the first girl that played in the boys' football team. When my sister went in it they kept winning, so they had this big thing about the men's FA banning us from

playing and all that. So she got on the telly and that about it. Now they've got a women's world cup. She might even want to do that when she gets older – professional football. She's quite good.

LUCY

It's mainly in sports, I mean, football is still mainly boys. I'm really interested in football and recently I was the only girl that was doing it. I actually forced my friend to do it with me. We had fun. Because we were the only girls there, we were expected not to know anything. When we started charging forward they were really surprised. But I still feel there's girls' sports and boys' sports.

HARWINDER

In encouraging girls and boys to make less stereotyped subject choices it would be helpful to have equal numbers of men and women teaching them. This takes us back to the subjects chosen for teacher training, and thus back to those subjects taken at school. It can be a self-perpetuating process. There is really no logical reason why men cannot teach child development, food technology and textiles or why there are so few women teaching craft, design and technology courses, manual crafts, and science in general. The question is why they do not choose to do so.

I think all of the CDT teachers are male. I think if we had a female teacher then there would be more people thinking, well if she's doing it it's all right. A lot of girls go into it anyway but there's loads of boys in those classes. But it's not their fault if women don't get into CDT or whatever. If they want it, they should really go for it. And male teachers should teach home economics. There should be both. It would be nice to see a male teacher doing it so that it's not seen as a woman's thing.

ALICE

Gender divisions defy logic, as we have seen, and are used to differentiate, order, and support a sense of contrast between the sexes. It would go some way to instil a sense of neutrality around these still sex-typed subjects if children became accustomed to both sexes teaching the same variety of subjects with equal status and capability.

138

Other areas of the school curriculum leave much to be desired in terms of their content. History, for example, has been basically represented as that of men, written by men. Women's history has been largely ignored, although there has been much published since the early 1970s to fill this gap.[42] Nevertheless, conventional attitudes and cutting school costs have no doubt conspired to prevent these books penetrating the schoolroom, apart from the more acceptable history of the suffragette movement. English literature may cover the better-known women writers, but often omits discussion of the position of women at the time, and may ignore many lesser-known female authors. The increase in feminist publishing houses; the publication of women authors from a variety of class and ethnic backgrounds; the republishing of novels by women written in the past; and recognition of the talents and importance of modern women writers (the black American writer Toni Morrison won the 1993 Nobel Prize for Literature), is helping to redress this balance. Many of these books contain heroines who are no longer portrayed as passive and ineffectual, and taking action only for personal or destructive reasons. However, they too may find it difficult to get into the syllabus. In addition, the cuts in funds to educational authorities have meant that schools can no longer buy many new books or other facilities, which obviously makes more egalitarian changes in curriculum content very difficult.

In the intervening period between the early 1970s and the 1990s, there was a significant expansion in the teaching of social science subjects in schools. School students were able to take, for instance, subjects like sociology at GCSE, O and A level, and some form of social and community studies have been a regular part of the curriculum in many schools. These subjects provide the space for discussion of the position and role of women, even if it is limited to examining aspects of work and the family. Many girls (and boys) have become aware of gender issues through these subjects. There is a danger that the emphasis of the National Curriculum on traditional subjects, and on science in particular, will result in less time being available for exploring more humanitarian issues in which young people can learn to question and challenge things that may otherwise be taken as 'natural', right and unchangable.

Teachers' Attitudes and Expectations

If it's moving furniture, they'd ask the boys. They'd pick the strong boys. There was an instance like that once. A teacher came in and said she wanted to move some tables or something, and said 'Can I have some volunteers to move some things?' A lot of girls put their hands up as well as boys, and she picked the strong boys, even though there were quite a few strong girls. They don't treat boys and girls differently in any major way, only little details that you can't really notice. If you think about it afterwards you realize that it was different.

CATHERINE

Every teacher is a former pupil. Every teacher has already been through the process of learning the roles for each sex. Therefore each reflects consciously and unconsciously their own attitudes and expectations in their treatment of their pupils. This has implications for both sex and class. If teachers ultimately expect less from girls than from boys, and less from working class than from middle class children, these expectations are picked up by pupils with devastating effects.

Research carried out on elementary school children in America showed that teacher expectations could have a crucial effect on pupil performance.[43] In this experiment a number of teachers were told at the beginning of a school session that certain of their pupils were going to show marked intellectual improvement in the coming year. Unknown to the teachers, these pupils were randomly selected rather than chosen on the basis of their ability. At the end of the year it was found that the children for whom intellectual growth had been predicted had indeed made dramatic gains against their measured I Q, as compared with a control group of children. Therefore, the teachers had successfully passed on their expectations to these children and had probably given them more attention and encouragement. Although such research methods are always open to criticism, the implications of the 'self-fulfilling prophecy' shown here cannot be denied, and the expectations of teachers at any level of education will doubtless have equivalent effects on those being taught.

Some of the Ealing girls talked in 1972 of ways that they had noticed their treatment differed from that of boys. Teachers seemed to be more sarcastic to boys, and more respectful to girls. ('Boys can take it better.') Girls were expected to be more tidy in their ways and in their work, neater in handwriting and the presentation of material. Boys, however, could get away with messy books and untidy behaviour. This is a subtle form of restriction of expression, and may develop into an obsession with form rather than content.[44] The Ealing schoolgirls in 1991 pointed out ways in which they too thought that boys were sometimes blamed and sometimes let off more easily than girls. Both consequences seemed to result from the feminine gender expectations that are applied to girls, such as being quiet and good:

> Boys can get away with much more than we can sometimes. If they're sitting in a lesson and something happens, they always say to the girls, 'How could you?' and give us a lecture, but they expect it with boys. We only get the lecture because they expect different from us. They expect us to be quiet and do our work.
>
> KIM

> Some teachers are like that. They say girls talk too much, or boys cause too much problems. Some teachers let the girls get away with it. I think they pick on the boys more. I don't know why because the boys do the same thing as girls but in different ways and they get in trouble.
>
> LEAH

Michelle Stanworth studied A level students and her research suggested that differences between girls and boys were emphasized more by male than female teachers.[45] Teachers tended to play on the contrasting features or characteristics of sex and gender roles in the classroom, and pupils suggested that teachers were more attentive and sympathetic to boys than to girls. Both male and female teachers gave more attention to boys' needs, whether this was in telling them off or helping them with their work. Many of the Ealing girls made similar observations:

> I think boys get a lot more attention in class, with both sex teachers, boys always do. Sometimes they keep shouting out and

the teacher thinks 'I'll go to them first.' It's true, you can really see it, boys get a lot more attention. There's teachers that give the girls more attention but in most classes it's the boys.

CAROLINE

Girls and boys are not really treated differently, but the boys can be a bit of a pain. Some of them need a bit more attention than what us girls do. They talk too much and the rest of it.

PAULINE

Male teachers usually favour the girls more. We are treated a bit more gently. The male teachers usually let us off. So I don't think the teachers treat us the same. The female teachers do though. They know how they are treated, so they try to treat everyone the same. It's mainly the male teachers.

HARWINDER

The relationship between any pupil and teacher can have important consequences for work performance, and one male maths teacher's treatment of girls appeared to be having such an affect:

He treats us different than the boys. He shouts at us for no reason. I just stay quiet in the lessons. I can't get on with him, then if I can't get on with him I don't want to take my book up to him. I can't ask him questions if I'm stuck or anything. I'm frightened he might shout at me.

MADHU

One of the Ealing girls, who wanted to do a degree in engineering, was taking the technology option and therefore in a traditionally 'boys' subject'. She commented on how the boys tended to dominate the class:

There's four girls in technology, I'm one of them, and about eighteen boys. Everyone did CDT in second and third year so I suppose the boys have got used to having girls in the lessons, so we don't get teased now. I don't feel isolated but I suppose they always get in, the boys, they ask questions. But if you push as well you're all right. The teacher said to my parents on parents' evening that I should ask more because the boys get ahead and jump out. But I'm quite shy so I don't. The girls tend to stay together. I think you get on better then, you get more done. Sometimes the boys are distracting. They chuck things round the room and try to hit you with rulers and squirt water. In technology the teacher is in and out so they get up to what they can. But you can still get on with your work, it's all right, everyone is at different stages and has got different things to do.

HARRIET

Rupinder was doing double science, and finding she was rather neglected compared to the boys in her class:

In my double science there's about three girls out of the whole class, which is a bit bad, and the boys just take over totally. Sir notices it as well, but he's just as bad. He's a really nice teacher. I like his lessons, but he likes messing around with the boys.

It is around adolescence that girls are struggling to find out what sort of people they are, and what they want to become. They are very tuned in to the things that will bring social approval, and quickly pick up cues from inside and outside school. Their composite expression of 'femininity' can change from moment to moment. However they view the advice, treatment and curriculum given by their teachers, they still absorb the form and the gender-differentiated assumptions that these contain.

Sexism, Racism and School Policy

Obviously, people's attitudes will find some expression in the classroom, and this will be the case with sexism and racism. Many schools, and certainly those I visited in Ealing, had taken on the anti-sexist and anti-racist policies instigated by the ILEA for schools in the early 1980s. They clearly worked positively in that there was a heightened awareness of sexism and racism which made any overt expression taboo. Whereas in the early 1970s the Ealing girls did not have 'sexism' prominently in their vocabulary, in the 1990s it has achieved common usage. Several of the Ealing girls were well aware of the nature of, and sanctions against, sexism:

I think they've realized that someone who is sexist, in these times, you get the name of being sexist, so I don't think they do it because they'd be called sexist. They've calmed down. It's not seen as being macho. They say 'Well, who does he think he is?' You get a name if you do that.

SALLY

Sometimes we have PE teachers coming in to train. We were playing softball with one of them and it's a really hard ball and it came to me and I tried to catch it but dropped it. He said 'Stupid girl!' I said it hurt my hand but he said that I didn't try. It was really weird. We had a sit-down as a protest.

FIONA

They're not sexist. If you want to try and do something that maybe wasn't a stereotyped thing for a girl to do, they'll give you all the backing up to help you to do what you want.

VANESSA

Research on teachers[46] found that women teachers were more sympathetic to sexual equality than male teachers; and that those working in London tended to be more feminist than those in other big cities.

As far as racism is concerned, incidence is going to vary greatly according to the area and the school. The black Ealing girls in this research could think of few incidences of overt racism in their schools.

I think the teachers, if they were racist, hide it really well.

Laura is a West Indian girl who is one of a minority of white and Afro-Caribbean girls in her school.

It's mainly Asians in this school but I prefer it, I get on with them more. The teachers weren't that bad at my other school, but the teachers in this school, because they're mixed, it's Asians and blacks, they relate to us more. In the other school they were all white teachers. They would teach the white children and forget all about me.

LAURA

For the Ealing Asian girls, racism was not an overt problem because children from Asian families made up the majority of pupils at school.

There is, nevertheless, a continuing level of racism expressed in different ways within schools, against different ethnic and religious groups. Research looking at racism against young people of mixed race found that racism was more often reported by boys and young people from working class families. It also revealed that 'Contrary to what is believed, racist abuse was reported to be more frequent and was experienced as much more wounding in primary than secondary school.'[47] There are also plenty of other ways, such as through the hidden curriculum of teaching processes, school organization and other factors, by which racist attitudes can infiltrate school life. In this respect, it has been shown how teachers' attitudes can discriminate against black girls by denying the validity of their own culture and experience and how this has contributed to educational institutions regarding them (rather than the institutions) as the problem.[48]

Mixed or Single Sex Schools

> My old school was a girls' school and we couldn't do things like woodwork because they were boys' subjects, and in all-boys schools they don't do cooking. But in this school, because it's mixed, you get a chance to do it, and the boys get a chance to do cooking. We can do woodwork. So we can get a chance to know what each other is doing. You learn more. You don't get to mix as much in a single sex school, so it's better going to this kind of school.
>
> LAURA

The majority of schools today are co-educational and employ men and women teachers, but the issue of mixed versus single sex schools remains unresolved. Both types have their advantages and their disadvantages and the evidence supporting either is inconsistent. In single sex girls' schools, for instance, it has been said that girls find it easier to concentrate, without the distraction presented by boys. Science is taught by women and is not so blatantly a 'boy's subject' as it is in co-educational schools where men usually teach the scientific and technical subjects. Women also hold all the positions of authority in contrast to the staff structure found in mixed schools which puts men in the top departmental posts and invariably makes them heads of school, and leaves women in the lower ranks.

However, there are many disadvantages: for instance, all-girls schools are often very insular and protected places, in which girls learn to perform well in their schoolwork, but are left inadequately equipped to deal with the mixed social world outside. Many girls recognize the artificiality of this environment and want to get out. Also, in spite of the increasing provision of science subjects for girls who wish to study them, the absence of boys leads school head teachers to assume that it would be irrelevant to provide the facilities for what are usually 'male' subjects like woodwork, metal-work and technical drawing. Therefore the opportunity for doing these does not even arise in all-girls schools.

On the other hand it is possible that co-education draws attention to and thereby reinforces the boundaries between the sexes. The continual presence of the opposite sex and of assumptions about the differences between the sexes implied by 'exclusive' subjects, at a time of self-consciousness and need for identity, may contribute towards maintaining the separation of the sexes. Also, the false incompatibility between female sexual attractiveness and intelligence may be emphasized in mixed schools. It has been suggested[49] that co-educational schools are more like boys' schools than a mid-way compromise between girls' and boys' schools. The debate around this issue still carries on, however, and it is difficult to weigh up whether mixed or single sex schools are of different and greater value to girls in pursuing their academic and social education.[50] The 1991 Ealing girls interviewed were happy to be in a mixed rather than a single sex school, because it is more like the real world, and they get to know better what boys are like. While educators and parents tend to be more concerned about the implications for their daughters' school performance, this is not an issue for the girls themselves, who only see the social advantages.

I'd definitely come to a mixed school. You've got to get to know how to communicate with men and boys, and how they work. If you went into a job where it was mixed you wouldn't know how to relate to them. At least I know how they work, how they think, and how to react to what they say.

KIM

I wouldn't like a girls school. You get a lot more bitchiness. I think girls like being around boys now. I think most boys and girls get on quite well. I'm not sure about other schools. As far as me and most of the boys go, we're just friends and that's it, and we get on well as friends. It's nice having boy friends. I've got a few close boy friends and if I'm going out with somebody and I wanted to ask something, I'll go and ask a boy who I think will give me the right advice. It's nice to know somebody's there with another point of view. From the way you're friends, you can know whether you can trust them or not. There's a few boys in my class who we go out with on Saturdays and it's nice because it's a laugh but you're not tied down or anything.

RACHEL

Parental and cultural restrictions on Asian girls talking and mixing with boys gives a sharper edge to their attending a mixed school. Many of the Ealing Asian girls in 1991 felt strongly that being in a mixed school is a definite advantage because it covers up the extent to which they are interacting with boys. If they went to a single sex school they would not be able to talk to a boy in the street without getting into trouble with their parents.

If I had gone to an all-girls school I don't think I would have had the opportunity to mix with boys. My dad would have said, 'You go to an all-girls school, so why are you talking to a boy?' Going to this school, there's a lot of boys around and I can talk. If they knock up or phone up, to see if we've done our homework, my mum doesn't mind. We're doing it in front of her you see.

REHANA

I reckon if I went to an all-girls school I'd be desperate to see boys. I'd be a little terror! But with a mixed school you learn to treat boys equally to you and the boys learn to treat you equally. When you go to a job you know how to treat them then. I prefer a mixed school. Girls at single sex schools end up running away

147

They're with girls all the time and as soon as they see a boy they want him, they become desperate, and run off with him. That wouldn't happen in a mixed school.

USHMA

I'm glad I'm in a mixed school, now I can understand boys' points of view. When we're in class I can understand what they feel as well as myself. It's better to know the boys' views so that I can act in situations.

INDERJIT

CONTRADICTIONS

There are a range of contradictions in the area of girls' education. The most overreaching general contradiction is that between the professed principle of equality of education for all pupils, when there is still a hidden curriculum in most institutions that discriminates by sex, race and class. Since this book was first published in the mid 1970s there has been a plethora of writing and research published that reveals and examines in detail the many ways that the school and education in general discriminate against girls and women.[51]

As we have seen, there was a clear contradiction after the Second World War between the traditional emphasis on a domestic education for girls, while there was an increasing stress on education for all according to age, aptitude and ability as expressed in the 1944 Education Act. However, the contradictions were different for girls depending on class. From the fifties, middle class girls were being encouraged (mainly in grammar schools) to go for higher education and careers. At the same time, these careers would come up against the barrier of marriage and motherhood, due to a lingering ideology that expected women to stay at home with their children. For working class girls, the contradiction was between the implicit academic nature of school, and the domestic role that they were officially being educated for. The concern of many of the 1972 Ealing girls with doing 'something worthwhile' was not provided within the curriculum.

Today the ideology that supported women's domestic role has been considerably modified. Education for girls is no longer officially linked with an assumption of their future domestic roles, to help them to become 'good' wives and mothers. It is no longer frowned upon for women with young children to work, it is seen as an acceptable aspect of women's lives today, and economically desirable. However, this is contradicted by the lack of help with child-care provided by the state which makes combining work and home a continual struggle, especially for lone parents.

At school, changes in the curriculum have increased the opportunity for both boys and girls to do subjects that used to be thought of as mainly appropriate for the opposite sex, like woodwork, technology, and home economics. Although the take-up is slow, this in theory would provide the means for both sexes to enter less stereotyped areas of work. However, this is contradicted by the contraction in the job market caused by the recession, so that, for instance, men will protect their traditional occupations rather than throw them open. Girls who have trained as carpenters and plumbers, or achieved an engineering degree find work hard to obtain. On the issue of co-education, more contradictions lie in obtaining better academic results through single sex schooling, at the cost of social benefits and increased facilities and opportunities for both sexes to participate in joint activities.

The National Curriculum emphasizes links with the labour market at a time when employment is declining. This combination has the effect of narrowing (rather than focusing) opportunities, and placing particular constraints by gender, class and race. Some researchers have already observed an increasing disjunction between school and work in the context of rising unemployment.[52] Whereas many of the Ealing girls have responded to the current employment situation by accepting the need for more qualifications, in other parts of the country working class girls may see training and qualifications as even more irrelevant if there are clearly no jobs to be had. However, if the Ealing girls are any indication, there is still determination and hope that they can find a way through the various contradictions that still characterize girls' and women's education.

NOTES

CHAPTER 3

1. Pearl Jephcott, *Girls Growing Up*, Faber & Faber, 1942.
2. Newsom Report, *Half Our Future*, 1963.
3. DES, The National Curriculum 5–16, A Consultation Document, Department of Education and Science/Welsh Office, July 1987.
4. This was discussed in much more detail in Bernard Coard's pamphlet on *How the West Indian Child is made Educationally Sub-normal in the British School System*, New Beacon Books Ltd, 1971.
5. S. Dex, *Black and White School Leavers: the First Five Years of Work*, Research Paper no. 33, Department of Employment, 1982.
6. Farrukh Dondy, 'The Black Explosion in Schools', *Race Today*, February 1974.
7. Farrukh Dondy, op. cit.
8. Alison Kelly, 'Gender Roles at Home and School', *British Journal of Sociology of Education*, 3(3), 1982.
9. J. Gaskell, *Gender Matters from School to Work*, Open University Press, 1991.
10. C. Griffin, *Typical Girls? Young Women from School to the Job Market*, Routledge & Kegan Paul, 1985.
11. G. Chanan and L. Gilchrist, *What School is For*, Methuen, 1974, p. 27.
12. See also Ann Oakley, *Sex, Gender and Society*, Temple Smith, 1973, chapter 5; Eleanor Maccoby, 'Sex Differences in Intellectual Functioning', in Eleanor Maccoby (ed.), *The Development of Sex Differences*, Tavistock, 1967; and Sara Delamont, *Sex Roles and the School*, Routledge, 1990.
13. J. W. B. Douglas, *The Home and the School*, Panther, 1967.
14. Current research shows that teenage girls smoke more cigarettes and take more drugs than teenage boys, which will, amongst other things, also impair their capacity for schoolwork. (H. Parker and F. Measham, at Manchester University, unpublished research reported in the *Independent on Sunday*, 10 October 1993.)
15. M. Mead, *Male and Female*, Penguin, 1950.

16. K. Clarricoates, *Gender and Power in the Primary School*, Polity, 1989.
17. Girls may therefore experience a 'fear of success' which hinders their performance, and interacts with the reinforcing belief that academic success is unimportant for a girl anyway. This kind of conflict was more salient in the sixties and seventies and was described by Matina Horner, 'Woman's Will to Fail', *Psychology Today*, 3, no. 6, 1969.
18. Cynthia Cockburn describes some of these reactions in her study of youth training schemes, in *Two Track Training*, Macmillan, 1987.
19. See also Eleanor Maccoby, op. cit.
20. L. A. Serbin, described in S. Delamont, *Sex Roles and the School*, Routledge, 2nd edition, 1990.
21. This parallels Brian Jackson's finding that fathers tend to differentiate more than mothers between sons and daughters, and to hold more stereotyped expectations from them. Brian Jackson, *Fatherhood*, Allen & Unwin, 1984.
22. J. W. B. Douglas, op cit.
23. Heidi Safia Mirza, *Young, Female and Black*, Routledge, 1992.
24. Also endorsed by A. Brah and R. Minhas, 'Structural Racism or Cultural Difference: Schooling for Asian Girls', in Gaby Weiner (ed.), *Just a Bunch of Girls*, Open University Press, 1985.
25. Alison Kelly, op. cit.
26. Ivan Illich, 'After De-Schooling – What?' *Social Policy*, September to October 1971, reprinted as a pamphlet by the Writers & Readers Publishing Cooperative, 1974.
27. See G. Chanan and L. Gilchrist, op. cit., in which this problem is discussed in greater detail.
28. See H. Rosen, *Language and Class: A Critical Look at the Theories of Basil Bernstein*, Falling Wall Press, 1972, for discussion of this and other questions.
29. Documented in research by Sue Lees, *Sugar and Spice*, Penguin, 1993.
30. J. Miller, *More Has Meant Women: The Feminisation of Schooling*, The London File Papers: from the Institute of Education, The Tufnell Press, 1992.
31. J. W. B. Douglas, op. cit.
32. N. Frazier and M. Sadker, *Sexism in School and Society*, Harper and Row, 1973
33. Sara Delamont, op. cit.
34. K. Clarricoates, op. cit.
35. P. Willis, *Learning to Labour*, Saxon House, 1977; D. Robins and P. Cohen, *Knuckle Sandwich: Growing Up in the Working Class City*, Penguin, 1978; P. Corrigan, *Schooling the Smash Street Kids*, Macmillan, 1979.

36. For example: A. McRobbie and J. Garber, 'Girls and Subcultures', in S. Hall and T. Jefferson (eds.), *Resistance through Ritual: Youth Subcultures in Post-war Britain*, Centre for Contemporary Cultural Studies, Hutchinson, 1985; A. McRobbie, 'Working Class Girls and the Culture of Femininity', in *Women Take Issue: Aspects of Women's Subordination*, Women's Studies Group, Centre for Contemporary Cultural Studies, (ed.), 1978; V. Walkerdine, 'One Day my Prince Will Come: Young Girls and the Preparation for Adolescent Sexuality', in A. McRobbie and M. Nava (eds.) *Gender and Generation*, Macmillan, 1984; C. Griffin, *Typical Girls? Young Women from School to the Job Market*, Routledge & Kegan Paul, 1985.

37. M. B. Ormerod, 'Subject Preference and Choice in Co-educational and Single Sex Secondary Schools', *British Journal of Educational Psychology*, no. 45, 1975.

38. R. Walden and V. Walkerdine, *Girls and Mathematics: From Primary to Secondary Schooling*, Bedford Way Papers no. 24, University of London Institute of Education, 1985.

39. J. Whyte, *Girls Into Science and Technology: The Story of a Project*, Routledge & Kegan Paul, 1986.

40. See Bob Powell, *Boys, Girls and Languages in Schools*, CILT, 1986.

41. At this time, one survey of 587 mixed schools discovered that 50 per cent had some subjects only open for boys, and 49 per cent had subjects exclusive to girls. C. Benn and B. Simon, *Half-way There: Report on the British Comprehensive School Reform*, London, 1970.

42. For example, Sheila Rowbotham, *Hidden from History*, Pluto Press, 1973; and *Women, Resistance and Revolution*, Penguin, 1974.

43. R. Rosenthal and L. Jacobson, 'Pygmalion in the Classroom: An Excerpt', in M. Silberman (ed.), *The Experience of Schooling*, Holt, Rinehart & Winston, New York, 1971.

44. See H. Rosen, op. cit., who criticizes this emphasis in middle class education.

45. Michelle Stanworth, *Gender and Schooling*, Unwin Hyman, 1981.

46. A. Kelly, 'Traditionalists and Trendies', *British Educational Research Journal*, 11(2), 1985.

47. B. Tizard and A. Phoenix, *Black, White or Mixed Race*, Routledge, 1993.

48. B. Bryan *et al.*, *The Heart of the Race: Black Women's Lives in Britain*, Virago, 1985.

49. J. Shaw, 'Some Implications of Sex-segregated Education', unpublished paper, given at the British Sociological Association Conference, 1974.

50. R. Deem (ed.), *Coeducation Reconsidered*, Open University Press, 1984.

51. Such as A. M. Wolpe, *Some Processes in Sexist Education*, Women's

Research and Resource Centre, 1977; E. Byrne, *Women and Education*, Tavistock, 1978; R. Deem, *Women and Schooling*, Routledge & Kegan Paul, 1978; R. Deem, *Schooling for Women's Work*, Routledge & Kegan Paul, 1980; D. Spender and E. Sarah (eds.), *Learning to Lose*, The Women's Press, 1980; D. Spender, *Invisible Women: The Schooling Scandal*, Writers and Readers, 1982; Whyte, J., R. Deem, L. Kant and M. Cruickshank (eds.), *Girl Friendly Schooling*, Methuen, 1985; V. Walkerdine, *Schoolgirl Fictions*, Verso, 1990.

52. Claire Wallace, 'From Girls and Boys to Women and Men: the Social Reproduction of Gender', in M. Arnot and G. Weiner (eds.), *Gender and the Politics of Schooling*, Hutchinson, in association with the Open University, 1987.

A NICE JOB FOR A GIRL

1972:

I think some girls don't want jobs what boys do, because you do not see women or girls driving buses nor trains, girls do not do anything mechanical. And you do not see women being butchers, nor being porters, etc., because women and girls are not strong enough to do men's jobs.

JEAN

. . . my exam results weren't all that good this year. I went to the [careers] adviser and they said, 'Well, what do you want to do?' – the big question. So I said, well I wanted to be a doctor. 'Oh,' he said, and we'd talked about it before, and I don't think I've got – I think I'd have to be really brainy to get in, because I'm a girl. My teacher suggested radiologist.

MARGARET

I've got a job already . . . I'm supposed to be an office junior, but it don't sound much like it. I take a few calls on the telephone . . . then I can make tea or coffee, whatever I fancy . . . I would have liked to have been an actress. I've always wanted to be an actress. I always wanted to go to drama school, but my mum and dad just couldn't afford it and I knew that, and really all the people I spoke to about acting as a career, they said really the best bet would be to get a place in drama school, but I couldn't get the money to do that, my mum and dad couldn't get the money to do that, so I just thought, oh blimey, if the only hope is a drama school, then it isn't worth it.

MICHELLE

1991:

I'd like to be a vet preferably, but I've been told that it's harder
for women to get into medical college than men, but I'm willing
to try. I was told that on the work experience. I've always
wanted from a young age to be a vet, but if it doesn't work out I
suppose I can be a veterinary nurse.

DEBBIE

I want to work in an airport, or travel or something – something
worthwhile, instead of sitting in a boring office doing nothing.
My mum works in an office and her manager asked me to do
receptionist, but I found it so boring, so I wouldn't want that all day.

SALLY

I think it's harder for us to get jobs because we're black and that,
but we're getting there and it's getting the same, with equal
rights. It is harder for a black person. And because you're a
woman it's even harder. A black man might just about get it, but
if you're black and a woman then it's harder.

LAURA

In the early 1970s the approach of school-leaving age found every
girl and boy looking around for a job or career. The grown-up
world of work that lay outside the sheltering security of the home
and school threatened some and enticed others with the promise of
money and independence. Girls accepted that they had to become
employed when their education was over. Even those who still saw
work as a time-filling activity before marriage were drawn through
an automatic process of careers advice and job selection. Many girls
who intended to work both after marriage and after having children,
were trying to align this with the traditional priorities of domesticity
and motherhood. They surveyed the apparent job market with
enthusiasm, anxiety or indifference, and their choice of work illustrated the way in which the range of careers open to them is
influenced by their treatment and experiences within school, and the
assumptions they made about the nature of their role. In the 1990s,
these assumptions and their occupational horizons have changed,
but much of the general landscape remains the same.

JOB EXPECTATIONS

In the Seventies

In 1972 the girls from the Ealing schools had already gathered some firm ideas about future careers, and why they thought they would like them. They covered a range of over thirty different jobs, although this is reduced if for instance the hospital jobs are considered as one. It is further reduced by the fact that just over four girls in every ten chose some sort of office work. The variations within this included personal secretary, ordinary secretary, shorthand typist, copy typist, clerk typist and junior office worker, but most girls specified shorthand typing and general office work. Office work was obviously the favourite work for girls especially in a dense urban area like London where opportunities were plentiful. The frequency of this choice is a reflection of the enormous growth in demand for office workers during this century. The popularity of office work points to its respectability and to the way it can accommodate a wide range of girls varying in their intelligence and qualifications. It may also be to some extent a characteristic of London, with its plethora of clerical and commercial work, and less dependence on industry. The next most frequently chosen jobs were as teachers, nurses, shop assistants and bank clerks – which altogether accounted for about a quarter of the job choices. Following these were girls who wished to become receptionists, telephonists, air-hostesses, hairdressers and children's nurses or nannies. The narrow range of careers so far selected took up over three-quarters of all the choices.

The West Indian Ealing girls had job expectations that were very similar to the white girls, except that they covered a narrower range. The majority chose office work and nursing, and the rest of the girls hoped to be bank clerks, teachers, social workers, children's nurses, hairdressers and models. None of them expected to work in a factory. Their distribution of job choices at this time was slightly different in that while clerical work was a similarly popular choice, none wanted to be shop assistants, receptionists or air hostesses. In the seventies the Asian community considered a relatively narrow range of jobs as appropriate for girls and women, but the Ealing

Asian girls gave job expectations that largely mirrored the choices made by their class-mates, for instance, a third said that they wanted to do some sort of office work.

The remaining job preferences, although quite numerous, were each made by only one or a few individuals, and included employment in the women's services, or as a ground hostess, kennel maid, laboratory researcher, fashion designer, computer operator, social worker, radiologist, physiotherapist, continuity girl, beautician, actress and model. Professional choices were rare and in this Asian girls were significantly different in their hopes to take up such careers as doctor, lawyer and barrister, teacher and pharmacist. These tended to be chosen by girls from India who were in the higher forms and often had fathers in professional jobs. In addition to the limitations placed on girls' working prospects in general through discrimination by sex, class and race within society, girls from Asian backgrounds could be further constrained if their family adhered to religious or cultural expectations which did not approve of girls and women working in certain environments, or at all.

All the Ealing girls' chosen careers were safely in the realms of 'women's work' (with the exception of being a doctor or barrister). There was little venturing into male or even neutral occupational territory. It was interesting that the choices bore no relation to the national distribution of women's work at this time which placed most girls and women (and especially those from working class backgrounds) in factory work, clerical work, shop work and service work (catering, etc.).[1] Working mothers in general and black women in particular have been concentrated in the worst jobs in terms of pay, conditions and status, and have provided a pool of unskilled labour for industry.

Back in the early 1940s, young working class girls would seek employment in the local factory, and move regularly from job to job within it, often covering as many as twenty jobs before they were this number of years old.[2] They did not consider office work then as this usually demanded a secondary school education. After the Second World War and during the period up to the 1970s, the occupational outlook had changed a lot for women, and girls had moved away from factory work. This was mainly the result of the availability and desirability of office employment (although opportunities differ a lot by region, and the subsequent decline in manufacturing industries has decimated many areas of production that would once have provided many jobs). In the early seventies I spoke to a careers officer with reference to this phenomenon and was told that: 'Girls who really should be working in factories making handbags and clothing are in offices.' But neither girls nor their parents would have agreed. Factory work can be dirty, and is usually given much less status than a clean, comfortable office job. Even if a girl's father or mother work in a factory themselves, they expressed hopes that their daughters would find something better. Overall, only two of the Ealing schoolgirls in 1972 expected to work in a factory. One explained 'It has good money. It is not too far away from my home and I know a lot of people who work there.' The work had little interest for her, only convenience and familiarity. The other girl was more concise. She anticipated liking 'nothing' about her future work.

In the Nineties

It might have been expected that by the early 1990s, the nature of jobs for girls might have changed a little from twenty years earlier. However, increased awareness of gender issues and equality of opportunities did not seem to have significantly expanded girls' job expectations. Like their predecessors, the Ealing girls in 1991 cited about thirty jobs they expected to go into, and the majority of these were in some kind of 'women's work'. There were, however, some significant differences. Firstly, the expectation or desire to do office work had shrunk to a fraction of its previous size. A minority of white or West Indian girls specified wanting to be a secretary or to work in an office, and jobs like receptionist and telephonist were noticeably absent. A number did, however, specifically mention that they thought they might 'end up' working in an office. The Asian girls made office work a more significant choice (14 per cent), although this was only about half the proportion of those who wanted to take up this work in 1972.

In keeping with the expansion in the financial sector in the past decade, there was a parallel increase in the proportion of girls wanting to work in banking and insurance. Perhaps they have become aware of this as an area where girls can now progress further than serving at the counter, or doing routine office work. This, however, is now another area of employment under threat as in addition to the general contraction in jobs, computer technology and the increasing use of credit cards and telephone banking are making staff cuts inevitable in the banking world. The Asian girls were the most keen on banking, as well as specifying careers in business and stockbroking. Unlike girls' choices in 1972, it was only Asian girls in the later study who expected to become a shop assistant or a hairdresser, and surprisingly, no one specified wanting to be a 'nurse', although this was probably disguised within a number of girls who said they wanted to work in the health services.

Working with children had been a frequent choice in 1972, and this was even more evident in 1991, in fact it was the most popular type of work for both white and West Indian girls. It attracted both working class and middle class girls for whom being a nursery teacher or nursery nurse, or just generally working with young children represents a realistic and enjoyable job that would serve them in the present and the future. It is a 'respectable' job, even if this kind of employment has remained relatively low paid and low status. Although a few men have entered this field, it remains a 'caring' job predominantly carried out by women.

Another relatively popular choice (by white rather than black girls) both in the seventies and the nineties was working with animals, more often specified as veterinary nurse rather than surgeon. Other jobs that were given in similar proportion at both times include air hostess, policewoman, beautician, radiographer and teacher. 'New' jobs mentioned include psychologist, psychotherapist, graphic designer, conservationist, photographer, and various media occupations, the relevant teaching and training of which entered the school curriculum in the intervening decades. There were a few girls who wished to become car mechanics or engineers (two Asian girls wanted to be engineers), which is positive in terms of their very existence, but also reflects the extremely slow movement towards entering occupational spheres hitherto reserved for men.

As in 1972, it was the Asian girls who were predominantly

represented amongst those expressing professional career hopes such as doctor, lawyer, scientist, etc. (One in five Asian girls wanted to be either a doctor, lawyer or solicitor, pharmacist, psychologist, or journalist.) For Harwinder, the ways her parents had had to struggle to earn money and the physical toll it took in their lives added to her desire to be a doctor, and for Amandeep her desire to be a physiotherapist had been fuelled by her father's illness:

They want me to be a doctor. They always did since I was young. They say 'If you be a doctor, that will be good', but they don't realize I have to study really hard as well to be one. I want to be a doctor because I want to care about people, but the real career for that is a social worker or something. I also want to be something that earns a lot as well, so I don't have to suffer like my parents — well my dad's all right, he's a manager [in a bakery], he brings in OK, but not that much. But he comes in with burnt arms and sometimes he has to take days off work. My mum works twice and she earns just as much as my dad, he's always going 'I earn as much as you and you work in two places.' They're always fighting about that, she works really hard. That's why I want to earn something. I'm not really sure what I want to do though. A doctor — first of all I don't think I'll make it, but I'll try my best. What I mainly want to do is talk to people and solve their problems and help them out, listen to them.

HARWINDER

I want to be a physiotherapist. After my dad had a stroke I went to the rehabilitation centre a lot and met a lot of physiotherapists there. I liked what they do. I helped a lot and they said 'You could be one.' I've got a part-time job there, I start in August. I like helping people, and I like to help my dad really. Mum thinks I'll never be able to do it. You have to train for four years I think. She thinks I won't stick it out. Shows what confidence she has in me!

AMANDEEP

Office Work

> I think there's less going for office jobs now. There are a few going for them but they don't specifically want to be secretaries. They want to do that kind of work in banks and stuff like that.
>
> EILEEN

> I'm hoping to stay on at [sixth form] college and do something, I'm not sure yet what. I don't particularly want to work in an office. But I think I will end up doing something like working in an office. Everyone else knows what they want to do: my friend wants to be a drama teacher for kids; another girl wants to work in a bank. I'll wait and see I think. My parents don't really want to push me into anything. My dad with my sister, when she was thirteen, he sent her off to night classes to do typing and shorthand and all that. And she's a secretary to a managing director now, quite good for her age, she's twenty-five. She gets quite well paid for it. So my dad thinks if I can do something like that, with the qualifications and skills I won't have much to worry about, which is true. I know, in a way, I'll go for a job like an office job for the security of it but not because I want to. I want to do something different.
>
> PAULINE

In the early 1970s, the great popularity of secretarial and general office work was based on its considered suitability for girls, and the relative ease of entry. It had many obvious attractions twenty years ago, and still has many today. It is a clean respectable job. It has some glamorous appeal because it may involve dressing smartly and the possibility of meeting and working with men. It does not need Saturday work, and could be relatively well paid, especially for girls proficient in typing and shorthand. It needs few qualifications and there is usually a demand for people prepared to do this sort of work. All things considered, it seems a nice job for a girl.

The Ealing girls were attracted by this work because they hoped to do interesting things, meet people, travel and earn good money. Some also mentioned their current enjoyment of typing. Here are a few of the ways that potential secretaries, shorthand typists, copy typists and office juniors in 1972 perceived their future work and the particular things about it that attracted them:

If I can work my way to a really good secretary I hope to be able to travel about (if the boss I work for travels).

Money. Working under a handsome boss.

Meeting different people and having an interesting and varied job.

The standard of work and dressing up as a new experience.

I like this job because you can get good wages and lots of promotion.

Working at an office is a comfortable place.

You are able to help different people and this is what I like doing.

I like typing and prefer to work in an office to a factory.

In reality, these hopes may have proved something of a disappointment. For example, a girl would not meet many men if she was working in the typing pool. If she worked in the office, it might well be that the number of new people passing through was very small, and the ones already there were not exciting. Secretaries and shorthand typists hoping to travel with their bosses would find themselves left behind, or merely transported to another part of town. It is clear, however, that this sort of work was, and still is, easy to slip into, for many valid reasons. One of these was expressed in other girls' answers to the question of why they wished to do this work: 'I don't know, but as I am doing shorthand and typing at school I think this job will be all right.' And, 'It is what I am learning mostly now. And it is really the only thing I could do.' In 1991, their reasons are more down to earth, to do with liking typing or working with computers, and getting a good salary.

At that time many schools were well-equipped with departments where girls learnt office skills and did courses in commerce. While the boys were being taught technical skills and expertise in woodwork, metalwork, technical drawing, etc., the only practical abilities that girls could develop, apart from cookery and needlework, were shorthand and typing. Therefore, at whatever age a girl decided to leave school, if she had taken these courses, she had these skills to sell. She had little need of other qualifications, except perhaps English, and she had already acquired an idea of whether she would like and could cope with a secretarial job. When a lot of these girls claimed that they liked typing and shorthand they were basing this on their own experience, and this avoided the trouble or risk of exploring new skills and occupations. The schools made similar assumptions, and office work was almost totally a 'girls' subject'. Today it has become more oriented towards business and management.

The expansion of business and administration particularly since the Second World War produced a constant demand for office workers. Demand usually leads to higher wages but in this case the parallel enthusiasm of girls for this work meant that in the main, female office workers remained as underpaid and exploited as they would be in any other women's job. Yet office work seems different from other women's occupations in that it contains so many variations in status and pay. For instance, secretaries may command very high rates of pay depending on where and for whom they work. In London young secretaries may start with a salary as high as that of a qualified nurse, while in provincial and rural areas and in some small firms and businesses in London the pay is much lower. Therefore secretarial work has also had the attractive and deceptive appearance of a career structure which can rise from office junior to executive secretary and yet seems to demand relatively little in the way of lengthy training or qualifications. This overlooks the fact that there is no guaranteed progress from one level to the next.

The popularity of office work with the Ealing girls seems to have fallen dramatically over the last twenty years. From its being the professed choice of a third of all the girls in the first study, it had dropped to about one person in twenty in the second study for both white and West Indian girls. For the Asian girls the proportion was higher (one in seven). This may of course be a finding peculiar to this area of West London, and in other parts of the country the nature of work availability (or lack of it) may preserve office work as a favoured occupation. However, I suspect that the pattern will be repeated to some extent. The apparent decline in office work as the most desirable female occupation may be explained by several related changes. One is linked to the technological changes that have occurred in the business world, and the way jobs are defined. Secretarial work is now done using word processors and other computing machines, and the relevant lessons taught in school are often called business studies rather than typing and office skills. It also reflects a change in attitude towards careers for girls. Office work was once seen as 'a nice job for a girl', that is, the sort of girl who wants a 'clean, respectable' job until she gets married and gives up full-time work to have children. This criterion has become rather old-fashioned. Girls now aspire to what they see as more exciting work, and many girls at this stage in their lives will dismiss this kind of work as 'some boring office job'. One girl (who wants to be a fashion designer) gave her opinion on the popularity of office work in the past:

> I wouldn't want that at all: I couldn't sit in an office. I'm a fidgety person. I like getting about. I don't mind computers, but I couldn't sit at one all day, I get annoyed with them. I wouldn't want to be a secretary or anything. I've always had my hopes too high!

NINA

It appears, therefore, that office work is moving from being a 'nice job for a girl', to being something that you do more as a last resort – several girls expressed this as, for example: 'I don't know what I want to do, but I don't want a boring day-to-day office job', or 'I haven't a clue what I want to do when I leave school. All I know is that I don't want to end up sitting in an office doing paperwork.' It would be wrong to suggest that there has been a general decline in the popularity of office work for girls. As suggested earlier, this will obviously vary according to the area of the country, and the reality of job opportunities. In London there are proportionally more opportunities available, or at least this appears to be the case. The number of potential careers for girls in general has expanded, but not necessarily into new areas or into the realm of 'men's work'. It is partly the developments in 'new' technology, and the introduction of 'media studies', that makes more appear to be on offer than twenty years ago, and certainly more innovatory work than secretarial or office work.

To the Ealing girls in 1991, discussing job expectations probably felt even more remote than it had to their counterparts twenty years previously. At fourteen or fifteen, the realities of working can be put into the relatively distant future, especially as the majority of these girls now planned to stay on into the sixth form or go to a separate sixth form college. Even many of those who would have preferred to leave at sixteen were staying on because there seemed little point in anyone, from whatever class background, leaving school at this time without any clear work prospects. Whether they would be retaking GCSEs, taking A levels, or a BTec, or doing any other qualifications in college, it still meant postponing the reality of working for a few years or more. Therefore, although some girls may well 'end up' in offices, this is not the vision they had at this time in their lives. A significant number claimed that they might do A levels and a degree, although some of the jobs they specified did not require this level of qualification.

As we have seen in chapter 1, the introduction of new technology in the form of computers and word processors was of limited benefit to many women working as typists or secretaries, who found that it de-skilled their work or put them out of a job altogether. But business moves with the times and aims to cut costs and make as much profit as possible, so all offices eventually have to invest in these systems. Resultant changes in the nature of office work have meant that many girls who would have looked to typing and shorthand to serve them in 1972, will today need to be trained in word processing, become familiar with using a fax machine, and probably have some additional computing skills. Accordingly, schools have renamed subjects, and what used to be called typing and office work has become, for instance, 'business studies':

Business studies is where you're on the computers and you have to pretend you're starting up a business. And you're on a computer most days, so you're learning typing, you have to use both hands. It's half and half girls and boys. My sister used to do typing on a typewriter but they don't do it now.

ROSIE

Lucy was one of the few Ealing girls who was still keen to get a job doing secretarial work:

It was because me mum got me typing when I was about eleven and I liked it from then, so that's what I chose to do. I want to be a personal secretary, you get a higher paid job and more prospects, get more promotion. I took my GCSE in typing one year early. I think we're learning word processing next year – every office has word processing. My mum says whatever you do, don't go into a typing pool so I'll avoid that. I've got another year at school, then two years at (secretarial) college probably. By nineteen I should be working.

Like Rosie, Lucy now shared these lessons with boys, something that would have been unheard of in 1972:

There's three boys in my office studies class, and about ten girls. Probably because boys think it's more of a girls' thing to do. But you see a lot of men doing it don't you – equal rights in employment. The boys are slow. They don't really concentrate. They probably think 'I'm not going to be doing this when I'm older anyway.'

It is more recognized today that men can and do go into secretarial work, although it is a small number that do. But learning to use a word processor is clearly an asset for anybody who wants to use a computer or take advantage of modern office technology, even if they do not intend to end up working as a typist or secretary. The machinery is gender-typed: a typewriter appears more 'feminine' than a personal computer, which has a more technological and therefore 'masculine' image. Therefore men can learn to use word processors without being labelled as doing something particularly feminine. As all the errors can be deleted without trace on a word processor, men do not need a high level of typing skills to use it, speed of working is the only thing they may lose without training. Therefore it is not such an innovation to find boys taking lessons in office skills.

I think it's changing. Office work is less popular now, there's so much you can do now. It's still slightly sexist, but I think the options are getting bigger. I think anyone who wants to do anything should go for it. If boys want to be secretaries and stuff, so they should be, it's up to them. I don't know any boys who actually want to be secretaries, but I was quite surprised with their work experience. And a lot of boys also went into schools and nursery schools and things. I was amazed at that.

LAURA

As Laura comments, although it is not unusual to find boys learning how to use a word processor, how many of them will be thinking in terms of using this as more than an additional skill for some more 'appropriate' type of work? Many are more interested in the business studies side of the subject. They have spent most of their lives under the entrepreneurial, enterprise philosophy of a Conservative government. In one school it was 'enterprise week' when I visited, and the fourth years (fourteen- to fifteen-year-olds) individually or in groups, had to set up some kind of business enterprise, usually involving selling either a product or a service. The money they made would be spent on a collective trip. Office skills have got mixed up with business and management skills but continuing gender divisions and sex discrimination ensure that it is men who will be more involved in business, while the servicing roles in the office are still taken by women.

Working with People

Part of the legacy of women's role is that they should be involved less with themselves than with caring and looking after others, and the upbringing of girls makes them dependent for identity and self-esteem on their relationships with other people. This was illustrated by the comments from the Ealing girls in 1972 on the jobs they expected to get. The jobs they chose reflected, of course, the jobs that were normally open to them; these, in turn, were usually extensions of their 'feminine' role and exploited some supposedly 'feminine' characteristic.

Many of those Ealing girls who then wanted to go into some kind of secretarial or office work spoke enthusiastically about the different people they hoped to meet, and for others the possible 'people involvement' acted as the determining factor in their choices. Here are some of the reasons the girls gave for other choices in the early 1970s. They show great consistency over the various types of work. (The expected job is given in brackets.)

I mostly like having to help people. I like to know what is wrong with them and would like to help in any way. (Doctor)

I enjoy having children around and I'd like to meet people and have their company. (Children's nurse)

I come into contact with people and the work differs from day to day. (Radiologist)

Helping people, meeting people, and sorting out their problems. (Social worker)

The thought of working with children appeals to me. I like helping children or people, and children are more willing to be helped than adults. (Teacher)

Meeting different people every day. (Bank clerk)

It seems interesting. You are meeting different people and helping them. The receptionists always look smart and kind. Also it is good money. (Receptionist)

I think being a telephone operator you come to know about many places and people and I like meeting people. (Telephone operator)

I like the idea of meeting people and of travelling and learning about the things in everyday life in other countries. (Journalist)

The travelling, meeting people from different backgrounds, being independent, money. (Air hostess)

You get the chance to meet a lot of people and a chance to travel. (Interpreter)

Meeting different people, seeing all types of people, helping people (an office job would bore me). (Shop assistant)

It is a friendly sort of job and you meet a lot of people. (Hairdresser)

During the intervening years between 1972 and 1991, the social and political environment has placed increasing emphasis on working for the individual, making money, and being seen to succeed and consume, for example by buying houses, cars and expensive household gadgetry. I was therefore cheered to see that the girls in the later study still demonstrated much of the concern for meeting or helping people in their selection of jobs and careers that their counterparts had shown in the 1970s. Over a third of the girls in 1991 also specifically mentioned 'people' as a significant factor in their job choices:

> Basically because of meeting new people all the time. (Courier on holiday coaches)

> I would like to work for the public and keep crime off our streets and also to be respected by most people. (Policewoman)

> The thing I like most about this job is looking after someone and knowing that they depend on you. (Nursery work)

> The idea of creating different styles and making people feel good. (Beautician or hairdresser)

> Meeting people and working with figures. (Banker or accountant)

> It's very rewarding and you're teaching and making other people happy. (Teaching drama to disabled people)

> I want to be able to help people and doing this I think I'd be able to; also it's something I've always wanted to do. (Firewoman)

> I would meet a variety of people and be working under my own initiative. (Solicitor)

> Dealing with the public and working on different things. (Airline or hotel work)

> I like finding out what makes people tick. I also like helping people with problems. (Psychology or counselling)

> Mixing with people and I also like to get dirty. (Aircraft engineer)

Being concerned with people is a very positive aspect of 'femininity' and it is wrong that this concern is so unevenly distributed between men and women. The stereotyped view of women sees them as naturally more adept than men at working with or for people and taking care of them. Nurture is supposedly based in the maternal caring role, and serving is contained in women's falsely assumed inferiority. The great investment in other people demonstrated by these girls' commitment to being wives and mothers in the seventies influences the vocational directions of their minds. Men, on the other hand, are supposed to be more concerned with proving their own individual success by individual strivings. They are seen as better with 'things' than people, and can cope with scientific and abstract problems.

I can remember finding conflict between the personal and the abstract in my own life. When I left school, I rejected any idea of continuing at university the pure sciences I had studied at A level. The thought of concentrating on such intensive abstract science frightened me and I was convinced that I was not good enough. I went to work as a technician in a medical research laboratory, and I specifically chose this sort of research because it had some ultimate connection with helping people and entailed working with other people. This gave it some tangibility and meaning. If, however, I had stayed there, I would never have acquired more than a limited autonomy, and would always have been carrying out someone else's experiments. Almost all the careers for women that involve intensive care and service of others contain the implicit contradiction that the very aspect of the job that makes it worthwhile can also wear away or suffocate women's sense of individuality. Continual attendance on the needs of other people at work, as at home, leaves little time or energy for self-expression. People are very demanding. Self-sacrifice brings its own rewards but it is unjust that only half the population should accept this as part of their basic personality and role. Men also should become more 'people-involved', instead of themselves making up a large proportion of the people that girls and women are concerned with helping, through, for example, nursing, teaching, typing for, cooking for, serving and waiting on.

In the 1970s, the acceptance of married women working was reflected in the Ealing girls' own changing attitude to jobs, and increased education for girls had led to a heightening of their expectations from work. As the long term possibilities of work were assumed, 'interest' (which includes meeting people) was accentuated as a job characteristic as important as or more important than other factors like convenience or money. This varied by region and according to the nature of available opportunities: for instance, if all local jobs were equally boring and uninteresting and marriage took on a high value then money would clearly be the most important criterion. 'Interest' was very important to the 1972 Ealing girls, whose counterparts in previous decades would hardly have considered this as a possibility as they moved from job to job, usually working in factories and workshops. Working class girls at school in the first half of the century might have vaguely hoped that the jobs they went into would be quite interesting, but it was usually far more important to earn money to help the family than to seek job satisfaction. Shop work, perhaps, came nearest to being interesting and unmonotonous, at that time.

Compared to the earlier research, there were proportionally more girls in the later study who said they wanted to go into a certain job or career because of the intrinsic nature of the work; because they thought they would find it interesting; or because it had good money or prospects. It was significant that for the Ealing girls in 1972, money was not considered to be the most important aspect of work, in fact this was specifically denied in several instances. Although this may be a London phenomenon, for the 1991 Ealing girls at least, the emphasis was more on the content of work – its interest and enjoyment, and the possibility of a girl 'making a career for herself'. That money had also crept a little deeper into their thoughts was to some extent a reflection of the business and consumer orientation of today's world, and the necessity of earning money whether you are male or female, to support yourself. As one girl, who wanted to work in a bank or a building society, wrote: 'I've always wanted to do this, I'm not sure why, but the money's good, and there are cheap mortgage rates, etc.' Considering the mundane, boring and dead-end jobs that were and still are the lot of many girls, there is bound to be some disillusionment. But it would take a lot of reverse pedalling to transfer their aspirations back to the home and family.

When girls in both studies were asked to name a job they would like to do if they had all the choice in the world, about a quarter declared, as they had in 1972, that they would do much the same sort of work as they had specified in their job expectations. The majority of the rest expressed desires to be famous actresses, models, singers, film stars, writers, etc. There was, however, a new thread running through these aspirations, which was contained in citing some kind of business venture. As in some of their job expectations, this too reflects the entrepreneurial nature of the Thatcher years in which they grew up, and perhaps the successful role models they had seen such as Anita Roddick (who created The Body Shop) and Debbie Moore (who set up the originally very successful Pineapple dance studios, etc., which collapsed during the current economic recession). They have also been exposed to many media stories showing young people who have successfully set up their own innovative businesses, many using a government enterprise grant. The ambitions of the Ealing girls included: 'own my own wine bar/ night club with them positioned all around the world'; 'own a posh hotel'; 'be a successful business woman'. In the 1970s, the enjoyment and hope of travel was particularly expressed in girls' choices of an 'ideal' job, but one girl in ten also mentioned travel in her reasons for liking the job she actually expected to take up. Such desires, as appearing in the later research, are far from real life, which for many of them will be constrained by routine work or the relative isolation and stationary nature of housework and child-care.

MOTHERS' WORK

Mothers go to work for all kinds of reasons and the acceptability of this might have been expected to influence their daughters' attitudes to working. In the 1972 research I found a tendency, although not very significant, for girls with working mothers to reject the home-based assumptions and satisfactions of women's role more than those with non-working mothers. Over two-thirds of the white girls, about 80 per cent of the West Indian girls and 43 per cent of Asian girls had mothers doing full-time or part-time jobs. Their own job expectations did not bear any relation to these jobs, however, because few of their choices approached the overall low-level nature of their mothers' work. A minority had mothers working as typists, secretaries and nurses (often at night), but the majority were involved in canteen work, cleaning jobs, shop or factory work. These jobs are even more stereotyped as 'women's work', and represent a narrow range of generally low paid and insecure jobs that can be done more easily part-time by mothers with dependent children.

In 1991, the picture had changed only slightly. Not surprisingly, a greater proportion of the mothers of the Ealing girls were working in full-time or part-time jobs (84 per cent white; 90 per cent West Indian; and 63 per cent Asian). This reflects both their economic needs and their personal choice to work full-time. Of those mothers with jobs in 1991, many were working full-time (white: 56 per cent; West Indian: 65 per cent; and Asian: 79 per cent) and the rest part-time. The range of jobs they were doing was slightly narrower than in the earlier study. However, there were some changes in the nature of this work which mirror some of the wider changes in occupational structure. For instance, in 1972 relatively more mothers worked in some kind of factory work: twenty years later the reduced numbers of girls' mothers doing this reflect the decline in the manufacturing industry. In 1991 there was an even higher proportion of mothers working in some kind of school work (teaching, school ancillary work, dinner supervision, etc.); and in jobs that involve caring for young children, such as nursery work, playgroup organization, and childminding. In a circular fashion, this illustrates the fact that more mothers are working and therefore there is an even greater demand for childcare workers. There was a slight increase in the representation of managerial work, but this was generally in the areas of nursing and cleaning. A significant minority in 1991 were doing secretarial or office work, or working as telephonists or receptionists. Apart from a few teachers, none of the girls' mothers worked in any professional capacity.

The mothers of the West Indian girls in 1972 had a slightly different job pattern. They were mainly employed in factory work or nursing, with a smaller proportion working as cleaners and home helps, or on London Transport. Clerical jobs were minimal and there were no higher-level jobs represented. In the decades after the Second World War women from other countries made up an increasing proportion of nurses. Long hours and low pay accelerated the decline in the numbers of indigenous women taking up this career, and nurses from overseas have come to provide an integral part of Britain's health service. Although there were fewer West Indian girls participating in the research in 1991, there was once more a significant number who had mothers in some kind of nursing work (several working with old people, which is one of the least popular areas of nursing), a few doing nursery or childminding jobs, and the rest in catering, caretaking, and sales work. Apart from one machinist, none did factory work. Once more, their occupational position was very different from their daughters' job expectations.

The mothers of the Ealing Asian girls in the first study were some of the large numbers of Asian women who came to Britain as dependents with little or no experience of working outside the home in the fifties and sixties. Some educated Asian women who had gained professional qualifications as teachers and doctors managed to continue practising this kind of work in Britain, although some found they were confined to the lower grades of their professions. Many women did not work immediately after they arrived here through the strict religious and cultural constraints on women's role, and sometimes because of not knowing the English language, but economic pressures soon drove many of them out into mainly semi-skilled or unskilled work. Like other women, they found it impossible to keep a family on the often low wages of their husbands. Frequently their workplace was limited to a predominantly female environment in factories and small workshops (sweatshops), laundries, etc., where they were open to overwork and exploitation. Asian families themselves may own workshops which use female relatives as cheap labour. This arrangement makes conditions harder to check and also makes it more difficult for women to improve their pay and conditions. This had happened in Southall, for instance, which was the home of most of the Asian girls that I spoke to, where local clothing manufacturers took advantage of traditional Asian skills and employed many women as sewing machinists. Outwork or 'homework' as a sewing machinist was also readily available at incredibly low rates for those who were unable or did not wish to go out to work.

This was the setting for the mothers of the Ealing Asian girls in

1972, of whom 43 per cent were working at that time (and of these 62 per cent were from India, none from Pakistan there were only a few girls represented from Pakistan – and 38 per cent from East Africa). Many had found work in the canteens and kitchens of Heathrow airport, and others were employed in sewing, ironing, laundry work and in local factories making sweets, rubber and chemicals. Their jobs were far removed from their aspirations for their daughters, and from those of the girls themselves. In 1991, the situation was very similar: the mothers of the Ealing Asian girls were working predominantly in catering and packing food, other factory work, shop work and cleaning, and a few working in some kind of nursing. There was little office work, and just one teacher.

Several of the Asian girls described how hard their mothers had to work, some even having more than one job. Like any other family, the struggle to survive economically is even more acute in a lone parent family, and for Geeta, whose mother was divorced, this added to her own desire to go straight into work:

> All day my mum works. One job in British Airways, and the other she makes samosas. She only has about half an hour break in between them. She comes home and goes off again at six. She packs the plates on the planes, she says it's hard, pushing trolleys and everything and that we should get a good education. I say 'I don't want to study, I'm not into education.' I hate it, but my sister is really intelligent, she gets good marks. And my younger brother and sister are always playing on the computer and looking up in encyclopaedias. Me, I'm always dancing, singing, making everyone laugh. I want to get a job, I want to grow up quickly and help my mum. I'm really close to my mum, I'm always talking to her. She's kind to me and she says 'I've got to pay this bill this week, and he wants trainers, and you want this . . .' and I want to leave school and help her. My mum says to me that the way I think is wrong, that it will be me who will suffer. She says education is really important. She wants us to be doctors and things, have really good jobs, but she needs help at the moment.

In 1991, the first group of Ealing girls would now have reached the age of thirty-three or thirty-four. If any of them had had a daughter of their own at the age of nineteen or twenty, it is theoretically possible that they could have been amongst the mothers of the Ealing girls who participated in the 1991 study. If we speculate on this further and compare the sorts of jobs expected by girls in 1972 when they were fourteen or fifteen with those being done by the working mothers of the girls studied in 1991, it is clear that they are very different in nature and status. There is some overlap between girls and their mothers in the area of office work, but still only 13 per cent of the girls' mothers were doing this kind of work, compared to the 40 per cent of girls who expressed it as their job expectation at that time. Proportions are similar for the West Indian girls' mothers, but very few Asian mothers were doing any sort of office work.

This illustrates once more the limited range of work available to women who wish to combine work with a family and, indeed, the majority of the Ealing girls in 1991, like their predecessors in 1972, said they would go back to work sooner or later, after their children had reached a certain age. They optimistically (and unrealistically) assumed they would return to their chosen line of work, having put the children safely into a nursery or with a childminder. The lack of good affordable child-care has not changed during the intervening period. Girls are planning to leave school later and to achieve jobs and careers that are higher level, and need more qualifications than those aspired to by their mothers when they were young. This was also likely to have been the situation expressed by the girls' mothers in relation to their own mothers. Each generation of girls, on reaching motherhood, finds her prospects curbed by the same constricted range of appropriate work for women with dependent children.

CAREERS FOR GIRLS

I've wanted to do this [research for history] for quite a long time but I don't know enough about the sorts of jobs you have to do for these sorts of things – you just get to know about things like air hostesses and teachers. They don't tell you enough about more unusual things. Careers officers come round now and again and ask what you want to know about but they tend not to know about that sort of job – just teachers and nurses and that sort of thing.

JENNY, 1972

We have a lesson and we do different things each month. And we have this computer that helps us choose. It told me I was creative and it told me what I wasn't good at. The computer feeds out what matches with you. In the careers lessons it's answering questions like would you mind wearing a uniform for a job or would you like to travel or whatever. They tell you about careers in general but not really any specific ones, you have to go to a library or something to find out for yourself. They have a lot on mechanics which is what a lot of boys want to do – a lot of boys want to do mechanical work and girls want to work in nurseries.

EILEEN, 1991

The sources for choosing a career that girls in the 1970s had to draw on were the images found in books and magazines, on television and through observation and discussion with the people immediately around them. These invited them to become nurses, teachers, telephonists, secretaries, bank clerks, and the rest of the familiar jobs for girls. Among the girls from the Ealing schools we saw that in 1972 this range, plus shop assistant, receptionist, hairdresser and air hostess accounted for over 80 per cent of their job preferences. In 1991, the range was quite similar although office work had shrunk in popularity and there was movement afoot: for instance, a few artistic (and therefore 'feminine') careers in aspects of design and theatre work had taken their places in a list that was still predominantly 'women's work'.

In careers books, then as now, there appeared to be an abundance of work opportunities for girls, some of which involved several subcategories of job. For some careers, further educational qualifications were necessary, but not for others. There was therefore an enormous discrepancy between what was supposed to be available and what was actually taken up. How many girls without high were thinking of becoming, for example, an architectural technician or a chartered surveyor, a dental ancillary, a cartographical draughtswoman, an interior decorating assistant, a dispensing optician, quantity surveyor, pharmacy technician, landscape architect, meteorological technician, or anything in horticulture or agriculture? If there is indeed such a wide range of possible choice, why do not more girls choose these sorts of jobs?

Girls needed, and still need, nerve and determination to enter what have been popularly defined as 'masculine' (or at least less 'feminine') kinds of work, especially if they do not appear very openly available. Many girls who have plodded fairly aimlessly through their school curriculum and have ended up amongst the 'girls' subjects', would treat the suggestion of pursuing one of these unfamiliar jobs with great reluctance. It is not easy to strike out on your own especially if conformity to convention and regulation is encouraged implicitly or explicitly within school. Some girls will step outside the predictable range of careers but may need help and encouragement to stick with their choice; many have long since held set ideas about appropriate jobs.

If for instance a job is labelled as a type of 'technician', this may be construed to imply some scientific (or potentially 'masculine') connection; an assumption not necessarily justified, but enough to frighten off a girl who has defined herself as non-scientific. The necessity of further training also scared away many prospective girl candidates, who in the early 1970s saw it as merely an extension of school, and therefore likely to be similarly authoritarian in form and irrelevant in content. Many were ignorant of the nature of further education, and on-the-job training. They did not realize that they could learn in an atmosphere which affords them more freedom and autonomy than school, and take subjects which could be more interesting or have more direct application to their jobs. It was often easier to drift into a factory or shop, or go into clerical or secretarial work in which training was either unnecessary or merely involved an evening class in shorthand, or short, intensive secretarial courses.

The Careers Service also has a role in schools of supporting and assisting with careers advice, which may include attending parents' evenings, giving talks in school, and having individual interviews with pupils in the fifth form. A fifth form leaver who has nothing fixed up on leaving school may use this careers service, but is unlikely to be encouraged to broaden their horizons. Cynthia Cockburn describes how many of the YTS trainees in her research 'found their encounters with the Careers Service useless, a "waste of time", and depressing. Several felt they had been deflected by their contact with careers officers from careers that appealed to them and that they had, often too tentatively, proposed.'[3]

In the early 1970s careers information was left largely to the discretion of the school, and the quality today is still dependent on the individual school policy and the education authority. Some may not have a specific careers teacher, some teachers combine careers teaching with other teaching and others have full-time careers teachers. Hence it is possible to widen the scope of career knowledge for girls, and hopefully for boys as well, by introducing a whole spectrum of possibilities at an age before views on sex and job separations have completely hardened. Careers and the nature of work should be a subject frequently discussed and explored. It should involve projects which cover an understanding of all sorts of work, and which examine the attitudes and values that are held about different jobs, and which, for example, downgrade many 'women's jobs'.

In 1972, the Ealing schoolgirls themselves wanted earlier careers teaching at school, and the provision of more activities like visits to places of employment.

> We don't get [careers] literature. We get the careers officer coming round about twice, and Mrs — talks to us sometimes. And we have films, but they tend to be about the same sort of things and not all on careers. I think we need more visits – I think the fifth formers do go on visits to factories and police stations and so on but I think we should have them younger because if you give them in the fifth form and that's when you want to leave, it doesn't give you much time to decide. They should give you a lot of this sort of thing, especially for boys because a lot of your life depends on what you do, so you should have a lot of time to decide what you want to do.

> If we did things like the fourth form leavers do – they go round looking at different jobs and things, and work in children's nurseries and things like that. If we could do that I think more people would stay on and they'd enjoy it.

Careers officers and teachers are not the only active influences in a girl's choice of job. Mothers are very important, as well as fathers, and female friends and relatives who are already doing certain sorts of work. A relative minority are absolutely swayed by one person, and it is reasonable to assume that most base their choice on their assessment and perception of themselves, their picture of what the world offers to girls, and their immediate opportunities. This invariably leads to a conventional career. Most parents, whether mothers were working or not, did not pressurize their children about jobs although some definitely wanted their daughters to stay on at school. As noted earlier, parental attitudes were usually either expressed through giving blanket support: 'It's entirely up to you, it's your life,' and 'Whatever you will be happy doing'; or in similar vein but specifying certain exceptions: 'You can do what you like, *except* work in a factory, shop, or anything not quite respectable.' Anything not quite respectable, at this time usually included the less traditionally feminine, less 'appropriate' jobs for girls, so even if the girls were to think about such jobs they would have faced parental opposition. Parents today may be more accommodating of less conventional choices, and profess that they would not mind if their daughter were to choose such a path, but have an implicit assumption that this is very unlikely to happen.[4]

Girls have always been excluded from certain male enclaves, from, for example, apprenticeships in crafts like printing. But apart from straightforward exclusion, they understandably lack the self-confidence to undertake jobs they had never heard of or which seem to be predominantly male preserves. In addition, girls have often lacked the opportunities for day or block release from their jobs to take further education, they are given little encouragement to try for unusual jobs and information has often been inadequate or not given early enough.

In the 1970s, there was less organized careers advice and information in schools for girls leaving school at fifteen, and what existed was generally very stereotyped for girls and boys. Twenty years later, many schools have improved facilities and some have adopted a more comprehensive and enlightened approach, despite the fact that many young people will find it very hard to get work in the present climate of recession and unemployment. Similarly, some have embraced a principle of at least attempting to challenge job stereotypes by presenting alternatives and encouraging girls and boys to pursue jobs or careers that may be thought inappropriate to their sex. This can, of course, vary considerably from school to school and from one careers teacher to another, as well as being affected by the nature of the area (whether inner city or rural, for example), and the type of opportunities available.

Most secondary schools usually have at least one careers teacher to inform and advise on different career opportunities, although this may not start in earnest until they are in their GCSE year. The Ealing girls of twenty years ago felt that their careers advice was often sadly lacking, or began too late. Although facilities have clearly advanced, some of their counterparts in the nineties had similar comments:

> We've had no advice on careers yet. Last year when we were choosing our options they had a careers teacher, but they said it wasn't worth giving us any ideas because we were too young yet. We're just starting now, they're just starting to bring in people.
>
> KIM

> I think they might start giving us careers advice next term, that's when we have to start thinking about [sixth form] colleges. So far they haven't. They should have done it this year, when we chose our options. If they advised us on what things we needed to do to get the jobs, we could take the options to suit the job. Without that we just chose subjects we thought we'd like. My dad thinks I'm going to change my mind about being a journalist so he made me take a mixture of options.
>
> CATHERINE

Careers teachers may take a more innovative approach, especially in schools where equal opportunities and anti-sexist/anti-racist policies have a strong profile. Evidence suggests that women teachers are more sympathetic to encouraging non-stereotyped careers for both girls and boys than men teachers.

Pupils may now also take advantage of the application of computer technology to the selection of their possible career choices, as one girl described:

> We're on a special thing at the moment called Jigcal, a computer-ized thing. There's questions that reflect your personality and what you're good at, then it files into the computer and picks out information on what you would be best at for your career, like art, science or English. Then you fill in job numbers and what jobs you'd like and it gives out information about those jobs, what grades you need and so on. It's fairly helpful to people that aren't sure, and it's good fun getting it all back.
>
> NINA

In 1972, the Ealing girls could leave school at any time between fifteen and eighteen years of age, with little experience of work apart from the jobs they might have done at weekends or after school in shops, etc., to earn a little money. Therefore a significant development in the careers field since then has been the introduction of work experience into many schools. This generally involves pupils taking two weeks at some point at the end of their fourth year or the beginning of the fifth (GCSE) year, in order to get some experience in an area of work as closely associated with their current career interests as possible. The way this is organized will depend on the school concerned, and the opportunities for work experience are going to vary considerably according to what is available in the locality. The Ealing girls had potentially quite a lot of scope for sampling different occupations, as their schools are situated in the Greater London area, and close to places like Heathrow airport, and the offices and television studios of the BBC. While most went into safely 'female' or neutral areas of work, a few girls had been found places in 'male' areas of work like garages, and some boys had gone to work in nurseries or offices.

Although career choices may be influenced by the quality of careers advice and the nature of available opportunities, these are also the product of the attitudes and aspirations of school students themselves and the way they perceive themselves. There are a multitude of interacting forces in their lives to which they respond and adjust. Simply telling them about new career possibilities and encouraging them to do them is not necessarily going to have any effect unless this desire arises from a conjunction of forces inside them at that time.[5] There has not been much widening in occupational scope for women in the last two decades, but partly through encouragement, and efforts by feminists such as Women in Manual Trades, and to a limited extent the opportunities offered by YTS, some young women have taken training in areas that are traditionally thought of as 'men's work'. These include carpentry, plumbing, engineering, painting and decorating, and bus driving; as well as professional careers in law and medicine. In the present climate of high unemployment and economic recession, however, men are likely to be very protective of their own employment in these areas.

GIRLS IN 'MEN'S WORK'

I heard that they don't really take women for mechanical work, they take men. Women can do the same jobs because they've got cars so they should be able to. I think it's going to be pretty hard doing an engineering job. For one thing, guys will probably say 'She's a girl. What's she doing here?' But if more girls get in they would probably accept it. There aren't a lot of girls going for things like that. They should. This is the twentieth century, boys and girls get equal opportunities. They should do it. It's probably hard for them to accept at first.

SHAZIA, 1991

My sister's friend wants to be a mechanic but she didn't get any jobs where she went because she is a girl. She trained, she did everything but she couldn't get a job. My mum says that where she works the men get paid more for jobs she's done. Some things have changed, not everything. Some jobs you can get women working but not in all of them. They don't think they're fit to do the job. They don't think they have the education to do the job like men have, and the physical ability. There's not really a lot that has changed.

DENISE, 1991

A boy has more power. It's probably in their voices, if a man says something and if I said something, I think the man would go further than I would, being a girl. There's more in them.

People think, he's a man, he can do the job. They'd go for the man if it was a mechanic's job and everything, girls can't go around fixing cars and things. There's nothing wrong with it, but it's a bit odd, the way other people look at it. It's not a feminine thing to do. It's like your question about being at home doing house jobs. I disagree with that, but women see it as their aim just to be at home with children, not in a garage.

HARPINDER, 1991

When the Ealing girls in both studies were asked to name a job they might have chosen to do had they been boys, they endorsed gender stereotypes, albeit a little less in the later study. In 1972, most selected the skilled male jobs that were frequently the hoped-for careers of their boyfriends and the boys in their forms, like mechanic and engineer. When they were subsequently asked, if the job was different from their own expectations, why they did not choose it as a girl, they were not at a loss to provide answers. However, these were mainly expressed in a succinct and dogmatic tautology describing the present situation. Here are some of their answers of that time followed by the job each refers to.

You don't often find women working in garages under the cars doing dirty work. (Mechanic)

It is a man's job, I'd look silly in a pair of dirty overalls under a car. (Mechanic)

Girls are not interested in engineering. (Engineer)

You do not hear of any female executives. (Executive)

Girls don't do pilot work. (Pilot)

Girls don't do technical drawing. (Draughtsman)

It is not right for a girl to be the same as a boy. (Engineer)

They had simply accepted that if a job was categorized as man's work, it was therefore not right, or suitable, or interesting, or appropriate for a girl.

There were other sorts of reaction and, for instance, some girls realistically recognized that 'male' jobs are often blocked to girls, either by entry requirements, or through the implicit preference given to boys. They showed awareness of the social restrictions but accepted them. For example:

They never want a girl to be a mechanic. (Mechanic)

This job is wanted by men mostly and they have more chance of getting it because a lot of people like men driving instructors better than women. (Driving instructor)

People would say it's not done for a girl to do this. But if I had guts I would. (Electrician)

Boys are much more approved of than girls, because girls are said to be liable to run off and get married thus wasting the ratepayers' money for their training. (Doctor)

Nobody would trust a girl as a pilot and I would never be given the time to prove myself worthy. (Pilot)

Other girls mentioned stereotyped female characteristics, such as being weaker, faint-hearted and less intelligent than men, as reasons why they would be incapable of coping with certain sorts of work.

A man is tougher, and girl journalists might have to see and report something that really upset them whereas a man wouldn't be so soft. (Journalist)

You don't have girl lorry drivers because usually the stuff inside the lorry is too heavy for a girl to lift. (Lorry driver)

It's unladylike. (Bricklayer)

I don't think I could face it as a girl but a boy is less squeamish. (Vet)

Boys should be able to put up with things a girl can't. (Doctor)

I think this job would be too complicated for a girl. (Computer science)

These old beliefs were repeated in spite of the everyday instances of women doing heavy or distasteful jobs. For example, nurses have to lift heavy patients, and witness many gruesome sights.

Another justification for girls keeping away from male-dominated territory was found in the acceptance and deference given to a boy's greater need for a good job because of his future necessity to support a wife and family.

Girls do not have to earn quite as much as a boy as he will soon support a family. (Banking)

There is more money in printing and boys need a steady bank balance if they're to get married. (Printer)

In the 1970s most of the Ealing girls found it fairly easy to think of a typically 'masculine job' they might have done. At the beginning of the 1990s, this question was harder to answer, because such crude stereotyping has come under criticism, and is not permitted within a philosophy of equal opportunity. Therefore, a lot more girls answered that they would do the same job if they were a boy as they had chosen as a girl, or that they simply did not know what they would do. Proportionally fewer girls than before – only about a third – specified a job they would do that was different. Their selection of jobs, however, was quite similar to the earlier study. It included jobs like mechanic, engineer, bricklayer and footballer, but also added several more 'business men' to the list. Other 'new' choices were: racing driver, dentist, designer, psychiatrist and psychotherapist. In their reasons for not doing 'men's jobs' as girls, they covered similar ground to those in the seventies, that is, they reject them for being intrinsically 'man's work'; they accept the operation of social restrictions; and endorse so-called 'feminine' characteristics that would make them unsuitable for this work. Here are a few of the replies in 1991:

Because I don't think girls are really accepted as mechanics. (Mechanic)

I would not be able to be a pilot, there are hardly any pilot women: and I think I might be too scared to be a policewoman. (Pilot or policewoman)

I don't have the intelligence. (Dentist)

Because it is difficult to be a successful business woman. Women are classed as weaker than men in the business world. (Business man)

Because I see it as more of a job for men. (Engineering)

I don't think they'd take me seriously if I was a girl and I think I could get further if I was a boy in that job. (Psychiatrist)

It is interesting to note that the only reason given in the earlier study that was not endorsed in the later one, was that a particular job was more suitable for a boy because he would have to support a wife and family in the future. Once again girls are implicitly recognizing that it is they as much as men who will one day be supporting a family.

For many, the acceptance of equal opportunities had made the question less relevant than twenty years earlier. Typical was one who said she would do the same job as a boy or a girl: 'because I do not think that a boy should have a different job necessarily than a girl.' Therefore, at least in girls' thinking, the gap between girls and boys' jobs has narrowed. In reality, the story is still rather different.

There were a few girls in 1991 who were seriously contemplating careers in traditionally male occupations. Melanie, for example, wanted to be a car mechanic, had already had a little practice in doing the work, and saw no serious opposition from her parents:

I've got a friend who's a mechanic and we do a lot of things together. He's got a car and we work on the car, I really enjoy doing that. I'm really fascinated by things like that. My dad is a carpenter and he does electrical work and things, and it really fascinates me, all these machines. I suppose I picked it up off him, because he works on his car as well, I help him, I love it. I love getting dirty! I don't mind getting my hands dirty. My mum's a bit so-so about it. She doesn't mind really what I want to do as long as its the right choice for me. My dad thinks I should go for it, same as my mum really. As long as I'm going to get paid for it they don't mind, I don't think! My parents aren't sexist.

Shazia is another whose aspiration it was to become a mechanic or an aircraft engineer. Her choice is more surprising because her family came from Pakistan, so she is potentially subject to criticism for working in an area that is full of men. For her work experience she had originally been assigned to a garage office, but managed to get transferred to the workshop after a week:

> For my work experience I went and worked in a garage for a week. I liked the mechanic work. They said I could come back for an apprenticeship. There were about four ladies there, including in the reception, cost office and workshop. I went to the office for a week, but that got boring, so I said could I go to the workshop and they said all right. They were surprised to see me there. The manager even said 'Are you sure you want to work in the workshop?' about three or four times. He said, 'If any of the boys misbehave, tell me.' But they were all right. They helped me a lot. The first few days they were edgy, they kept taking the mick, 'Your nails might get dirty, or your hair', that sort of thing. But after that they accepted me. They actually saw I was there to do some work. They all helped me out if I didn't know what to do . . . I'd asked my mum if I could work in the garage and she said 'No', so I decided to go in the office. Then I worked in the garage, and then told my mum at home. She goes, 'It's OK. Make sure you don't do anything stupid.' I want to work with planes, at the airport and everything. My uncle works there. I though it might be a good place to work. My mum goes, 'It's a boy's job.' I like football as well, and cricket. My mum says, 'You'd be better off being a boy.' She says, 'Can't you get a decent job working in an office?' I go, 'No!' It's not for me.

While Shazia was looking towards some kind of apprenticeship, Harriet wanted to do a degree in some kind of engineering:

> I like fiddling around with things at home, electronic kits, and I've been doing Meccano since I was about six. I want to work backstage on telly, anything fiddling around with cameras or lights. I'm doing that for work experience. I want to do a degree in engineering. I know a guy who is an electronic engineer and going round his house is really good fun, he's got all the stuff there and you can muck about. He says it's what he does at work!

She had strong views on how girls like herself should go for such jobs because they really want them, not just because it's men's work, and that companies should not employ women just for the sake of equal opportunities:

> I think you should just do what you want to do. If you really want to do it, then great, but if you do it because you want to be a woman who does a man's job, then that's wrong. You've got to want to do it. Like I really want to do it. I think it will be a bigger achievement if I got a job, because not many women do it. I suppose it wouldn't be because they are taking on women just for the sake of having women in their companies. I would do it because I wanted to do that job, not just to achieve getting a job that most men do. I didn't realize at first, I just said I wanted to do it and then everyone said, 'Oh, most men do that don't they?' But I thought more girls would take technology classes. I thought there were loads of women doing that in television but there aren't. I talked to a guy that works at the BBC and he says there's one woman in the whole maintenance. He said they now take on women just to have the numbers of women, so they can say they're equal opportunities. I don't know if that's right or wrong — just to take her because she's a woman so that it would look good on the numbers, if there was a guy who was better. That's unfair as well.

While Harriet was determined to do engineering, and Melanie was keen to learn to be a mechanic, Rosie was having a little more trouble deciding whether or not to be a firewoman. She had held this ambition for many years, but was finding there were plenty of people ready to deter her:

> There's these programmes on TV, documentaries about the fire service. There was one where they were saying, 'We had a woman come in and it was horrible because we had to look out for her, make sure she was OK.' They were worried she would get hurt. I thought, 'Oh God!' It's been on for five or six weeks now and in every one there's a man saying, 'I don't think it's a woman's job, they shouldn't be doing it.' There was only one programme that showed a woman, but they showed all the hassle she had to get in, all the things she had to go through, people

thinking she wasn't good enough and pushing her out of the way saying, 'You stay back and hold the hose.' But now they are used to her, she's won them over and they're all friends. But at first they were all saying how could she leave her baby, because she'd had a baby the year before, so she had to talk them round.

Rosie's mother had always been encouraging, but not all her family were so positive. The male members of her family had predictably more negative reactions:

My dad's worried, he said he'd never be able to let me do it. He's so possessive. My mum says, 'If you want to do it you should try.' My dad's like that too, but he's also a bit scared and worried. One of my brother's girlfriend's friends is a fireman and I was talking to him and he was saying it was a good job. It can be really bad some days but really good other days, so he made me interested as well. But he was saying to me, 'I don't think women should do it.' He's really sexist. He said only men could do it. I didn't like that. I argued with him about it. Then my sister got involved too, then my brother – he doesn't think I should do it, but he's always been like that. My other brother tells me I should do it.

This prejudice against women going into this line of work has also fuelled her own doubts about being able to cope:

I don't really think I've got the guts to do it, although I really want to. I don't think I could handle it. I'm really emotional and I wouldn't be able to take seeing people hurt and injured. If it was just putting out fires I'd be OK, but if it was getting people out of trapped cars and stuff I'd be no good at that. I'd be more panicky than them. I suppose I'd probably get used to it, but it would take a long time. Most firemen say you get used to it, it doesn't bother you after a while, but I'm not sure if I could get used to it if I saw someone trapped as an everyday thing.

Unfortunately, it looks as if Rosie may end up in an office, just as she did for her work experience, unless she can overcome her own and others' doubts:

I've liked it since I was about ten. It's something I've always wanted to do. I always read up about it. For work experience I was going to go, and I went to see the careers teacher but he said it was taken off the list as there were no insurances to cover me, so I couldn't do it. I'll probably end up in an office, but I would like to be a firewoman. I've always been interested in doing something different. I don't want to do something that every woman does. It's only women on the typewriter – I don't want to be like that, but I probably will in the end. That's what I ended up doing for my work experience because there was nothing with the fire service.

The girls described here benefited to some extent by having had friends or relatives who did the sort of 'men's work' they were interested in doing themselves, who could give them some idea of what was involved. Work experience can help them even more. What is significant about them is that they already have a lot of interest and motivation, and with encouragement and support this may be sustained. For those girls who have no particular interest in crossing such boundaries it is hard to create these desires simply by providing information and encouragement. In this respect the Girls and Occupational Choice Project (GAOC)[6] demonstrated how girls' choices narrowed and became more conforming as they progressed through their secondary school life. One area that does seem to have attracted more girls through doing CDT (craft, design and technology) lessons is design, a job choice made by a significant number of girls in the 1991 study. While this is not the epitome of 'men's work', it has attracted more girls into taking and becoming involved with this whole subject option.

Journalism is an area in which women have been increasingly represented, but they are rarely found reporting from the more exciting or dangerous places. One of the Ealing girls said in 1972 that she would not do journalism, which she saw as a boy's job, because men are tougher and women might have to see and report something that upset them. However, from the 1970s and through into the eighties and nineties, female journalists have taken a higher profile, reporting on wars in areas like Central America, and the Arab countries. Women like Kate Adie, a television reporter based in dangerous trouble spots, confound traditional prejudices. It was significant that her name came up amongst those named as the famous person girls would like to be. Several of the Ealing girls wanted to go into journalism:

> I like the idea of getting information what people need, I like to think that without me people wouldn't know what was going on. I'd like to get the news. I'd like to be like Kate Adie, travel everywhere, like if there's a war going on she's right in the middle of it, she's actually saying what she sees, she's reporting from the spot. I'd like to do that.
>
> CATHERINE

> What I like about being a journalist is being with the public, working with the public, getting and finding out things. You have to go out and get things. I want to feel that I've gone out and got something and done it. If it wasn't for my parents I wouldn't have thought of being a journalist. I kept telling them I just wanted to be a sports teacher, or in some profession of sport, but there's no money in sport.
>
> KATE

Journalism is not truly 'men's work', as women have always written for newspapers and magazines to some extent. But there are certain male-dominated areas of journalism that women are now challenging, and beginning to make significant inroads.

Once again I have not described these reactions in 1972 and 1991 in order to provoke either surprise or pessimism but to show how gender divisions need to be questioned, and to indicate whether and how these may have changed. The reasons behind girls' avoidance of male-defined jobs may sometimes appear simplistic and irrational but they are entangled with much deeper feelings of 'feminine' identity. Simply providing increased opportunities will not induce girls to take them. The same applies to any efforts to persuade boys to enter 'women's work', but this would also be complicated by the fact that this sort of work would be seen as not only inappropriate, but of lower status.

It takes self-confidence and courage for girls to break through the prejudice that surrounds entry into male-dominated careers. Throughout their school life, they have experienced many counter positionings of sexes and subjects, they have absorbed the siting of male and female as opposites, and have moved towards the safer 'feminine' areas of interest. They have learnt that much of the work men do is associated with so-called 'male' characteristics such as aggression, strength, stamina, competitiveness, ambition, and a technical or analytical mind, which are qualities that conflict with the myth of 'femininity', and probably where they have positioned themselves in relation to this. Therefore bricklaying, as one girl said, is obviously 'unladylike', and contradicted her sense of her own femininity at that moment. If girls are not well equipped with these qualities, it is at least partly related to the nature of their upbringing, and if they are, they are reluctant to use them to advantage and may prefer to see themselves as ultimately unable to succeed. In many cases it is less anxiety-provoking to opt for work in which girls are welcomed: it is not appealing to forge a path into areas that may be hostile and competitive. Although girls see working with people as an important factor, it is often as important that these people should be friendly and welcoming. As it is, the vast majority of the Ealing girls are not yet frustrated mechanics, engineers, lorry drivers, electricians, plumbers, pilots and veterinary surgeons. Nor are the boys frustrated nursery nurses, secretaries, hairdressers, telephonists, language translators and so on, and are even less likely than girls to have aspirations for these, due to the traditionally lower pay and status of 'women's work'. If they did enter these jobs in any number, then pay and status levels might well rise, but men would also tend to colonize the higher levels, and 'professionalize' the area if appropriate, as happened with social work in the 1970s.

Both boys and girls are capable of undertaking a much wider spectrum of skills and occupations, but where sex has become an organizing principle in society, working men and women at home and at work have had to accommodate themselves to separate slots within the system. Unemployment has disturbed the equilibrium but has mainly left gender roles intact. Even if it were possible, it would be a mistake to think that a female invasion of male work or vice versa would seriously challenge gender roles and discrimination. For a start it is complicated by class and race. Disentangling and resolving all this involves not only challenging male power, but making fundamental social and economic changes, which is not impossible but is hard to envisage at present.

For decades there has been a familiar call for more people, and especially women, to go into careers in science and industry. This achieved less than moderate success, and one study done in the 1960s[7] revealed in detail the attitudes of girls at that time to science in general and to engineering as a career in particular. This bias against industry was due to: belief in prejudice against girls; ignorance about the range of work involved; acceptance of the common view that engineering means having dirty and disagreeable working conditions; a wish to avoid stiff male competition; and a preference for work to which they could easily return later in life. Although the research was done a long time ago, such comments as girls made about engineering have held true through the years.

For those that have followed careers in industry, it has not been easy, as when they have succeeded in entering such an occupation, employers may then try to channel them down a different route from their male counterparts.[8] Now that there has been a small movement of women into some of the more traditional areas of male industry such as engineering, we find that there are no longer enough jobs to go round. The economic recession and the contraction in industry means that young women with excellent qualifications in science and engineering, for example, are unable to get a job. Today, graduates are finding it harder than ever to find work, and graduate unemployment in 1993 reached the unprecedentedly high level of 15 per cent while the national average is 10·4 per cent. (This represents a combined figure which includes the 'new' universities.) Taken separately, the 'old' university unemployment rate is nearer the national average while the 'new' universities show a much higher rate. These former polytechnics recruit from a far wider and more working class based selection of potential students; a significant number of them are women who enter as mature students (often with children) who have a hard economic struggle to survive. With little support, it is many of these students who will find themselves without work at the end of their courses.

FURTHER EDUCATION

I saw a careers officer when I left school. It was so boring you know, I can hardly remember. They said I could be a clerk. Ever since I was a kid I always wanted to teach, always. But I never knew anything about further education. All I knew when I was fifteen was that I wanted to get out of there. I found out about further education by chance, from my teacher at night school. Further education changed my life coming here, I'll tell you that. So different from school. But I still think they ought to offer more courses. I mean, I wouldn't want to do engineering or anything, but that's only because of the way I've been taught.

JANE, FURTHER EDUCATION STUDENT, 1972

Careers advice is obviously important in helping girls choose their subject options for GCSE, and the choices they make to study for A level, BTec, or any other further educational qualification they wish to pursue. In the 1970s a great many working class girls who would have benefited greatly from further education neither knew of its existence nor felt encouraged to find out about it. They were very anxious to leave school and did not realize that further education could be very different from school. At that time, the provision of further education, day release and block release was inadequate for both girls and boys, but particularly for girls. There were a lot more girls than boys taking day release; many more boys with apprenticeships than girls who were predominantly employed in hairdressing.[9] Opportunities for further education at that time were seldom offered from clerical and other office work apart from large institutions like the Civil Service and the then nationalized industries. Girls either made the best of the learning and skills they gained at school, or they embarked on a training course at their own expense.

The attitudes of employers and girls too often coincided to hinder any solid demand for more further education opportunities. Employers were content to see girls as short-term investments, on whom it was not worth spending money since sooner or later they were bound to leave for another job or for marriage. They also assumed that girls themselves did not wish for further education.

This might have often been the case at this time since many girls were so pleased to have left school that they perceived further education as a step backwards in freedom and maturity. Girls had no chance to realize that further education colleges could be much less restrictive than school, and need not interfere with their financial independence. The situation might have been different if employers had been compelled to make these opportunities available to all girls and boys. Also, if a wider variety of subjects had been offered to each instead of rigid sex-defined courses. Apart from the usual O level and A level subjects, the main courses that girls were found in at further education colleges at this time were business and com-merce - which included a disproportionate amount of shorthand and typing - and hairdressing. A whole range of technical subjects was available to boys, and they also took business and commerce but their courses were oriented towards management and they did not learn the 'feminine' skills of typing and shorthand.

In the 1990s, moving into further education by going into the sixth form at school, or in a sixth form college, or any other college of further education, is very common. Going to such a college at sixteen now is generally a different experience from staying on at school twenty years earlier. The relative autonomy it appears to offer, such as students only attending the particular courses they are doing and having their free periods to study or not as they prefer, is very attractive to many girls who are fed up with the way they feel they are treated like children at school. In the early 1970s pupils who stayed on into the sixth form predominantly took A levels, whereas nowadays they may take or retake GCSE exams as well, or do vocational subjects, or courses in subjects like theatre studies that they were then unable to do at school. Encouraging commitment to education is positive in principle, but education perhaps should take better account of today's realities for young people at the end of it, when many will face a much more disjointed trajectory into and through work than they have been promised.[10]

In 1983 the Conservative government set up the Youth Training Scheme (YTS, now called Youth Training, or YT) as a way of providing unemployed young people with some training. The idea was to help any sixteen- or seventeen-year-old leaving school to get skills, work experience, and qualifications, and also to keep the increasingly large number of young people without a job off the unemployment figures. Since 1988, unemployed sixteen- and seventeen-year-olds have been expected to take a YT course unless they have other means of support, since the government removed their entitlement to income support until they are eighteen. The course programmes normally last for one or two years and vary in subject from vocational courses such as painting and decorating, car mechanics, child-care, theatre studies, to general training in social and life skills. The scheme has been a mixed success as there have not always been enough courses available for those who need them, or they have not been available in the desired subjects, and there is no guarantee of getting a job afterwards. They have simply kept youth unemployment figures down a bit, and often provided firms with cheap labour. Although available for those leaving school without a job, none of the Ealing girls mentioned this even as a remote possibility. In her study of sexual inequalities and the YTS, Cynthia Cockburn describes and illustrates the ways that young women are discriminated against. She found such processes operating at an unconscious level and sometimes a conscious level, and that some very sex-specific selection occurred at the recruitment stage.[11] She also found evidence of racial discrimination in the process, for Asian and Afro-Caribbean women.

In the nineties, economic recession has eaten away at traditional occupations. It has made men (and women) redundant who would never have thought they would find themselves in that position, such as those working in banking and insurance. In many ways it has thrown a lot of things up in the air, to be caught by whoever is there waiting to take advantage of the moment. There is a polarity in society at present between those who are doing very well and have benefited from the Conservative policies of the last two decades, and a larger section of the population who have less than ever before, many of whom are lone mothers. There have been considerable changes in the lives of girls and women over this period, which have raised their expectations rather than the reverse, both at work and in the home. Boys' lives have also been affected, but more in terms of a decline in their work prospects than significant change in the type of work they expect to do, or their role in the family. Despite talk of shared roles and the 'new man', research on social attitudes still shows that women still do the bulk of domestic work within the family.[12] In this area there are a great many more changes needed in the lives of boys and men. But the nature of real life never quite matches people's attitudes and future expectations, especially when they are young teenagers. The generation of women that includes both the Ealing girls of 1972 and the mothers of the girls studied in 1991 will have discovered this. It is likely, too, that these teenage girls expressing their expectations in the early 1990s will also eventually find themselves faced only with the familiar and narrow range of jobs that accommodate the needs of women with dependent children, like their mothers before them.

CHAPTER 4

1. In 1970 women formed 71 per cent of service workers, 48 per cent of sales workers, 67 per cent of clerical workers, 38 per cent of technical and professional workers, 20 per cent of production workers and 7·5 per cent of executive and managerial workers. M. Galenson, *Women and Work*, figures from the International Labour Office.
2. Pearl Jephcott, *Rising Twenty*, Faber & Faber, 1948.
3. C. Cockburn, *Two Track Training*, Macmillan, 1987.
4. A. Kelly, 'Gender Roles at Home and School', *British Journal of Sociology of Education*, 3(3), 1982.
5. J. Whyte, *Girls into Science and Technology: The Story of a Project*, Routledge & Kegan Paul, 1986.
6. See J. Holland, 'Girls and Occupational Choice', in A. Pollard, J. Purvis and G. Walford (eds.), *Education, Training and the New Vocationalism*, Open University Press, 1988.
7. N. Seear, V. Roberts and J. Brock, *A Career for Women in Industry?*, Oliver & Boyd, 1964.
8. C. Cockburn, op. cit.
9. In 1970 there were 15,801 girl apprentices altogether, 11,336 being in hairdressing and manicure. There are no figures available on apprenticeships as such for 1991.
10. Claire Wallace, 'From Girls and Boys to Women and Men: the Social Reproduction of Gender', in M. Arnot and G. Weiner (eds.) *Gender and the Politics of Schooling*. Hutchinson, in association with the Open University, 1987.
11. C. Cockburn, op. cit.
12. 'Men and Women at Work and at Home', in *British Social Attitudes: the 9th report*, 1992/93 edition, Roger Jowell *et al.* (eds.), Dartmouth, 1992.

CHAPTER 5

SOPHISTICATED MYTHS

Eventually when I quit the Royal Air Force, I'd like to have a kid who I could bring up and who I could have all my time with. But the second kid I'd like to go back to work. I'd like to see them both grow up but I think you need money and after all the years you have at school and all the exams, I think you should get something out of it, get a career. Then I'd get a nanny or a childminder, someone I could really trust. I think in a way women still have to choose between a career and a family but today I think you can have both, more than a while ago. There's more jobs open to mothers who have children. And jobs have crèches and things for children, or they pay for their nursery fees or the nanny. And working mothers get more encouragement to go back to work after their child, not stay at home. After all you've done at school, staying at home – well, you should get out again, go back to work. The one thing I'd never be is become a housewife. I couldn't. I think people that do it, nowadays, who've had all those years at school and exams, and then to go home and staying home – I will never do that. I think you should get out and get a career. If you fail exams, you've got to try again. You shouldn't just give up.

CAROLINE, 1991

The sexual division of labour has always seemed a monumental fact of life. It has history on its side and has been accepted as an essential condition for the survival of society. But it appears to rest on a number of very doubtful assumptions, the grounds for which have been seriously questioned, and have been further undermined by the practical consequences of changes forced by unemployment and family breakdown.

Many of the differences assumed to exist between men and women have been generated from the biological fact of women's capacity for reproduction. Their subsequent preoccupation with pregnancy, childbirth and child-rearing has been seen as excluding them from many other sorts of activity. A belief, for instance, that 'proper' women (i.e. middle class women) are incapable of, or unsuited to, heavy or physically demanding work was expanded to keep them from doing many other things outside the home. Their nineteenth century status as the property of men, the sign of male affluence, and the producer of future heirs, contributed to their devaluation and to paternalism. This view of men and women was the dominant ideology for many centuries and still receives some support today, an anachronism hanging on in the midst of modern scientific and technological progress. Despite the expansion of women's role, a significant number of people, especially men, take a fall-back position that it is really men who should be out at work and women who are 'naturally' more suited to looking after the home and family.

That a woman's place is at home looking after husband and children has been a myth which has helped to validate the continued cheap reproduction of workers and, therefore, the maintenance of business and industry under a capitalist economy. Nowadays, the public assertion of this belief has been largely put to one side, rather than totally replaced. The increased economic need for women to work, the recognition of this by men and by (mainly male) employers, together with changes in girls' and women's own attitudes and expectations about their lives, have all served to question and partly dismantle it. The Ealing girls in 1991 soundly rejected the suggestion that 'a woman's place is in the home'. But however little support is given to this idea, it is still implicitly endorsed within an acceptance of women's double role. And in real life, the home is certainly where many women still find themselves working long hours, whatever attitudes and beliefs they may ascribe to. Although acknowledged to have an acceptable and legitimate part to play in the work-force, many people see a 'normal' distribution of roles as men in continuous work and women in broken periods of work while caring for home and children. The fact that the present economic situation renders this 'normality' impossible for many families is not seen as permanent, and allows women's crucial economic role to be implicitly treated as temporary.

Every society tends to believe that the division of labour it has adopted is a 'natural' one, or one most ideally suited to the social or physical conditions of that society. Thus it was that a capitalist society gave primary roles to men as workers and women as family carers. Even when women were very visible in the work-force, such as the many working class women who worked in factories, shops, etc., throughout the past two centuries, this was ignored since the people who represented 'normality' were the middle classes. The belief that under capitalism and other economies in the developed world the condition of women springs from something universally true of women is contradicted by the existence of cultures which do not contain the same division of labour. Much anthropological evidence illustrates this.[1] If, however, anthropological evidence seems rather remote and one is tempted to dismiss such societies as 'obviously not like us', there are closer examples to be drawn from women's situation in our own society both past and present. For instance, the idea that housework and child-care are light jobs has been used to suggest that women as housewives and mothers have a soft option. But this is far from true. Although housework has become easier over the years, it used to be very hard work, and remains so for those today who cannot afford modern household aids. In the earlier part of this century, and long before that, domestic servants worked an endless round of drudgery, doing things which the most physically fit person would find tiring. Child-care can be even more exhausting, needing seemingly endless amounts of energy. Children are physically and mentally demanding at all times, even when they are asleep, for mothers learn always to stay alert for the sound of crying, and it is no light task to carry round a two- or three-year-old child.

Many other kinds of work also provide ample evidence of women's physical strength and stamina. The hospital services are one good example, where not only do nurses have working hours and shifts that are in themselves exhausting, but they are also required to do a lot of heavy lifting. Physiotherapists are continuously involved in physical activities, doing exercises, massages and supporting people. In another area of work, women cleaners working in offices and industry have to move large machines around from floor to floor, and room to room.

The emergency substitution of women in men's work in the past has provided further proof that women have a vast reservoir of abilities. The two World Wars showed this very clearly, when women were drawn away from their homes and children to fill the gaps in industry created by men joining the armed forces. Heavy work was often carried out, requiring the same strength needed for tasks at home:

> At many jobs that they had rarely or never done before, women proved to be quicker and defter than men, with their small fingers used to knitting and sewing. Women were easily trained for welding, which gained much ground in British engineering during the war. But even the jobs that required sheer physical strength were not always beyond middle-aged housewives who had been used to struggling with shopping baskets and small children up several flights of tenement steps. No women went down the coal-mines, but in most jobs beneath that level of sheer strength and stamina, a few could always find a place.[2]

No one cried out then that a woman's place was only in the home, but when the war was over, it was conveniently packaged and labelled as a temporary crisis. Women were applauded for their special efforts, but were encouraged to return home, or were automatically made redundant.

Myths about women's role and abilities still persist in spite of past and present illustrations to the contrary, and now a superficially egalitarian ideology. The reasons for this were discussed earlier, and linked the economic and social structure with ideology and women's psychological sense of identity. It is still economically necessary that women provide their free services in the home, maintain a family and pass on their own example to future generations. Today, nearly half of the work-force are women, and 68 per cent of married women are working. In real economic terms, a woman's work role can no longer be regarded as secondary to her domestic role. Yet this has been a traditional belief which both men and women grew to accept with unfortunate consequences for women. Many women have always worked out of the sheer need to make ends meet, and there are other equally valid reasons. For instance, the need to find social companionship, to break the isolation of the home, create a separate identity outside the home, and to gain economic independence are all very important.

The division of home and work activities into primary and secondary served to saddle women with two jobs. Even if they are out at work all day, the household tasks and child-care are still made their responsibility and women's guilt is easily aroused by the possibility of child neglect. In the 1960s and 1970s, inaccurate and often horrific accounts of 'latchkey' children made many mothers either stop work or feel torn with anxiety. In the 1980s and 1990s, there has been even more need, and acceptance of this need, for mothers to work and, for lone mothers in particular, the practical pressures and psychological stresses have been even more intense.

MOTHERHOOD

Two aspects of the demands of motherhood have reinforced each other to preserve the importance of woman's mothering role. The first is concerned with real conditions, and the second with ideology. In this country every mother with young children is still faced with a widespread lack of nursery facilities. In the 1990s, as in the 1970s, if she wants to work she often has the choice of putting her children in the care of any available and willing relatives; leaving them with a paid babyminder who may lack adequate facilities for the care of more than a few children; or trying to get a place in a day nursery, either private (which are generally expensive), or state-run (which are usually over-subscribed). Day nurseries are still relatively few, and most have permanent waiting lists. A young mother needing work who is without access to any of these has no choice but to stay at home, or be exploited as an outworker.

There were plenty of nursery facilities during the Second World War, when state-sponsored nurseries were crucial to facilitate women's employment, but there has been relatively little increase in nursery provision to cope with the expanding female labour force in the ensuing decades.[3] In the absence of adequate or affordable child-care provision, mothers have to stop working for significant periods of time. This contributes to the discontinuity that characterizes women's working life. It frustrates those who want and need to work, and reinforces any underlying prejudices held by employers that women are a temporary or surplus labour force, worth less than men and treated accordingly.

Supporting this is the myth surrounding the importance of motherhood. Girls have been brought up to believe that the most fulfilling thing in life is to have children, and to be good mothers. Women who cannot have children are pitied, those who do not want to are considered peculiar and unnatural, and mothers who are indifferent or unenthusiastic about their own children are condemned. It is taken for granted that a child needs its mother, and the mother needs to have her child. These assumptions have been inextricably bound up together, and in many modern societies this is thought to be 'natural'.

Today, girls are less sure about the potential joys of motherhood. In the later study, about two out of five of the Ealing girls considered that having children was not as important for a woman as it used to be. (Fewer girls from Asian families agreed with this, but a lot of them were not sure.) Half of them also disagreed that a husband and family is the most satisfying thing that a girl can have, and a third of these girls remained unsure about both issues. This reflects their ambivalence over the place of marriage and family life in the general landscape of their lives. Family life is still very important, as indeed is their concern with people in general, but at this stage, it is placed within the context of other needs that they recognize as important, such as forging their own identities in work and any other potentially fulfilling area of their lives.

Motherhood is another subject that can be questioned by looking at other cultures. It is true that women have to undergo the biological process of reproduction, but it is not only women who can care and provide for children. This has been shown by the Australian aborigines, for instance, and the Arapesh, who involve both sexes equally in child-care. The Matabele in Zimbabwe were shown to operate a system in which a child has a 'Big Mother' and a number of 'Little Mothers'. These were all called 'Mama' by the child, and: 'It is thought unnatural for the biological mother to show more interest in "her" child than in those of her sisters and cousins.'[4] This freed many Matabele mothers for work in the fields and in the towns and enabled them also to have their children looked after independently. Another example can be drawn from Victorian England, when upper class families usually provided nurses for their children from birth. This left the mothers free to carry out their social duties, and to visit the nursery as often or as seldom as they liked.

The emphasis on exclusive mothering has been a relatively recent one. The developments in state education this century have meant that children now remain dependent for longer than before, and the expansion of psychology and Freudian theory laid the responsibility for a child's personality and behaviour firmly at the door of the family home, focusing on parents and mothers in particular. This served to tie women more and more to the home, making their whole lives an investment in and a sacrifice to their children, and making them feel guilty if they could not adapt to such a life easily or willingly.

But many other arguments were used to support the idea of a special mother–child relationship. The belief in a maternal instinct is one, and although this instinct is present in many animals and is necessary for their species survival, it has no proven physiological basis in human beings. A mother's love and protectiveness for her child need be no more intense than that of its father, or in fact any other person who becomes very involved with it. Another belief is that women innately possess the 'right' characteristics for motherhood. The way girls develop their so-called 'feminine' personality and identity is often through the caring roles and relationships they have with family members and other people, and this can nurture an apparently 'natural' predisposition for motherhood. Girls have many rehearsals with dolls and through observing their mothers, and may often be responsible for the care of smaller brothers and sisters. There is also the knowledge that they are the sex capable of having children, which is a positively creative thing to be able to do.

At the time I was originally writing this book in the mid 1970s, the organization of work made it more economically valid for most men to be out at work and for women to stay at home with children, or for women to combine part-time work with child-care. Despite changes in work styles, and increased unemployment, this is still the case. As women will probably always be the ones having babies, so some people will always make a case for this division of labour, at least when children are very young. This is, of course, also predicated on the assumption that women are the most naturally appropriate people to look after their babies. But if we subscribe to the view that either men or women are capable of caring for babies, and if it is possible for a family to live on one income (often difficult), then either mothers or fathers could stay at home. The fact that it is mainly mothers at home is due both to prejudice against full-time fatherhood, and an occupational structure which still makes it likely that 'men's work' will pay more than 'women's work'. It was significant that several girls in the 1991 study described how their fathers had spent some time at home looking after them or their brothers or sisters to enable their mothers to go to work. These men inevitably had some flexible work arrangement to facilitate this, such as Fiona's father, who was a self-employed accountant:

> When the twins were born Mum had this job and they asked her to come in when they were busy, so my dad used to take the twins to work. They had a little playpen in his office. He used to take them quite often, he doesn't mind. He does take days off to take them out and stuff, or if my mum's got to do something, so it's not bad. He does help with them and he makes us help with them as well.

Since women have historically lacked an officially acknowledged place in the external world of production, they have had little alternative other than to sink their identity into their ascribed role, into caring for those closest to them. Motherhood has become an integral part of this. But changes in the economic structure, in the nature and availability of employment, and in women's lives and expectations have made it impossible to deny the importance of women's work outside the home. However, the economic need to use them more efficiently by overtly tampering with the mothering role is an issue which has been carefully avoided. Ironically, the social and economic conditions necessary for 'good' mothering have become increasingly difficult.

The growth of psychology in the twenties and thirties and the subsequent recognition of the importance of a child's early experiences resulted in much theorizing and research. The consequences for a child of early separation from the exclusive and continuous care of its mother were scrutinized. The doom-laden concept of 'maternal deprivation' was formulated, predicting delinquency and personality defects. This condemned mothers who were separated from their young children through work or for any other reason. One of the earliest proponents of this view was John Bowlby, who in 1947 declared: 'It appears that there is a very strong case indeed for believing that prolonged separation of a child from his mother (or mother-substitute) during the first five years of life stands foremost among the causes of delinquent character development and persistent misbehaviour.'[5] He later modified this, but the essence: that there was an 'autonomous propensity' by both mother and infant to develop a deep attachment towards each other[6] remained through subsequent decades. Many of his followers carried this further by extending and misinterpreting his and their own findings. Bowlby's early research, and the central theories of exclusive attachment and mothering were much criticized.[7] Soon after Bowlby and similar researchers had made their theories public, these began to be used against mothers who worked. For instance: 'It has been claimed that proper mothering is only possible if the mother does not go out to work and that the use of day nurseries and crèches has a particularly serious and permanent deleterious effect.'[8] Numerous studies that tried to test these only produced inconclusive or contradictory results, and indicated the complexity of the concept. In spite of this lack of evidence, working mothers became inevitably linked with child neglect and have been made very responsible for the future development of their children. This continued into the 1970s, when Penelope Leach, for instance, advocated that mothers with pre-school children should stay at home. While defending the rights of children to good quality child-care, she was also nurturing the guilt of countless women for whom full-time motherhood was neither a desire nor a possibility.[9]

Ideas about maternal neglect have subsided somewhat with the increase in proportion of women working and leaving children in some sort of child-care. But the belief in a special mother–child bond is still very strong and its spell has yet to be broken. It is a debate that quietly festers on. There is always someone prepared to stir up people's emotions by making assertions about child neglect and how broken families are caused by mothers working. The incident in 1993 of a young single mother being jailed for leaving her two-year-old alone at home while she went to work because she could not afford to pay for child-care evoked widespread reactions ranging from condemnation of her as a mother, to criticism of the government for making it so difficult for women in her position to survive. It served to highlight the plight of many lone mothers and the continuing lack of child-care facilities.

It is undeniable that a child needs to make close bonds with at least one person that she or he can trust, love and depend on. What has been incorrectly claimed, however, is that there is one exclusive and primary relationship between mother (or a specific mother substitute) and child, which must remain virtually unbroken during the child's first few years of life. This was particularly strong in the post-war years and at the time I was doing the first study for this book, and the consequent reluctance to remove children from mothers had even kept some children in very unhappy family situations in preference to going to a 'good' foster or children's home. A child that is badly treated, or who grows up with a background of instability, insecurity or rejection does have a greater probability of developing problems. But this is just as likely to happen in a family home with a full-time mother who cannot cope or who may not be suited to devoting herself to domesticity and child-care.

The myth of maternal deprivation and neglect remains rooted within a deceptively simple concept of motherhood. It would perhaps be better to abolish the terms 'motherhood' and 'father-hood', as they serve to isolate responsibility for children. Although a substantial amount has been written, attempts to produce general theories about maternal deprivation have not proven very meaning-ful. Research has shown that the satisfaction felt by a woman towards her position, whether it be a working one or not, has a more positive effect on her children than her blanket acceptance of the need for all mothers either to stay home, or to work.[10] Dissatis-fied mothers can produce the same 'harmful' effects as negligent ones. Too often the happiness and satisfaction of a mother are neglected in the theories and research lavished on the needs of her children. Concentration on the possible bad effects on children resulting from their mother's working has ignored the possible benefits to both mother and child. Many positive effects on children from socializing with others, and on mothers from developing a

separate and economic identity outside the home have been documented.[11]

Unfortunately it takes more than counter-evidence to permeate
and erode such a monument to women's subjugation, and one that
is so much a part of social structure and beliefs. There is a perennial
scarcity of good, economical nursery facilities; many jobs available
to women, and especially part-time jobs, offer relatively low pay;
and most women still place a deep investment in caring for their
families. A combination of social, economic and psychological
factors and processes interact to prevent women from sharing the
mothering role with men as well as other women out of mutual
choice. Probably neither children nor their families have heard or
read much about maternal deprivation research, but they learn
through the way that families are organized and from books,
magazines and the television, that a mother and her children have a
'special' attachment, and it is seen to be more appropriate for
women to stay home or juggle work around their children's needs
than it is for men.

By comparison, the importance of the father's role has been
relatively under-researched, but all the indications suggest that a
father is equally able to have as intense a relationship with a child as
its mother. But for men to participate fully implies entering the 'less
valued' world of women. Research on men who looked after
motherless families in the early 1970s found that:

> Those fathers who continued to work had to regard their work
> in a new light. No longer could they look at it from the point of
> view of its economic rewards, the satisfactions, if any, which it
> brought and the other criteria by which most people assess their
> job. For many, a new and over-riding criterion asserted itself –
> the compatibility of work with the care of children.[12]

Those men who had had to give up work found this particularly
disturbing and felt that 'without a job they were less than men.'[13]
This research also found little support for the claims of maternal
deprivation in these circumstances. Since that time there has been
more research around various issues of fathering.[14] But even if male
reaction to increased 'fathering' had been favourable, the division of
labour by sex at that time, with its emphasis on efficiency, would

not permit working men to include this in their role. Unemployment did not then present such a problem and therefore men were usually in work that occupied all the day; they could also be working late on shift-work or overtime and have little opportunity to spend much time with their children. Today, the picture has changed significantly, as men have found themselves increasingly at home, either through the rising level of unemployment over the last twenty years, or through more flexible working arrangements and self-employment. In conjunction with this, there have also been changes in the way men and masculinity are seen. The attempt to mesh together aspects of the 'new' man and the 'old' man have been illustrated in fashionable photographs or advertisements showing a semi-naked muscular man cradling a tiny baby in his arms. It implies that men are moving into child-care, and that they can be both 'masculine' and tender at the same time. Other changes during this period put men as fathers into greater relief: for instance, within the rise in lone parenting, there has been an increase in the number of lone fathers, who make up over 9 per cent of lone parents; and it has become more commonplace and even expected for fathers to be present at the birth of their children. Over the same time, the proportion of women in the work-force was still slowly increasing, leading to many men participating more in domestic work and child-care through necessity as much as inclination, although there has been more emphasis on sharing in modern couple relationships. It is, however, girls and women whose ideas and expectations have been changing, more than their male counterparts. They are now setting the agenda for the roles within marriage or cohabitation but are finding their raised expectations of future partners often result in disillusionment or conflict.

In 1972, several of the Ealing girls with full-time working mothers specified that they would make their home and family different by making sure they were at home for their children after school. They did not expect father to be there, or other friends or relatives. Although it is undoubtedly reassuring to come home to somebody, after school or work, there is no rational reason why it has to be the mother. But once again this is a difficult pattern to break, since it is with their mother that many children have already had to form their closest attachments through the isolating circumstances of the nuclear family. Their dependence on her makes her presence hard to find a substitute for and has reinforced the belief in this as the crucial relationship. If care and responsibility for children could be more consistently (but not confusingly) shared amongst more people, and other attachments were made and nurtured, there would be less pressure on mothers, and children would be able to benefit from a number of different relationships with adults of varying personality and role. But it is hard to construct a different and shared way of child-rearing in the midst of an established system that emphasizes privacy, property and possession of people as well as things.[15] Experiments in raising children in communes and similar environments have consequently encountered problems as well as having advantages.[16] In my research nearly twenty years later, this concern for a mother to be at home for her children was not expressed. This is not because there were fewer 1991 girls' mothers working, but because there is less of an expectation that mothers of children that age will be at home. The common assumption now is that women work, whether or not they have children, and certainly by the time their children are in secondary school most will be thinking about taking at least a part-time if not a full-time job. Many will have been working from a much earlier stage in their children's lives and mothers at home are no longer the norm.

FEMININE OCCUPATIONS

In her role as a housewife and mother, a woman is still regarded by many as someone who 'doesn't work', whose activities, although necessary, are not 'real' work. This attitude has traditionally been extended to any work she does outside, and consequently 'women's work' has been undervalued, underpaid, and very exploited. Women 'do work which is both dirty and physically tiring when it appears as an extension of housework. Indeed, the more closely work resembles housework, the less it has the status of "real" work. Cleaning is a clear example of this. Also secretarial work often involves little more than being a "substitute wife" to bosses, carrying out all the low-level menial tasks and drudgery.'[17] Running personal errands has always been implicitly accepted as part of a secretary's job. Secretaries are often treated as sexual decoration for the office and the male ego, and the crucial part they play in their bosses' success goes largely unrecognized.

'Everyone knows that if something is called women's work it means it will be low paid, probably very essential, often uninteresting, and unpleasant, and men don't want to do it.'[18] These words, written in 1973 by Labour MP Audrey Wise, still apply in the mid 1990s. A vicious circle is set up in which women's work, like the status of women themselves, reinforces their own devaluation:

> In our money economy, women have relatively little money in their own right. They sell their labour in the bargain basement, at cut prices, and so they are given a cut-price valuation in all spheres of activity. When you sell your labour power you are also selling your time, your life-time, the stuff of life itself, and if it fetches low prices you are yourself valued low.[19]

There are many reasons for the persistence of this circularity, and for the continued separation of jobs according to sex. Employers, for instance, have little wish to change the situation, because they benefit from women as a cheap labour force. They, and most other men and women, accept many assumptions about women's suitability for particular jobs. In male-dominated areas of work, there is strong opposition to women's entry from the men who are fearful of lowered wages, and, especially in the recession throughout the eighties into the nineties, the very real threat of unemployment. Opportunities vary greatly by region, and outside the highly urbanized centres, women wanting to work choose from the limited jobs available. In the recent past, many women took on the boring repetitive jobs that they were supposed to be so well suited for, because there was nothing else, or because with their double work load inside and outside the home, they could not cope with jobs needing concentration and responsibility. The decline in the manufacturing industries meant that men were thrown out of work while women continued to move into jobs and professions, many in the service industries, which took longer to feel the effects of the recession and have declined more slowly. This has also contributed to what has been called the 'feminization' of the work-force.

One characteristic of many jobs that have proved popular for girls in the past is that they have been one-level occupations. They contain little opportunity for moving into anything different or higher. Most 'women's work' remains 'stationary' apart from certain professions in which the proportion of women has been slowly rising, and jobs like teaching and hospital work. In these a rise is possible, but there are still significantly less women in top positions than men. Movement has tended to be horizontal, from job to job, with little progression to anywhere except marriage or old age. Office work, for instance, which still represents a good, respectable but less popular job for a girl than previously, has a very low ceiling in terms of prospects. This is especially so for working class girls who often go into it with lower qualifications, or merely lack some of the refinements of accent or manner acquired by middle and upper class girls. Office work has built up its own status hierarchies and discriminates accordingly. In the 1970s, office work was seen as a good choice for girls, and as one writer on the subject noted at the time:

> Within this vast cross-section of the female population, there are many distinct gradations of social class, which are translated into distinctions at work. It is often assumed that an office girl slowly progresses from the typing pool to the carpeted office of the 'executive secretary'. But in fact few girls seem to make much progress once they enter the office. It reflects enduring social distinctions as faithfully as does the school system ... The selection goes back as far as birth and is reinforced by the prestige gradations of secretarial schools.[20]

Therefore, a secretary or shorthand typist usually progresses only to a position where she is working for a more important boss. She is unlikely to become anything other than a secretary herself. In work such as television production[21] and publishing, secretarial work has been traditionally used as a side-door for women into positions that men would apply for directly, and there is no guaranteed promotion. Similarly, receptionists, telephone operators and shop assistants do little more than swap jobs. Female bank clerks are generally viewed differently from male bank clerks, every one of whom is 'a potential bank manager'. Women as 'rank and file', and in servicing roles to men's occupational superiority, have been taken for granted in a view that places men at the top of a hierarchy of power and women at the bottom and disregards the real usefulness of their work.

In the years since the first Ealing study, more women have appeared to be entering 'top jobs', an impression created by the media publicity given to a small number of successful women in the business world. In fact, there has not been much significant movement of women into 'top jobs'. Nevertheless, many of the Ealing girls in the later study mentioned this as proof that things had changed and that equality was well on the way. However, it is no solution to changing women's situation by getting women into management and top jobs, for this does nothing to remove the inequalities everywhere else. It is more important to give all girls the opportunities to learn various sorts and levels of skills and to give them self-confidence in their abilities, instead of exploiting them through myths of femininity that imprison them in the 'bargain basement' of work.

We have seen that since feminine characteristics are not ones that are highly valued in this society, women's work has historically been treated as inferior. Often, women are seen, and see themselves, as not having the appropriate qualities to cope with certain aspects of 'men's work'. But this does not necessarily constitute a criticism of women. On the contrary, men can be seen as sacrificing themselves to the acquisition of more money, either through desire to make profit, or simply to make enough to feed and clothe a family. In the early 1970s the overwhelming concern that the Ealing girls showed about people and about interest in a job reflected their emphasis on 'human' aspects rather than money. Working men have often been willing or forced to surrender to a de-humanizing rat-race, agreeing to productivity deals which make work more unpleasant in return for promises of increased wages, which soon get swallowed up in inflation. Women have traditionally been excluded from this at home, and those who worked, although more exploited than men, have been generally loath to follow men's example in their demands. In the seventies, the emerging militancy of women in jobs such as teaching and nursing made many aware that they must demand better conditions as well as pay. This militancy has since subsided, lost in the declining power of the unions in the context of high unemployment and the depressing conditions of a continuing economic recession.

As far as men have often accepted working under almost any

conditions for more money, women have generally been more sensitive and resistant to such compromises. Up until relatively recently their actual or ideological exclusion from total involvement in work preserved in them a sense of being apart from the system. Even today, when so many now take the financial importance of their working lives for granted, they are less willing to exchange conditions for cash.

HOPES FOR THE FUTURE

The fact that women now form a crucial part of the work-force is no longer at issue. There may be those who believe or hope that this is a temporary phenomenon, but it would take a lot to persuade or force women to return to a full-time life at home. In the present economic situation and high level of unemployment, both girls and boys potentially face a fragmented working life. For women the discontinuity has always been through child-bearing, whereas for men it is now due to the current precariousness of their jobs. The combination of effective contraception and abortion, smaller size families, and the greater longevity of women means that women now have a large proportion of their lives potentially free for other activities, such as taking a paid occupation. Assuming an (albeit) ideal situation of good and available child-care, a woman with two children need only spend about three years of her life preoccupied with pregnancy and lactation. This represents a tiny proportion of her life-span. If she wants to be a full-time mother until her children are well into school, this still leaves between thirty and forty years of her life when she is able to work. Of course not every woman wants to work, but the important thing is to have the choice, and not just the choice of low level and boring jobs.

There is still a lingering prejudice against women because of the possibility that they may leave work to have children, but this is just one of many breaks within the general fragmentation of people's working lives today. Research studies in the seventies showed an increasing tendency for girls to anticipate working certainly until having children, some returning soon after, and most returning when the children went to school. There was an emphasis towards part-time work as a compromise between work and family commitments. Although part-time work is notoriously exploitative, it remains attractive for enabling women to seemingly fulfil their role both in the family and at work.[22]

Adult life may prove far removed from the hopes and expectations expressed as teenagers. We have already seen how the jobs done by the mothers of the 1991 Ealing girls are in generally low level areas of work that may fit in best with family needs, while at the age of fifteen, like the 1972 girls, they may well have expressed high hopes for something quite different. The reality of most women's lives is that they usually want or have to put the needs of their children first, and a meaningful job or career takes second place (or disappears altogether) unless they have the sort of work that can accommodate a more flexible working pattern, or they can afford full-time childcare. The 1991 girls were equally as hopeful as the 1972 girls. In drawing an initial outline of their future hazy horizons, most endorsed the importance of getting established in a job or career and then having children a bit later. Real life will doubtless be a lot less predictable. Nevertheless, work is now seen as having an acceptable and semi-permanent position in their lives, and whether for personal, professional or financial reasons, girls and women will continue to work, unless the employment situation dictates otherwise.

If we look a little deeper we can see how the reality of the lives of their mothers and other women have been absorbed into their attitudes and expectations. I asked the Ealing girls in 1991 what they thought was the most important thing about a job for a girl, and almost everyone (95 per cent) said it was 'making a career for herself'. When asked to write anything else they could think of that was important about having a job, they had a lot more to say than the girls in 1972. In the earlier study, girls were more content to simply endorse that either meeting people, getting money before getting married, making a career, or a combination of these, were important, and relatively few added other aspects of their own. Almost twenty years later, their contemporaries have absorbed the 'individualization' that has become a feature of our society, and the instability within it, and are well aware that women can no longer rely on a husband. This is reflected in their expression of other necessary or individually fulfilling ways that working could be important to them. In general, they strongly endorsed the ideas that girls and women need or want to work in order to support themselves; to give them independence; to fall back on in case their marriage does not work out; to stop them being stuck at home, etc. Here are some of their responses:

Freedom and Independence

Not to be stuck at home in the kitchen. I want to meet people and travel.

Securing a career with money to support yourself with.

Being able to cope on her own, stand on her own two feet.

It gives her independence and gives her a focus other than the family.

I think everyone needs to be independent and that is a quality that you get from a job.

To get some money and be able to live a good life on your own with a car and a flat.

She should be able to have her independence, do her own things, be her own boss, and enjoy herself at work.

By standing on your own two feet you are able to get respect from people which to me is very important.

Being independent, not relying on her husband.

In Case of Marriage Breakdown

They should have money set aside in case something goes wrong in the marriage.

Being able to stand up for herself if she has any problems with her arranged marriage.

Prove Themselves Independent from Men

Not feeling dominated by men and able to make a life for herself.

Supporting yourself and being independent – not really needing a man to support you.

Show men you can be as good as them.

To show women can have a good superior career, just as men.

Getting confidence to do jobs that men only think they can do.

To prove to herself and other people that she can do whatever she wants if she's determined.

Enjoyable career and not feeling inferior to her male associates.

Confidence, Self-respect, Achievement, etc.

Achievement, feeling good about what you do and knowing you do it well.

A girl needs to develop as a person.

That she can get a name in whatever she does and tries to get to the top.

Establishing herself as a person.

A career is a stand for the women and getting more respect in the public.

So I feel secure and proud of myself.

The Asian girls were particularly concerned with the importance of a career to gain self-respect; self-confidence; to show that they were not inferior to men; and to stand on their own feet. They more than the other girls expressed a preoccupation with proving themselves to their families or to men, which can be understood in the context of the traditional status of women in Asian cultures and religions, and the relatively restricted lives that many of them consequently lead. Here are some of their comments:

So people look up to you, especially the opposite sex and your family.

Just showing parents that we are capable of doing as much as boys or better. I hate being compared to them.

To gain self-respect for herself as well as her parents and to become confident of the job she is doing.

To show my husband if I had one that I am not a slave or housewife and that I have the right to work too.

I really intend to be an independent person mainly because female sex people always have to prove themselves as not being a second class citizen.

Overall, girls' responses suggested a more assertive approach to their lives, and recognized the real possibility that in the end, they may have to provide for themselves. This could be seen as a depressing reminder of the fragmentation of family life, but it also has a feeling of determination, assertiveness, and desire for independence that is refreshingly positive. Even if girls see life as potentially a bit of a struggle, they are more prepared to challenge this and are not looking to be left helpless. They are also looking to challenge men, and want the sense of achievement they may find in work. It is difficult to predict how far strong statements like these will be translated into future behaviour. Intentions are always easier than actions, but their consciousness of these issues and potentialities at least prepares the ground for doing something about them.

Combining Work and Family Life

The girls who were contemplating the world of work in 1972 viewed it with fragile and incomplete images of their future lives, but with hope, and with some awareness of the changing ideas about women and their role as they expressed in their ideas about combining home and work:

I think [work after marriage] is important because I think you tend to vegetate a bit if left at home doing housework all the time.

I think it's important for a girl to work as well as being married unless she's got small children. Apart from the extra money, if anything went wrong with the marriage she would have to support herself, fall back on her job. If you're too dependent on one person, the husband, it's very tempting for the husband to make the wife more the slave.

At this time, over 80 per cent of these girls said they would definitely carry on working after they married: by 1991, the girls in the later study were almost unanimous on this. In 1972 most expected to stop work when they had a family, and stay at home while their children were very young, but many also expressed strong views that women should go back to part-time or full-time work as soon as they could put their children into nursery school.

. . . when you have a baby you don't say, right, now I'll pack up working and be a housewife. I don't agree with that at all. When they're small, OK, but once you can get them into a nursery, then, when they're about three, go back to work again.

If you're indoors all the time, you can get bored and fed-up with it. I don't think they should leave their children when they're ever so young, but when they're about four they should be back at work.

In 1972 I said it would be rash to make wide assumptions about these findings, and caution is also necessary when trying to infer action from stated attitudes and intentions, especially for girls at this age whose real futures may be hazier than the impression given by their answers. This has been so. The continuing lack of adequate child care facilities, and the high level of unemployment has kept some women who want to work at home; while other mothers with young children have been forced to take jobs before they may wish to, because their husbands are in low paid jobs or out of work, and they have to take whatever work is around. The girls' ideas did, however, reflect their own absorption of a general and changing opinion about women and work. Twenty years later girls' professed intentions to work at some point after having children was empha-sized even more. Once again there was an optimistic assumption that child-care would be available. They also endorsed even more strongly that being a full-time housewife and mother was a boring prospect. In some cases, girls' anticipation of the tedium of being a housewife seemed not to recognize the added dimension of child-care, which is qualitatively different, and makes demands that can sometimes leave women with barely enough time for the housework they might actually like to do:

> I'd carry on working, definitely. I wouldn't give it up and just become a housewife. I'd take some months off when they are first born and everything. When they're about one, then I'd start, with a babysitter or something. But I wouldn't give up work. I wouldn't become a housewife, it's boring, just sitting at home and cooking and cleaning. No.
>
> KIM

> When I have children I'll still keep on working. They can go to a nursery or get a babysitter, but I want to carry on with my work. You can combine them, a job's important because you'll be getting more education in a job. Being at home with kids you aren't doing anything. Women who do stop at home aren't really learning anything, just getting bored and they won't be able to get any money.
>
> DENISE

With the elevated importance given to women working, the status of housewives and mothers has dropped even lower. For girls at school, the idea of being a full-time mother has been tagged as boring. Girls and women may accept more and more that they have two roles, one at home and one at work, but the one at home is denigrated compared to having a job. This, of course, reflects the persisting values in our society that consider paid employment as having the most status, while any unpaid labour is not 'proper' work. In asserting their rights and desires to combine work and home, girls and women must beware the trap of colluding with these values. The cleaning, feeding, washing, general maintenance, and care of a family take up a large proportion of time, but are crucial to keeping society going.

Some girls also saw not working as a waste of their qualifications:

> Most people who have kids go back to work after. I don't think

it's right just to give up your career just because you've had kids. You've obviously been through a lot to get that job so you're not just going to throw it down the drain.

LEAH

Commitment to a career still leaves women having to make all the adjustments, juggling domestic life and work life as they have always done, within a society still organized around the anachronistic assumption that work is primary for men and secondary for women. This was implicit in some of the Ealing girls' ideas and beliefs:

I think it's important to have a career, rather than just wait to get married. And I love children. I don't think women still have to choose [between a career and a family]. I think if they really want a family they can work round it. It might be a bit of a struggle at first but I think they can do it. My mum did it. A lot of my friends want a career, they're set on careers. I think more girls now want careers, and families later, which I think is good.

MELANIE

My mum doesn't want me to be a housewife. But they [parents] wouldn't stop me doing anything – they want me to do what I want to do. If I want to do something and she won't let me, I say 'I'll be a housewife!' and then she lets me! Silly, but she does. She doesn't mind being a housewife herself, but she doesn't want me doing it, she thinks I'm brainy. I want to be a scientist. She says they weren't taught what we're taught now, in her day. She wants me to do something I want to do. I want to have kids, but I want to be something as well, but apparently you can't, at least that's what we're learning about in media studies at the moment . . . you can be a mother and have a job, but you have to neglect one I think. I don't know which I'd neglect, it depends on your husband as well, whether he's got a job as well.

FIONA

Many have the example of their own upbringing during which their mothers were at work, and if it has been reasonably successful, they assume this as an appropriate model to follow:

I'd carry on with my career, definitely, wouldn't give it up for anything. I'd like to have children but I'd like a career that I can go back to. Sports is one of those things. I think when they're nursery age I'd like to do part-time. Then when they're ready to go to school, I might go full-time. I'd like to be there when they're growing up but not all the time. It's better for them to be with other kids, at a nursery or playgroup. That's what my mum did with me and my brother and it worked out OK.

TERESA

For Catherine it was important to continue to prove to her mother that this combination was possible:

I'd like to have a good career, then get married and have a family, but at the same time I want to carry on with my job. I'm not going to give up my job just to get married. If my husband thinks I'm going to stay at home and do the housework then I'd probably divorce him! If I had a young child maybe I would take a year off but I'd always go back to my job, maybe when they were older and going to school during the day. I wouldn't like them to be alone with a childminder because they'd get too attached to her, they wouldn't feel close to me ... I'd like to show my mum that I can have a career and have a family. She's got old-fashioned values, saying that I should do all the cooking and things. I want to make a point and say I don't have to do all the cooking, I can have a family that will do everything, that I can have a life with both my husband and I cooking or something. It's just me and my mum who do all the cooking. She thinks that's how it should be, I'd like to show her that it should be both.

Rachel has adopted a pragmatic attitude to combining her family aspirations with her job expectations:

I've always wanted five kids and I've always wanted to be a policewoman, so I'll have to try and make up my mind what I want. There's not much point in being a policewoman if I'm going to be off every year to have a baby. If I don't find the right man then I'll be a policewoman, but if I do then perhaps I won't. It all depends who comes along.

For Tracy, who did not believe in combining work and children, a career was still important, so she would have to do it at the beginning of her working life. Economic necessity might not allow her to do this.

> Children won't come till later on because if I have them early in my life then that's my life gone, the whole life would be dedicated to the kids as I wouldn't have a child and leave them with a nursery nurse or whatever.

For some of the Ealing Asian girls in 1972, there was little contemplation of combining a career with marriage and family because of the certain knowledge that they would not be allowed to work, even after taking their studies into the fifth or sixth form. Parents from Pakistan in particular were very cautious about letting their daughters work in this country, and often either kept them at home after they had left school, or sent them back to Pakistan to be married. Some still do, although many have modified this practice, often through financial restriction as well as any social changes and other pressures. Obviously, Asian girls do not represent a homogeneous group: there are cultural and religious differences according to the family's country of origin, as well as individual family differences by class, caste, education, occupation, and the length of time the family has been in Britain. One girl at school in Ealing in 1972 knew that she would have to return to Pakistan for her marriage, but she had every intention to take up work over there.

> When I get married I can go on working if I like, and I will. I will work at dressmaking because ladies can do this sort of work. Women can do teaching or dressmaking, and they have to go for a six-month course if they want to be a dressmaker. There are lady doctors. Can't do factory work because there are men and women together. In teaching and in hospitals, have to work together, but not in dressmaking, don't get any men dressmakers.

NASEEM

Then, as now, Asian women were working in many low status occupations in Britain in factories and as machinists in sweatshops. Older women were often found working in the textile industry, which is an all-female work-place where they work long and hard for little remuneration in company with many others. Meanwhile, girls at school were being encouraged by their families to qualify for certain professions that are considered respectable and carry high status such as teaching and medicine. Jobs in which the relationships between the sexes were clearly defined were preferred, and when possible courses were studied at all-girl day colleges. Office-work was often regarded with some suspicion as it involves social contact with men, although bank work was an exception to the rule. Some technical and scientific work was also acceptable. As well as the preference for a female working environment there may also be restrictions by caste. More conservative Sikhs, for instance, would consider it wrong for a Jat woman (one from a caste of peasant farmers) to work for someone who is not a Jat. Families in which wives or daughters were working sometimes kept this knowledge hidden from relatives at home in India, where it would be considered a loss of status. Thus it was described in the early 1970s:

> There are, in fact, two classes of Sikh working women: girls who have been to school in Britain and are waiting to marry (in the Punjab, such girls would generally have to stay at home), and older married women whose children are at school or grown up. Newly married brides or wives with infant children are expected to stay at home, often under the wing of mother-in-law. However, if they have professional training, they are more likely to continue working. It seems that young wives whose husbands' families have shops are allowed to work in these.[23]

In the same way as girls' desires to stay on at school can postpone marriage arrangements, so also working and earning their own living could offer them the chance of becoming slightly more independent of their parents. Surinder, one of the Ealing girls interviewed in 1972, enjoyed school for the autonomy it gave her, and was also very keen to go to work after she left school, since if she were to stay at home her parents would arrange for an earlier marriage. She would still have to be accompanied to work, however.

I want a secretary job if I pass my shorthand and typing, but

I don't want to work in a factory, I really don't. I want to pass my exams ... they want me to get married – straight away if possible. If I go to work then I don't have to but if I stay at home then I have to get married in two years ... Some husbands do let ladies go to work. My dad won't let my mum go to work. About five years ago no Indian women used to work, but now they've started working. I think it's nice. It's a good idea, instead of staying home all the time. Once you're married you can't talk to another man. My dad says you can't. My mum can't.

After marriage, the authority of the family is replaced by that of the husband, and in the earlier research, many Asian girls spoke about hoping that their future husbands would let them work, and planning to persuade them if they were against it. For some, the restrictions on many aspects of their lives were great, while for others, such as the wealthier middle class Asians from African countries like Uganda and Tanzania, there was, for instance, more likelihood of continuing a career after marriage. For instance, Gita, from Tanzania, who was not going to have an arranged marriage, said:

I'd try to talk to [my husband] and make him understand that it would be better if I did work. I think boys have changed their ideas. They don't really mind girls going out to work after they're married and after they've got a family – so I hope I'm a lucky wife ... If I got married early I'd like him to keep on with my training because I really want to be a doctor and I'd like to go on with it, so if he understands and he wanted me to get married quite early, well I would but as long as he let me do my training. [My mum] doesn't work. You don't have these sort of things in our families. They wouldn't let mothers go to work. The girls do now but mothers usually stay at home. I think this is a bit stupid – ladies, girls, can work if they have a family; not when the kids are very young but when they are about two or three and they start going to school. I think a mother should work because the father can't support the whole family.

Another girl was even more assertive in her view. Her family had come from India and she had been born here. Like Gita, she too wanted to become a doctor:

> Definitely all for it [women working]. When you've got your kids into a nursery and that, go back to work. That's what I'll do. I don't want to stay at home doing nothing. I'll talk to him [my husband], get him to see that I don't want to stay home and do nothing. I don't want to stay at home waiting till he gets back. That's old-fashioned. Girls can get married and just come back to their work – nothing stopping you.

To other girls from Asian families, however, the obstacles preventing this may have seemed insurmountable at that time. Today, it is quite common for Asian women to work, and 63 per cent of the mothers of the Asian girls in the later study were in full-time or part-time work (compared to over 80 per cent of the mothers of the white and West Indian girls). Many acknowledged that it could be awkward if the husband did not approve, but said either that they would hope to sort this issue out before marriage, or that their husband would have to accept their working. As one girl said: 'In Asian families women probably do have to choose between a family and a career. But you should just not get married to that type of person.'

Shazia's aspirations to be an engineer in 1991 were described in the previous chapter. She felt determined that her future husband should not only accept her being an engineer, but would accept her continuing to work.

> I'd carry on. My husband will have to accept it. I don't want to just sit at home doing nothing. If you've got qualifications, you can't sit at home. My mum had the chance to get a teaching job here, but she never knew. She was seventeen then, and she could have done something with her life. She could have gone to evening classes. She had the qualifications and the brains.
>
> I'd carry on working. Probably for a year or two I wouldn't work, because of the kids growing up, but then I'd start again. I'd probably get a babysitter or send them to playgroups. Men might say engineering isn't a suitable job for my wife, like the people at work, but I think they'd start accepting it. I'd say that before I got married. I'd say 'I'm working here and I want to

carry on, so it's up to you, if you want to marry me.' Probably most guys would accept it though. If they like you and want to spend their life with you. Nobody can be absolutely sure the marriage will work out. If you've got no job or anything, you can't do something. If you've got a job, you've got something to keep you going.

In common with all the other girls in the 1991 study, the Asian girls endorsed that being a housewife would be very dull and boring, only a minority disagreed with this.

I don't know how long I'd stay at home after I'd had the children, but I wouldn't give up my job and become a housewife. I'd go mad if I did that. Plus I want my mum and dad to look after my children!

RAJWINDER

In 1991 almost all the Ealing girls, from whatever background, assumed that they would carry on with work after having children. Whether this would be the job of their choice is another matter, and not one that they gave much thought to at this stage. Debbie was planning to do GCSEs, then hopefully A levels, and then train as a veterinary nurse:

I think it just depends what the women want to do. If they want to look after the children and not have a career, then that's up to them. Hopefully I'll carry on. When I was in work experience the woman that worked there fitted the job around picking up her kids. I'm hoping I could do that, shift the times around.

She was planning to do what women have been doing for many years, fitting their jobs round their families. Despite the often more optimistic hopes of this set of girls, it seems likely that they too will end up doing just this. In 1991, like 1972, realism is mixed up with idealism, and there are remarkable similarities between the two groups. But whereas the earlier intentions showed an awareness of how women's role was in the process of change, those of the girls in the later research were underlaid with the mistaken assumption that women's role and opportunities had already significantly changed. In spite of the movement of women out to work this century, they have not developed the same kind of separation between work and home that men have always had, and still preserve. While this research shows girls' superficially strong endorsement of the importance of work and maintaining their jobs and careers, in the end they will generally put the needs of the family first. They will be working for their family more than for themselves.

Sharing Housework and Child-care

The double responsibility of working women has always officially gone unrecognized. With the increasing demand for and supply of women workers, the turnover of ideas in the 1960s and 1970s, and the public attention given to women's changing status, I was wondering in the mid 1970s how far this atmosphere of change had influenced ideas and expectations about the domestic division of labour. If the Ealing girls were any indication, equality had not got very far where housework was concerned. Although it was thought useful for a man to be handy about the house, and fair for him to help with the washing-up, domestic work remained largely exclusive to women. As Oakley observed at that time: 'During childhood an identification with the mother or other female adult who cares for the housewife-to-be instils a sense of housework as a feminine responsibility. The mother is not only the female child's role model for feminine behaviour but for housework behaviour also.'[24] An orientation towards housework then becomes bound up with the rest of the female personality. At this time housework was still clearly women's work, despite some husbands being willing to help out with peripheral things, like washing-up and doing the vacuuming and occasionally going to the launderette. The emphasis was very much on 'help' rather than share.[25]

Housework is low status and menial work and the separation of the sex roles at this point has been and still is very resistant to change. Some people have considered it unmanly for men to take more than a token and circumscribed part in housework, and social judgement may even condemn a woman whose husband appears to be exceeding his share. Even in the late 1970s, some men would go to great lengths to avoid its being known that they did housework.[26] Men's own avoidance of housework has been complemented by an equally strong reaction by women themselves to protect their role from male intrusion. Women whose identities are bound up with being indispensable wives and mothers do not always welcome the knowledge that their work can be diluted and shared. They may also be frightened of being judged as 'bad' wives if they fail to do certain things for their husbands. The sexual division of labour has again made some sense of this through the traditional assumption that men should be at work all day and women should be at home or in 'easier' or part-time work. Although both may be equally tired by evening it has seemed unreasonable to many women in the past that they should now persuade their husbands to help with 'their' work. For women who are at home all day with children this is reinforced by the assumption that theirs is not 'proper' work.

In 1972, more than half of the Ealing girls disagreed with a suggestion that being a housewife would be very dull and boring, and implicitly accepted housework and child-care as being part of their rightful role:

> If I get married, everything bar housework will be on a mutual setting, bank account and everything shared. Housework – I don't expect him to do it although I don't like it much. I'm hopeless at cooking. I hope I can find someone who can cook!

> I think they ought to help. My dad helps my mum quite a lot you know, washing-up and things, but I think my mum works harder on the whole.

> I expect him to wash up now and then, but I wouldn't lay everything on him. I wouldn't say – right, I'm going out to work, you get on with the washing-up.

> I don't agree with the wife going out to work and the husband staying at home and looking after the kids. I'd rather stay at home all day if it was that way, really. I think there's a certain bargain in the home and for the woman that's her children and they need her more than the father.

Attitudes towards women's role at work and in the home have changed significantly over the last few decades. As more and more women have moved into the work-force, through financial necessity or choice, it has become much more acceptable and desirable for both economic and psychological reasons that women go out to work, both before and after they have children. Accordingly, in 1991, only 15 per cent of all the Ealing girls disagreed that 'being a housewife would be very dull and boring'. They no longer took housework and child-care to be an implicit part of their future role: many had high expectations from their future partners. Some just wanted help, while others expected equal shares in the domestic tasks at home:

> I'd definitely expect my husband to share things. Not too much. I wouldn't want to make him a househusband, but he's got to help me out, I can't do it all.
>
> • KIM

> Last year I went out with a boy for about eight months, and he was like, 'Girls shouldn't do that'. I don't know why I went out with him. He wouldn't have wanted me to be a firewoman, he would have wanted me to be at home cooking. He expected me to do everything for him. He'd just sit there while I made dinner or something, he'd sit and watch telly . . . I'd expect a partner to do exactly what I do – take turns in doing the housework, turns in making dinner, ironing. I wouldn't expect him to do all the ironing or washing-up but I'd expect him to do it equal.
>
> ROSIE

Some had seen the positive examples from their own father and mother sharing in the home, and this had reinforced their own expectations:

> I think my husband should do his fair share of work, it shouldn't be all down to me – cook, wash, clean. My parents' marriage is very much like it. My dad cooks when mum's at work, and he washes, they really share it all. I think that's the way it should be.
>
> MELANIE

> I'm not going to marry someone who says, 'You're tied to the kitchen sink'. That's not right. If it's both your child, they've got to look after it as well, half the responsibility . . . My dad is quite good. He's out of work at the moment, he's self-employed

and he does most of the housework, and cooks. My mum's lucky in that, a right little housewife he is! And he loves it.

LUCY

It is questionable whether their expectations will be fulfilled, as it is girls and women who have changed their attitudes, ideas, expectations, and the nature of their lives much more than boys and men have done. Although it is much more acceptable now for men to share in housework and child-care, this is not as common in practice as it is made to sound in theory.[27] Traditional attitudes and expectations die hard, especially when it appears to some men that they may be losing some of the 'privileges' of the male role in the family by sharing the domestic labour.

I would expect him [husband/partner] to do half of it with me. I think most men don't mind that now. They wouldn't be really excited about doing it, but I think they'd do it if they had to now. We had this discussion in media studies, all the boys were saying 'women's place is in the home', but they were joking. They were laughing, trying to get on our nerves. But you don't know if they were really joking or not.

FIONA

There are many resistances to men and women sharing housework and child-care equally, and one aspect of this is the way men have been brought up in their own families. If it has been taken for granted that boys help equally, and the boys themselves accept this, there is more likelihood that the Ealing girls' aspirations for their future family lives will be fulfilled at least to some extent. While it is girls who help with housework or the care of younger brothers and sisters and while boys are excused these activities, there is less chance of change.

They expect me to do more cooking and stuff. My brother can cook quite well, but they expect me to do more things than he does, he doesn't do a lot. He'll lie in bed on a Saturday morning, we'll get up and help with the housework. I suppose he's a boy so we're not that bothered, but we'd like him to do things as well.

EILEEN

My mum's a bit difficult to accept because she thinks I ought to be around helping out with the children. My brothers don't do very much.

PAULINE

However, some girls were more optimistic about the possibility of changing this and other aspects of the traditional masculine role:

I do think men have changed, and especially when I went on my work experience, the last couple of weeks. I was with men all the time and it really shocked me when one of them said he wouldn't mind staying at home being a househusband, taking the child to school, going home to Hoover, cook the dinner ... I don't know about the boys at school though. A lot of them are macho when they're round their friends, but when you've got them on your own and talking to them, they're totally different. I think some of them would stay at home and share the housework and whatever, but of course they won't say anything like that when they're with their mates, only when you talk to them on their own, they really change.

CAROLINE

My dad doesn't help in the house, but my mum doesn't either. My mum's at work, we do quite a bit. She comes back about six o'clock so we do everything, clean the house and everything so she has nothing to do. When there's a lot of children they can do the work. My brothers were brought up like that, they have to cook and clean just as equally as the girls. So they'll still do it when they go. My brothers say they prefer to cook and clean and look after the children than go out and work!

LAURA

Laura's parents are from Jamaica, and she shares her home with her five brothers and sisters. While her brothers may share, there are plenty of other boys who will follow in their father's footsteps, as Vanessa, indicated:

Some boys just carry on family traditions. I think my brother will be like my dad. He'd like to do the work but he'd like the mother to look after the children, seeing like he didn't do too much of the housework, only things for himself. I think he'd be that type. I think with white families it's slightly different. Black families have always known, especially in my mum and dad's country, that the wife always has to do everything for the husband. The husband goes out and the wife stays at home and does the cooking. The man brings in the money. Most of my white friends say it's a different thing. Both of them co-operate more.

Of the Asian girls who were saying earlier in the chapter that they would expect to work after they had a family, many were also agreed that a husband should share at home. For example, Rajwinder had a good example in her father:

My dad does quite a bit, for an Asian father. If my mum's working a late shift, my dad cooks, and he's also very good at things like Hoovering the house. He does the shopping as well. Mum does cooking and things like washing clothes. I don't want to marry some guy who says 'you've got to do the cooking, do this and that'. If I say to my mum or my aunt that I want a guy who will do half everything, straight down the middle, they say 'Where are you going to get a guy like that from?' They don't think they exist. I used to think they were right but now I see a lot of the guys who go to university who have learnt that you've got to look after yourself and they're a bit more open-minded. I want to marry someone who will do everything half and half. I'm not going to spend my whole life running after some guy. You must stand up for yourself. I think maybe if the boys started at a younger age. I think it's the mothers' faults as well. A lot of Asian mothers are running around after their sons doing everything for them. When the son gets married he thinks his wife is going to do the same thing for him. So I think the mother has to start from a younger age. And us girls at school should start showing boys we're not a pushover. We're not their mums mark two! We're equal to them. I know for a fact that Asian boys get treated better than the girls do, and I think it's up to the mothers to change that. Someone's got to tell them!

RAJWINDER

I think both should share the responsibility. I know in the past people have said that the lady's position is in the kitchen, but it's not true. I think they both should do the same things. It shouldn't be just the lady cooking at home, it can be the husband cooking at times too. While the wife goes out to work, he should share the household. I think men these days are sympathetic, as long as you've discussed it with that person, then I think it's OK.

MADHU

It was already being thought of as quite normal to work after marriage in the 1970s: to give up work on marriage in the 1990s is almost unthinkable – even if you were to marry a millionaire! Now it is thought equally normal to plan to work after having children, too, although this varies in time from a year or so after birth to when the children are at school. For the Ealing girls real employment opportunities do not necessarily relate closely to expectations at this stage in life. The idea of choosing not to return to work sooner or later is not seen as a real option, or desire. Lack of jobs may force this reality, but the vision of their lives at this point includes a working future, whether or not they have a partner and/ or children. They are well aware of many important practical and personal reasons why having a job or career could be important for them. So what has happened to the myths I was describing in the mid seventies? Twenty years later girls are less hampered by fears of maternal deprivation but guilt can still be provoked, and nursery provision remains sadly lacking. The belief that strict divisions exist between the activities that men and women do inside and outside the home has been somewhat eroded, but there is still sex segregation in the job market where class and race inequalities also remain strongly intact. And although some men have been forced into, or have chosen to take, a more active part in housework and looking after their children, domestic inequality remains, and men still only help rather than share in these responsibilities.

NOTES

CHAPTER 5

1. See for instance Ann Oakley, *Sex, Gender and Society*, Temple Smith, 1972; Ann Oakley, *Housewife*, Allen Lane, 1974, chapter 7; M. Mead, *Male and Female*, Penguin, 1950.
2. Angus Calder, *The People's War*, Panther, 1971. (The Second World War.)
3. In 1974 London boroughs provided day nursery places for only 1·5 per cent of children under five years of age. Between 1976 and 1991 there has been little change in the provision of local authority day nurseries. There has been a great increase, however, in the number of private day nurseries.
4. Edgar Moyo, 'Big Mother and Little Mother in Matabeleland', *History Workshop Pamphlet*, no. 12.
5. John Bowlby, *Child Care and the Growth of Love*, Penguin, 1947.
6. John Bowlby, *Attachment and Loss, Vol. 1: Attachment*, Penguin, 1969.
7. See for instance Lee Comer, 'Myth of Motherhood', *Spokesman Pamphlet*, no. 21, and her book *Wedlocked Women*, Feminist Books, 1974; Michael Rutter, *Maternal Deprivation Reassessed*, Penguin, 1972; Ann Oakley, op. cit., chapter 8; and R. P. Wortis, 'The Acceptance of the Concept of Maternal Role by Behavioral Scientists: Its Effects on Women', *American Journal of Orthopsychiatry*, 41(5), October 1971.
8. WHO Expert Committee on Mental Health, 1951, quoted in Michael Rutter, op. cit.
9. Penelope Leach, *Who Cares?* Penguin, 1979.
10. M. R. Yarrow, 'Maternal Employment and Childrearing', *Children*, 8, 1961.
11. Sue Sharpe, *Double Identity: Lives of Working Mothers*, Penguin, 1984.
12. Paul Wilding, 'Motherless Families', *New Society*, 24 August 1972.
13. Paul Wilding, op. cit.
14. For instance, Brian Jackson, *Fatherhood*, Allen & Unwin, 198 ·· Charlie

Lewis, *Becoming a Father*, Open University Press, 1986; Charlie Lewis and Margaret O'Brien, *Reassessing Fatherhood*, Sage, 1987; Sue Sharpe, *Fathers and Daughters*, Routledge, 1994.

15. June Statham, *Daughters and Sons: Experiences of Non-sexist Childrearing*, Blackwell, 1986.

16. See for instance C. Bookhagen, E. Hemmer, J. Raspe and E. Schultz, 'Kommune 2: Childrearing in the Commune' and G. Zicklin, 'Communal Childrearing', both in H. P. Dreitzel, 'Childhood and Socialisation', *Recent Sociology*, no. 5, 1973; also *Children's Community Centre – Our Experiences of Collective Child Care*, published by a group of people involved in this in Dartmouth Park Hill, London, July 1974.

17. M. Benet, *Secretary*, Panther, 1972.

18. Audrey Wise, 'Women and the Struggle for Workers' Control', *Spokesman Pamphlet*, no. 33, 1973.

19. Audrey Wise, op. cit.

20. M. Benet, op. cit.

21. Liz Kustow, 'Television and Women', in M. Wandor (ed.), *The Body Politic, Stage 1*, 1972.

22. Sue Sharpe, *Double Identity*, op. cit.

23. A. James, *Sikh Children in Britain*, Institute of Race Relations, Oxford, 1974.

24. Ann Oakley, op. cit.

25. Sue Sharpe, *Double Identity*, op. cit.; British Social Attitudes, 9th Report, 1992/93 edition, Roger Jowell *et al.* (eds.), Dartmouth, 1992.

26. In *Double Identity*, op. cit., I describe a husband who Hoovered the sitting room on his knees so that the neighbours would not see him.

27. In the early 1980s, the children in Alison Kelly's research reported that 84 per cent of their mothers/14 per cent of the fathers regularly went food shopping; 87 per cent mothers/17 per cent fathers regularly cooked meals; 85 per cent mothers/4 per cent fathers washed clothes: and 80 per cent mothers/8 per cent fathers cleaned the house. This was in the face of parents' ideology that housework should be shared especially if the wife worked and demonstrates how far behaviour can stray from belief. 'Gender Roles at Home and School', *British Journal of Sociology of Education*, 3(3), 1982.

THE CHOSEN SEX

Is it Better to be a Girl . . .?

1972:

I like being a girl and being feminine. I also like boys. I think being able to have a child is wonderful, whereas boys can only help.

I think it is better to lead a girl's life because girls don't get hit because they are feminine. Also they don't get told off as much as boys do. Girls can wear sexy clothes.

Boys can't wear pretty things and be emotional over a film or book, etc., and if you're a girl you like boys and little children and if you were a boy you wouldn't be able to do this.

It's easier and nicer to be a girl — boys have so much responsibility.

1991:

I wouldn't like to change the way I am. When you're a girl, you can be like a boy as well, but if you're a boy, you can't really be like a girl. Girls get away with a lot of things: girls can wear trousers or skirts. Boys can't. They have to keep up their macho image.

Because you can show your emotions, have kids, and you can just have a good life without having to put up a front. Boys are immature!

Because boys have more of an image to live up to and are not so sensitive.

Because looking at the boys it takes me only five seconds to think that I'd like to be a girl!

. . . Or a Boy?

1972:

> I'd prefer to be a boy, because they have a much larger choice of jobs than we do, also they seem to have far more fun.

> Boys can get out of doing things round the house, and it is natural for a boy to get into trouble, not a girl.

> [Boys] don't have to wear skirts, and parents let boys do more things than girls.

> [What I dislike about being a girl is] having to have children, why can't men have them. Having a period, we have to go through pain where the men don't. Girls do the housework and cook when she comes home from work, where the men have everything waiting for them when they come home, and then they laze about.

1991:

> Because they don't have to worry about things as much as girls. They don't have to be a 'pretty' boy.

> Boys have better job opportunities.

> Because boys don't have a lot to worry about. They don't have to worry about getting pregnant or getting raped, etc.

> They have an easier life, they don't have periods, they don't have children, they usually get the job they want.

Boys' and girls' satisfactions with being male or female are one part of a constant self-evaluating process, and the mirror into which they constantly look for self-appraisal is framed with the comparative values and standards set up through their activities and social interactions. It is hard to question being male or female at birth but not so difficult to assess and criticize the gender consequences that follow from it.

Their perception that femininity and the feminine role are often considered less important or meaningful than equivalent areas of masculinity lies uneasily alongside women's enjoyment of them. The ambivalence that this can produce has questioned the happiness derived from feminine activities. This same unequal value system has explained the acceptance of tomboys and the rejection of 'sissy' boys. Girls have traditionally been envious of boys' attributes and perceived advantages in life but the reverse was rare. This attitude seems to have changed, often moving in the opposite direction as girls get older.

When boys and girls are young they differ in the amount of preference they have for activities associated with the opposite sex. Girls have generally shown as great an enthusiasm for boys' roles, toys and activities as they have for 'feminine' things, whereas most boys firmly adhere to an appropriate 'masculine' role and activities and often contemplate those of girls with derision. The nature of such gender preferences in young children was documented in traditional psychological research.[1] One such study showed how young girls liked both traditional masculine and feminine activities and roles, while boys were much more enthusiastic about the masculine ones. The differences widened with increasing age when six- to nine-year-old boys and girls showed a greater preference for masculine choices than for feminine ones.

This is the time in life when it is quite permissible for girls to be 'tomboys'. But as they move towards and into adolescence, they feel and respond to pressures that point them in a more 'feminine' direction. They internalize much of their role without even being aware of it and there are many models readily available. Increasing age and experience has given them an idea of how life is organized and they begin to structure their present and future perceptions accordingly. The tomboy preference for masculine activities gives way to an emphasis on appearance and the recognition of a future status that has traditionally depended on becoming girlfriend, wife and mother. The switch from masculine preferences to feminine ones can be rationalized through shared involvement in the social trappings of femininity and through acknowledging the more enjoyable aspects of being female. This has already started happening for many children before they reach their teens, aided by earlier puberty and easy access to information about sexuality and womanhood.

GENDER PREFERENCES

'I'd Rather be a Girl'

In the Seventies

In a study of twelve-year-olds carried out in the 1960s[2] girls and boys were asked what sex they would have chosen to be if they could have chosen for themselves: 93 per cent of the boys and 81 per cent of the girls chose their same sex again rather than preferring to be the opposite sex. The reasons given by the boys for their choice were mainly connected with physical superiority and the claim to have a 'better life', whereas the girls most frequently mentioned appearance and clothing as the attraction of being female.

The Ealing girls were also asked this kind of question in 1972, and a similar proportion (75 per cent) of the white girls replied that they would have chosen to be born as girls. The rest would have preferred to be born as boys. The reasons given by the white girls were various and those who favoured being girls were mainly concerned with the traditional activities of the feminine role. They had progressed beyond the earlier twelve-year-olds' emphasis on clothes and appearance, and although these were still important aspects they were superseded by the anticipated joys and satisfactions of becoming wives and mothers and caring for homes and children.

Girls at secondary school were then already very aware of their feminine role especially where it concerned reproduction and mother-hood, and this necessarily affected their future hopes and ambitions in other areas of life. As we saw earlier, the undervaluation of femininity has skirted deceptively around motherhood in terms of ideology, while the real conditions for instance for working or unsupported mothers are discriminatory and oppressive. Glorifica-tion of motherhood has always concealed the amount of sacrifice and the struggle that this involves for women. Nevertheless, mother-hood remained one of the most positive aspects of the feminine role for many girls.

I'd rather be a girl because I love young children and I think a mother is closer than fathers to young children.

Girls have more happiness in life, bring up a family, wearing nice clothes, and not having to go out to work when they're married.

I like being a girl and would like to be a housewife and have children.

A girl may have her own home and cooks and cleans for her husband if she gets married and she may not have to work all her life.

There appeared to be no conflict in their minds between their futures as housewives and mothers and the generally low social value associated with this role. Their love of children made motherhood a very attractive and worthwhile goal. The sexual division of labour has placed women primarily at home, produced the discontinuity in their potential working lives and reinforced their assumed 'inferiority' as workers, but it is this very factor that enhances the feminine role because it seems to imply greater choice. For instance, 'Girls can do more things, they get married, have children. They can stay at home or go to work. Men cannot.' It is an attractive proposition not to have to work all your life, as men appeared to have to do, and they were pleased that being girls excused them from this, as well as from other sorts of responsibilities.

I enjoy being a girl and I hope to get married and have a family of my own. I don't want to be a boy because they have horrible jobs to do for fifty years.

I like feminine things, and boys; and boys, when they grow older, have to support a wife and child.

It is part of the traditional male role to assume responsibility and to take the initiative, at work, at home and in developing personal relationships. This has equivalent drawbacks and advantages and there is no reason apart from custom for boys to do this rather than girls. Girls sometimes mentioned the fact that boys have to ask girls out as being something they did not envy while others complained that waiting to be asked was just as bad. For these Ealing girls, these and other feminine activities, such as wearing fashionable clothes and make-up, being sensitive and emotional, and being treated more gently and respectfully, all enhanced a picture of frivolous irresponsibility against a background of future maternal responsibility.

> I would prefer to be a girl because most boys are rough, don't have a very good reputation at school. If you were a good-mannered boy, you are normally laughed at. I also like being feminine, I don't want to be rough.

> Girls have better clothes and bright colours suit them.

> I think it is better to lead a girl's life, because girls don't get hit because they are feminine. Also they don't get told off as much as boys do.

> Girls can wear much prettier clothes, can have children, can be emotional over books and films, have a gentleman to pay for you and go out with.

> I think a girl can have a bigger choice of fashion, and when they're upset a girl can cry and let it out but a boy keeps it inside him and makes it worse.

West Indian and Asian girls in the study were far less enthusiastic: only 50 per cent and 20 per cent respectively would have chosen to be girls. Those West Indian girls who preferred to be girls gave a similar mixture of reasons, and many just enjoyed the way they were. Clothes and fashion got a particular mention, but the future joys of being a wife and mother which were so popular for the white girls, were not as much in evidence. Like them, the relatively few Asian girls who said they would have preferred to be born as girls gave reasons that were more concerned with clothes, and also with potential job opportunities than with marriage and family life.

It is easy to identify with the way they felt and understand how attractive women's role appears compared to that of men. At that time it seemed that women's lives were not as directly tied down to earning money. They potentially had a husband to pay for their upkeep and although in real life it has become far less possible to keep a family on a single wage, this has been the assumption made by the state in all its rules and dealings with married women. Although women may seem separated from production through being at home, this is deceptive as we saw earlier, and women have a crucial part to play in organizing their own domestic labour so that their housekeeping money can be stretched in every possible way to make ends meet. Working class girls in particular are well aware of the struggle that maintaining a home and family can involve, and are also conscious of working class women's traditional need to work. Many of their mothers exemplified this and worked in badly paid and unsatisfying jobs. Work was then not seen as attractive but as an unfortunate necessity of life and therefore the apparent opportunity to avoid it seemed one of the advantages of being a woman. When we consider girls' reactions to questions about being girls, it is relevant to take socioeconomic conditions and ideologies into account. We also need to keep in mind that 'girls' are not a homogeneous group of people but different and changing individuals. 'Femininity' is not fixed either, and their perception, attitudes and behaviour to being a girl (or to boys) depend on their position relative to what is going on in their lives at that moment.

There are other inducements favouring a woman's life. For instance, children are more worth spending time and energy on than many boring and alienating jobs, since they actually respond and grow. At the time of writing, the apparent choice of whether to work or not after marriage and after children, and the ability to organize life in the home without supervision gave an illusion of freedom and greater choice of action. If girls accepted that their life would be fulfilling by having a husband and bearing his children, then this could provide a defined and tangible goal, one that could be reached without too many qualifications or too much competition or training. Inasfar as their role was concretely defined as being at home and with children and still only vaguely defined in terms of work, it provided girls with a necessary framework in structuring and organizing their lives. Girls' lives had so far traditionally been set out for them, the major question often having been *who* they will marry rather than what they may become. This could be interpreted as 'easier' to the extent that they would not have to bear (in theory) the major economic responsibility for family survival. In practice this is belied by the relatively high proportion of women who are heads of their households.[3]

There are many other errors and deceptions in this picture. What seems like 'freedom' and 'choice' has its own confining limitations. The value of being able to choose whether or not to work is diminished when it is realized that the only available jobs, for someone without qualifications and training, may be uninteresting, without prospects and underpaid. Part-time work, which many women want, was and still is often hard to find and may be almost full-time work for a half-time wage. Housework may have seemed to offer freedom to be your own boss and organize your own day, but it produces its own monotony. Although it has become less time-consuming with modern aids, housework offers little permanent satisfaction and technology has removed most of its skills or made them redundant. Freedom becomes isolation and autonomy condenses into a choice of radio programme.

Many of the forty housewives interviewed by Ann Oakley claimed that 'the "best thing" about being a housewife is that you're your own boss, you don't have to go to work and you have free time.'[4] However, this 'freedom' becomes compromised by always having to be enjoyed in the place where work is to be done, and as Oakley comments:

> The housewife is 'free from' rather than 'free to'; the absence of external supervision is not balanced by the liberty to use time for one's own ends. The taking of leisure is self-defeating . . . Housewives experience more monotony, fragmentation and social isolation in their work than do workers in the factory. Somewhat predictably perhaps they have more in common with assembly-line workers than with those whose jobs involve less repetition and more skill.

Motherhood offers a more meaningful role but ironically this is also one which is in perpetual conflict with that of the housewife. Children bring dirt and untidiness and constantly create housework. Caring for them has many rewards but it can also become overwhelming and intermittently depressing, as their constant demands leave women no time to themselves, no time to think, no time to give expression to their own individuality. When at last they do have time, their early youthful enthusiasm and capacity for self-expression may have drained away. But whether the satisfactions which come from looking after a home, husband and family are great or small, they do not have to fill a lifetime. For those mothers who have stayed at home caring for a family, when their children have grown up and are self-sufficient, their 'primary' role is apparently over and time may stretch into the future filled with nothing but housework. The thought of working again can be frightening after so many years at home, and without skills the choice of work may now be rather limited.

In 1972, the Ealing girls showed little feminist consciousness, if this is taken to mean criticism or rejection of any of the traditional features and expectations of the feminine role. However, their endorsement of traditional features of femininity does have positive and optimistic aspects that should not be overlooked. They were responding in a realistic and rational way to a social structure over which they had little individual control. Most recognized only a distortion of feminist ideas at that time and if they were to reject their role as women there appeared to them to be nothing to replace it. Women's oppression has always been characterized by isolation at home – producing a lack of solidarity which has hindered the development of any women's movement. The pleasure and confidence that girls express in being female are a stronger basis on which to build solidarity than are a preference to be male and a rejection of women as inferior or unimportant. From this basis the good aspects of the stereotyped feminine role can be emphasized and the onerous and oppressive ones can be challenged and changed. People do not have to be worn down and discontented before they become militant. It is often when people are growing strong and confident in themselves that they are able to examine their situation and demand change.

In highlighting what girls saw as the more positive features of the 'feminine' role, the perceived disadvantages of the 'masculine' role also came under scrutiny. For instance, these girls' reluctance to have 'horrible jobs for fifty years' was very reasonable and was seen as one of the many drawbacks of being male. The fact that fathers are often less close to their children than mothers, and are not generally found in many jobs that involve child-care is a major gap in their meaningful experience. Furthermore, the development of 'manliness' has usually demanded the public suppression of all but the more destructive emotions.

Many of the Ealing girls were enthusiastic about the things they liked about being female and feminine, and glossed over the realities and hardships. They were well aware of the pain and struggle that can be involved but accepted this as the way things are and should be. At that moment they had little idea that change might be brought about by themselves rather than imposed from outside and so continually tried to compromise and adjust.

> I'm not really sure. I like a lot of things about being a girl, like clothes, but I think at the moment boys get a fairer deal in a way, so maybe I'd prefer to be a boy. At present, a lot get more money for what they do and get better positions in their jobs, and more politicians and things. I suppose it's partly because girls don't go in for things like that but they do tend to get on easier than girls. I think girls have to fight harder to get better jobs.

> PENNY

Some expressed a preference for girls' jobs and said that these were more interesting, or that girls had better opportunities. The correctness of their assumptions about opportunity and prospects is dubious, but it is true that the 'women's work' that involves personal interaction, in places like hospitals or offices, does seem more relevant than, for instance, producing parts for cars.

It is hard to make the necessary connections between women's role at home and their role at work, between their personal and sexual lives and the parts they play in production. If girls and women still see themselves as separated from the mainstream of productive work in society they will emphasize, as did many of these Ealing girls did over twenty years ago, that theirs is the 'easier' and more enviable position. And although they were right in some of their reasoning, this serves to camouflage the way that the social and economic system separates and restricts the lives of both men and women.

In the Nineties

Looking back from the 1990s, it is clear that many changes have taken place in the last twenty years to alter girls' views of themselves, and of the role of women at home and at work, and in society in general. As Melanie observed in 1991:

> I think there has been some change in boys, but not as much as in girls. I think girls have got a much wider range of thinking. Where boys think, 'I shouldn't be doing this, I should be doing this,' girls think, 'I can do whatever I want.'

This should, therefore, be reflected in how they feel about being girls. As described above, in the first study there were significant differences between the white and black girls on their professed preferences for being born a girl or a boy. Nearly twenty years later these differences have become less pronounced. There is an overall increase in endorsement of the pleasures or advantages of being a girl rather than a boy. If we compare sex preferences between the girls in 1972 and those in 1991, even more of the white girls in the 1990s (84 per cent) preferred to be girls, as against 75 per cent in 1972. Correspondingly, only 16 per cent expressed any preference to be a boy, compared with 25 per cent in 1972. There was little difference between 1972 and 1991 in the preferences expressed by the West Indian girls, in that they were more or less split down the middle. The later study shows a slight movement towards favouring girls. For the Asian girls, so many of whom would have preferred to be boys in 1972, the picture had significantly changed, and only just over half (56 per cent) preferred to be boys in 1991, compared to 80 per cent in the earlier research.

For everyone, the reasons for choosing to be girls in 1991 were quite similar to those expressed in the earlier study, but illustrated an increased range of positive attributes: as a girl you can potentially do everything a boy can, as well as be able to wear a wide variety of clothes; feel free to show your emotions; get away with more; etc.

> People expect boys to be tough. And if you didn't play football or be tough with the boys, you would look like a poof or something. With a girl it doesn't matter what you do. It doesn't

make you more feminine or more masculine, so you can do anything you want.

VANESSA

As before, women's capacity to have children was seen as a significant advantage to some, but motherhood was less emphasized as a reason in their choice. Significantly, no one in 1991 said they were glad to be girls in order to get married, unlike in 1972; nor did they say they were glad not to have to go to work all their lives like boys had to do; nor that they did not wish to be a boy because boys would have to support a wife and children. Clearly they implicitly recognized the decline in popularity and certainly in the security of marriage, and the changes that have occurred in the division of labour within the family, and in men's and women's roles in general. The apparent attraction of being 'feminine', which was frequently mentioned in the 1972 responses, was only specified by one person, although obviously some traits such as being emotional and wearing pretty clothes were implicitly categorized as part of 'femininity'.

Other reasons reflected changes in women's role and girls' positive attitudes towards this and towards themselves. These included assertions that girls are more intelligent and interesting; they have stronger characters; mature earlier; they are more caring; they have better relationships with people; more challenges; more experiences; more fun; they find it easier to get jobs and have more choice.

Girls mature earlier than boys, plus they are very good company, easier to talk to and understanding.

Because I am happy with my life and I think girls are more intelligent and interesting.

One Asian girl saw an advantage in girls being more sensitive and responsible with family issues than boys:

I prefer to be a girl. The majority of boys are very careless, they don't care about their parents, how they feel and what they think of you. I think if I upset my parents I'd feel very bad about it. I think it's better to be a girl. They have more responsibilities than boys, taking care of the home and family.

SADIA

There was a sense that girls had acquired some knowledge and certainly a recognition of the historical inequalities between men and women. Several specifically talked of wanting to confront the challenges facing them:

> Because I want to show them people who think that girls cannot make it to the top, that they're wrong.

> I'm happy being a girl. I don't know what it would be like to be a boy, but I think you get on easier if you're male. But I like a challenge because you have to work extra hard if you're female.

> I wouldn't mind being a boy because they've got life so easy, they don't have to compete against women, or worry about things like sexism, they get everything put in front of them. However, I would like to be a girl so I can show men that women can do things like that. I plan on making men see. My brother's always making comments like, 'You'll never make a journalist, you can't compete with all those men.' So I want to show him that I can do better.

> CATHERINE

These kinds of feelings were also fuelled by the negative things they felt about boys' lives, for instance that boys are less sensitive than girls; they get too much hassle; they fight too much; and they moan a lot. A significant minority of the girls did not feel the need to give specific reasons but said they were simply quite happy to be girls.

If this is taken together with other of the girls' expressed attitudes and expectations, it suggests that girls were being more assertive in describing themselves and their future role as women. They no longer saw themselves predominately in terms of becoming wives and mothers, but were more aware of themselves as individuals, who have their own needs outside their traditional role, with their own independent identity. This is similarly reflected in the reasons they believed that a job or career is important for a woman (as described in chapter 5), which emphasized aspects like having something for themselves, standing on their own feet, and being independent. It is also endorsed in some of their other attitudes, and whereas, for example, girls in 1972 had implicitly endorsed that a husband and family were the most satisfying things in a woman's life, by the early 1990s this had been greatly undermined. (A minority – 15 per cent white; 25 per cent West Indian; and a third Asian – agreed, while the rest disagreed or were unsure.)

Girls also expressed a rejection of the macho nature of masculinity, and recognized that many boys and men have to put up a front, and give themselves a tough image for their mates. It may not be how many boys and men wish their lives to be, but they cannot afford to be seen as a wimp or a sissy.[5]

> Boys always have to put up a front. If something happens they can't cry because that's too sissy for them. They've got to be strong and macho. I couldn't do that. But it's a difficult question – we have our downs and they have their downs. If you asked boys the same question they'd want to be a boy. If any of them said girl it would only be one or two out of the whole school. They enjoy being macho, they're big and strong, and bringing in the money. I don't think they'd like the idea of having kids either. I don't think they could cope.
>
> KIM

> Because boys as I see it are always trying to act as if nothing hurts them, they do not have any emotions. Girls do show their emotions and I need to do this as I am quite emotional.
>
> INDERJIT

One girl saw being male as a disadvantage because they were at greater risk of being the objects of aggression, at least around school:

> I think boys get a lot more hassle, there's a lot more fighting between boys. Girls stick together more. They are a bit more bitchy. But boys get more hassle and people are always after them. Girls aren't like that. It's better to be a girl in this school because there's always a lot of trouble between boys, every boy in this school has someone after them somewhere. Not many girls get mugged but a lot of boys get mugged at this school.
>
> DIANE

Girls have implicitly absorbed the idea that women have, or should demand, equality. This is reinforced by the existence of at least some women now working in occupations previously seen as 'male', and occupying a few conspicuous positions in the media and in politics, which gives the impression of movement towards a more equal status. Girls' and women's sense of their own status has also risen. Any hint that women are less intelligent than men is unacceptable. Girls have moved more into previously male-defined areas: there is less assumption that there are things that girls 'don't do' or 'can't do', or that they will put up with any opposition from boys.

> I prefer to be a girl because I'm happy being me. I think it's fine being a girl. I don't feel put down or pressured by boys, or that I can't do something because boys do it, or I can't go on the field because the boys are there. If I want to do something I won't let a bunch of boys stop me.
>
> LYN

'I'd Rather be a Boy'

In the Seventies

Only a quarter of the (white) girls in 1972 would have preferred to have been born as boys, and they placed a different interpretation on 'feminine' characteristics. The joys that were anticipated by other girls in housewifery and motherhood were retranslated into pain, inconvenience and lack of freedom. Their general contention was that 'boys have it easy because they have better jobs and opportunity in life, no periods or pregnancy, less responsibility and more freedom.'

> A boy does not have the worry of staying home all day and looking after the children. He also has the chance of a better job. Boys have more chance of getting on in life than girls.

> Boys do not have as many problems as girls have.

> I have always wanted to be a boy and am always dressed in jeans, etc. Boys always get on better, they can just go up to girls and talk to them. Girls have to wait until they are approached. Boys get all the pleasure and girls get all the pain.

253

Boys do not have to worry about leaving their jobs because they do not have children.

Boys seem to be a lot freer than girls, and parents don't worry about them as much as they do to girls.

Boys – the way I look at it, they get away with a load of things we don't get away with. My mum and dad don't worry about them the way they worry about girls, and they seem to trust them more.

Girls have a long history of restricted mobility. Middle class girls in particular have for several centuries been tied very closely and protectively to their homes. For working class girls this has happened more gradually since their home situations were often so cramped that it was a relief for parents to have them out of the house. But at the turn of the century their restriction was accelerated by the increasing awareness of 'respectability' amongst certain areas of the working class. 'Respectable' families did not let their daughters wander the streets.

There are also all the other ways in which freedom has been constrained. For instance, there has been little encouragement within women's role for exploration and adventure, and girls' upbringing has not allowed them to develop much confidence in doing this. The traditional conception of women as property and producers of 'heirs' ensured their close supervision in the past and the 'weakness' of their sex has made them prey for the sexual desires and superior strength of men. Despite the so-called permissiveness of society today, girls are still kept under quite a strict family control. In the last couple of decades the increasing level of street crime, and the violent and often sexual acts committed against women have made parents even more wary about their daughters' 'freedom' outside the home.

If freedom was a general issue at home, it was particularly salient in the minds of the West Indian and Asian girls. The restraints described by many of the West Indian girls, often imposed through parents' fear of sexual exploits, cause many of them to yearn for more freedom and independence. Boys are certainly not subject to such restrictions, and recognition of this was reflected in the response to questions asking whether they would have chosen for themselves to be girls or boys.

Half of the West Indian girls in 1972 replied that they preferred to be female, while the rest preferred the idea of being male. Those who preferred a boy's life were often very conscious of the problems, burdens and 'pain' that were part of their feminine role. But instead of extolling positive virtues of masculinity, they were more concerned with describing the negative aspects they perceived about being female, the struggles involved, and the fact that boys did not have to go through these.

> [If I was a boy] I'd be allowed to go out more like my brother who is younger than me. I wouldn't be able to have illegitimate babies and get into trouble with my parents.

> A boy don't have to do so much housework, and they go out more often, and mothers don't nag about them all the time.

> I choose to be a boy because if you are a girl, you have to go through a lot of trouble such as pain and all different things. Although boys have pain but not as girl.

A few thought that girls had an easier life, but this reason, and the anticipation of the joys of being a wife and mother, which were so important for the white girls, were minimized.

Parents fear for the safety of their daughters if they are out at night. But rather than equipping them with knowledge and confidence about 'the facts of life', many of them prefer a method of strict control. However much they do trust their daughters it often seems to girls themselves that parents have little trust in them and that ways have to be found to get around this. The Ealing girls were conscious of their relative lack of freedom, often made explicit by the comparative treatment of their brothers.

> My brother, he can go out any time of the night he likes – come in any time of the morning he likes – and if I did that, there'd be hell to pay. It's just not fair. My mum still thinks my time is at half-past nine. I think that's ridiculous!

For many of the Asian girls in 1972, it seemed that the difference in freedoms and general life-styles that they observed around them created resentment towards the restrictive boundaries that surrounded their own lives. This surfaced in their 'chosen sex'. If they had been given the choice at that moment, only 20 per cent would have preferred to have been born as girls. Even in the closeness of their own community, the relative independence of boys showed up only too clearly. And this longing for greater freedom ran throughout the reasons they gave for preferring boys' lives.

A boy has more feeling happy than a girl because the boys can do everything but girls cannot do it. A boy gets better jobs than girls.

A boy has a freedom of doing anything he wants but the girl has just to be tied in the house.

Life is easier for boys than girls, they can come in as late as they wish and have more fun than we do.

A boy don't get pregnant and the girls do. And anyway our Indian people don't let the girls to be free same as with boys.

I would be a boy. At least you can go to places and all that. They can go anywhere that we can't go to ... you can't go alone anywhere. I mean, when I get home and I want to stand in the road for a minute, she tells me to come in, sit down, don't answer the door. If someone comes, she says don't answer it. At least boys can go out and enjoy themselves. I don't mind about boyfriends so much but I do want to enjoy myself.

In the Nineties

If we look at the reasons expressed by the relatively few white girls (16 per cent) and those West Indian girls who in the 1991 research would have preferred to be boys, they described similar reasons as in the earlier study, stating, for instance, that boys have better job opportunities; an easier life; boys don't have periods; they don't have to worry about pregnancy or rape; and they have more freedom. Some girls from West Indian, and Afro-Caribbean families in general, still laid slightly more emphasis on lack of freedom, and the risk of pregnancy.

My brother's allowed out everywhere. When he was my age he

was going out a lot more than I do. But you get used to it. They say boys are less likely to get raped and stuff so they're allowed out more. I don't think anything would happen to me but you can't be sure. It's how my mum was brought up so she's bringing me up like it.

EILEEN

I reckon boys have more advantages than girls because, for example, if a boy gets a girl pregnant, the boy can sod off and the girl is lumbered with the baby.

By the 1990s the discontent voiced by the Asian girls in the earlier study seemed to have cooled a little, although freedom was an ever-present concern. The proportion of Asian girls who said they would prefer to be girls had risen to 44 per cent (and those who preferred to be boys had fallen from 80 per cent to 56 per cent). The issues, however, remained much the same, and of their reasons for preferring to be boys, nearly two-thirds were because of the greater freedom afforded to boys in their religion (regardless of whether they are Sikh, Hindu or Muslim).

My culture stops me from doing what I want to do. My dad thinks I'm rebellious but I don't mean to be. I just like to do a lot of things.

SOPHIA

My parents worry a lot because I'm the only girl. They think if they let me out there could be trouble, so they don't let me out, only sometimes with my brothers. I feel trapped. I'm not allowed to go anywhere.

SADIA

I think I'm pretty lucky when I think about it, as an Asian girl, with the freedom I have. With some girls' parents, once they're home from school they have to be at home and that's it. They can't experience what's out there. Some of my friends wouldn't even dare to ask their parents, but we're lucky. I think freedom is important. We go to the movies. They ask a hundred questions and it shows they care, but they never say no. A lot of my friends, if they want to go somewhere they have to lie. They say they're going to their friend's house to do work, but they're really out somewhere else. A lot of parents are scared their daughters will lie. We can tell the truth, which is better.

HARPINDER

Several girls told me that they had to lie to their parents, either in order to go out with friends, or see a boyfriend. Ayesha said: 'I admit I lie sometimes, when I have to. I regret lying to my mum and dad, that's what hurts me.'

The concern with preserving a girl's reputation was also a continuing complaint, and the double standards involved. Asian boys can and do go out with girls, and many of their (Asian) girlfriends have to keep this well concealed from their families.

> I would be a boy. I think boys get a lot more freedom. If it was any other religion, then I'd probably stay a girl, but in this religion I prefer to be a boy. Boys are more wanted by the family. Parents favour a boy more, and they can do what they want. Most boys get away with whatever they do, even if they're naughty, because they're boys. If a boy's walking with a girl it's all right. The boy doesn't get anything done to his reputation, but the girl does. '*That* girl was walking with a boy!' They think they're more likely to get in trouble, just because they can get pregnant. If they did that would be really bad. It's their reputation that they're mainly worried about.

KULJIT

In this, the Asian girls suffered the same sort of situation as any other girls, for whom social and sexual control is exerted by the threat of gaining a bad reputation.[6] But for them in particular it can have even worse implications for the family name, and affect a girl's chances of making a good marriage. While sex is something not discussed at home, and is supposed to be saved until marriage, some Asian girls are sexually active, and it is a subject of concern, and one of the reasons why Ayesha would prefer to be a boy:

> Boys have sex, right? You don't know if they've lost it or not, their virginity. You know when a girl's lost it. Boys have all the freedom they want. They can come and go as they please. They don't mind if he's had sex, but with a girl it's 'Get out of the house. I don't want to know you'.

For Harwinder it is partly her home situation that makes her wish she was a boy, as her household responsibilities prevent her from working as hard as she feels she could have done:

> When I was younger I always wanted to be a boy and I still want to be a boy. I would still want to be a doctor, but I feel I would have been able to do more studying and be much more clever and be allowed out more if I was a boy. If I didn't have to do all this [house]work, then I would be able to study. My brother has all the time to study but he doesn't want to. If I could, I know I would have studied. So I've wanted to be a boy. I still do, if I could change right now.

The girls who were denouncing their lack of freedom and opportunity, and their future domestic responsibility were right to do so, just as other girls were right to contemplate their anticipated enjoyment of raising children and a freer expression of emotions. What they are doing is describing the unequal advantages and disadvantages experienced by both women and men. Each has a life that is circumscribed and justified by current social beliefs and economic conditions. Each bears the consequences in different ways but under a patriarchal society, women have traditionally borne these in not just one but in every area of their lives.

BOYFRIENDS

> At the moment I'm going out with a fantastic guy and I'm really enjoying being a girl.

Over the period since the first edition of this book, various feminist researchers have looked at the nature of girls' lives, the culture of femininity and the importance of aspects like boyfriends, love and romance in their lives.[7] Boyfriends feature heavily in the thoughts and activities of teenage girls whether or not they have actually got one. They may represent social success and status, a secure symbol of acceptable femininity, someone with whom to share experiences and explore love and sexuality, someone to take them out and give them a good time. Girls are surrounded by constant reminders of the importance of attracting boys. Two-thirds of the Ealing girls in

1972 said that they had current boyfriends, most of whom were older than them and working, mainly as mechanics, electricians or in similar jobs.

Just under half (45 per cent) of the white Ealing girls studied in 1991 said that they had a current boyfriend, compared with two-thirds in the early 1970s. Of those that did, most of their boyfriends were still at school, rather than being in the traditionally male working class occupations that most of the 1970s girls' boyfriends were in. This too reflects the trend for both girls and boys to remain at school after school-leaving age rather than moving immediately into employment. Several said their boyfriends were unemployed or had part-time jobs.

In 1972, nearly three-quarters of the Ealing West Indian girls said that their parents never or seldom allowed them out with boys. Nevertheless, over half of them had claimed to have a boyfriend then. At the time of the second study, in 1991, almost two-thirds of their counterparts said they had one. Many of the West Indian girls in the earlier research had described how strict their parents were about boys. This was particularly enforced by religious parents. In their daughters' eyes parents drew a simple equation between boys, sex and pregnancy, and adopted a preventative solution that tries to deny their daughters opportunities for social and physical contact, rather than explaining, discussing and working out other alternatives. Some felt that it implied an absence of trust and understanding.

That's one thing I disagree on, the fact of having boyfriends. They both think that when you have a boyfriend, the only thing you're going to do is have sex, which you're going to end up, you know, in a sticky position kind of thing. If they hear that one young girl about the age of fifteen, is pregnant, they say, well you're going to do the same and they don't seem to find out by letting me have a boy. They just jump to conclusions and that's that for them.

AUDREY

When we go out, she reckons be back before 10 o'clock – I don't understand it because when my mum was back in the West Indies she used to be out late, and she reckons how it's more safe over there, because over here, London's so big you know what I mean, and I just can't understand it. If she had freedom why can't she let me have freedom . . . It's just their minds – probably what *they* did they think we will do, when we go out – know what I mean. It's just their minds 'cause there's no part of the Bible say you can't go out. No, there isn't and I always say that to my mum.

VALERIE

Nearly twenty years later there were fewer complaints, but they sounded rather familiar:

My dad is strict, he doesn't like girls going out at all, he thinks we should just stay at home, but he lets my brothers go out. The girls have to stay at home and do the housework. He's old-fashioned, he's really strict. He doesn't like me going out. He doesn't even like me talking to boys. If he found out he'd kill me!

LAURA

My parents expect me to get my career first. At the moment they won't let me have a boyfriend because they think I'll slack off from school. They want me to get a career first and then get married later . . . They think I'll just get carried away and concentrate only on him and not do my schoolwork. And the other thing is they think I'll be stupid and go and get pregnant. They don't trust me. They think I'm stupid. My mum says one or two things, she'll say, 'Just be careful what you do.' And, 'Don't go and get yourself pregnant.' That's about it she doesn't detail it. Just the one statement: 'Don't get pregnant.' I learn from school or magazines. She doesn't tell me.

CATHERINE

She'll say, 'I just hope you don't get into this.' What she does, she doesn't really talk to you, like saying, 'If that happened I'd be very annoyed.' She'd say, 'I'd break your bones' and everything. She doesn't want it to seem a very light matter to get over. If she made it light it would make me feel that she didn't mind. But if she really makes it that you could be really scared of her if you did that, then I think – 'Oh my god, I will never do it!'

VANESSA

Many of their feelings are shared by the Asian girls, but their situation differs because of specific cultural conditions and expectations. The frustrations expressed by the Ealing Asian girls that I talked to in 1972 lay mainly in not being allowed to go out when and where they wanted and often not being allowed out at all; also in not being allowed to associate with boys; and in not having much control over their future lives. Of these, the most salient dissatisfaction at school was the taboo on boys. This could threaten girls' future school lives since if they were suspected of or discovered to be having any sort of relationship with a boy, however innocent, this could jeopardize their future educational prospects, as parents might take them away from school. (One of the 1972 Ealing Asian girls was subsequently taken away from school for associating with boys, and put to work in a laundry – an all-female environment.)

> Sometimes my mum says 'I hope you're not going out with boys.' Some girls go to school and go out with boys and talk to them. She says 'I hope you're not like that or I'll stop your school straight away.' She didn't go to school. In India there wasn't any school for girls – only boys went to school. If I go to work probably I'll have to go to work with my aunt or someone, I can't go to work on my own. They won't let me travel alone. They take me in a car and make someone go with me, an elder aunt or somebody. But if I come to school I come alone. They think you will talk to boys on the road. You must not talk to boys until you get married. Don't know what they'd do with us if we did. I've got [a boyfriend]. He comes to school and we talk together. Some of my friends have got boyfriends and their parents don't know. Some go away with them and their parents can't do anything – they go to another country. I think it will change. We don't want to be like this when we get older, it'll change.

SURINDER

Parental power commands great respect among the Asian community. There is a tradition of close mother–child relationships in Asian families, but it would be hard to discuss issues of freedom, boyfriends and sex with someone who had never experienced similar conflicts, who is likely to uphold restraint, and who may herself speak little English and rarely mix with English people, as was the case with a significant number of the girls' mothers at that time. For instance, it would be difficult to talk rationally about the problems of relating or not relating to boys at school when parents have made the implicit assumption that girls must mix with boys as little as possible. Sisters and girlfriends are more likely to be confidantes.

Although only a small fraction of these Asian girls in 1972 said that their parents ever allowed them to go out with boys, twice that number said that they had a boyfriend. And from their various remarks it would seem that in spite of the severe consequences of discovery, many girls inevitably talked to boys and some occasionally went out with them, although most would not admit it to their parents. In 1991, despite Surinder's hopes for changes, the strong restrictions on associating with boys continued. And, similar to the earlier study, a significant number of them (27 per cent) said they had a boyfriend, usually without the knowledge of their parents.

The boys that go out with girls in our year, I don't think the parents are very happy about it – well, most parents don't even know. But you don't know who's right. A girl and boy, if they're just going out with each other that's not so bad, but if it's their parents' fault that they're lying to their parents, I don't know.

KULJIT

Geeta lived with her mother as she and her father were divorced, and although she was close to her mother on most things, boys were one issue that they could not talk about. She had a boyfriend, he is Sikh and she is Hindu.

She goes, 'You can cut your hair, wear make-up, do whatever you like, but don't ever go out with a boy.' I'm the first in our family to have a boyfriend, he comes round to our house and sits and talks. We're really close. He's Sikh, but said, 'I would change my religion for you.' But if she found out I don't know what she'd do. She wouldn't talk to me probably. She thinks it's all right talking to boys as friends but not to go out with them. I just say to my mum that he's my friend from school. I hate lying to her, but that's the one subject we can't talk about. My brothers and sisters think we're just going out and we haven't done anything, but we have. He even asked me to sleep with him but I said not yet, I'm only fifteen. If they ever found out – oh my God! They think he's an angel and wouldn't do that. They don't know.

For some there was no conflict because they respected the wishes of their parents:

When it comes to boys I can't talk to anybody except my cousin's sister. My parents trust me but they don't trust the outside world. They try to keep me locked up as much as possible, to protect me. I don't have a boyfriend but I don't think I'd want one either. I'd only be putting myself at risk. It goes against my parents. If I do I'd be in trouble if I was caught, so I don't take the risk.

INDERJIT

It is such restrictions on freedom that each generation of girls promises to change, but these aspects are embedded within a strong and cohesive Asian culture which will continue to resist such loosening of controls around the lives of girls and women.

MARRIAGE

The View from 1972

In the early seventies, the importance and seeming inevitability of marriage turned every boyfriend into a possible marriage partner. Most of the (white) Ealing girls wanted to marry (82 per cent): a third of them hoped to be married by the time they were twenty, and three-quarters of them by the 'critical' age of twenty-five. At the age of fifteen, ten years hence seemed almost another lifetime away, and the occurrence of marriage during this time was almost taken for granted.

For some girls, the failure or miserable conditions of their parents' marriage made them hesitant about the prospect of their own, but it was hard to reject it for this reason alone. Fictional romance and the rosy glow that was portrayed surrounding young married couples helped to foster the hope that it could all be different for them.

> In ways I don't want to get married because me mum and dad's marriage ain't worked out all that good and I wouldn't want mine to work out the same, but I expect I will get married. I'm going out with me boyfriend at the moment and I wouldn't mind him really. He's dropped a couple of hints but I pretended not to pick 'em up, you know, be a bit difficult.

> I do think about marriage and I don't want to – I'd like to but not for a very long time. You'll see my mum at home, and children, her depressions and frustrations. I don't think I could put up with that. I think if I get a career I might not get married. Everyone says I shall but I'm not so sure.

> Since my father left, I've had it sort of drummed into me that, well, never trust anyone, and things like this, so I don't think I will get married, not yet anyway. I got a couple of boyfriends but I don't go with anyone steady or anything. Just a different one every night or every time I go out.

By their attitudes, many of these girls had implicitly accepted that a husband and family were the most satisfying things in a woman's life. They thought having children was still of great importance, but they found the old cliché that says that women's place is in the home to be far less acceptable. The ideological climate concerning women's equality exposes the implied put-down in this statement as male-defined and offensive; other aspects of women's role, like marriage and children, could not be so easily rejected

In comparison, only half the West Indian girls and a quarter of the Asian girls said they wanted to marry, 40 and 50 per cent respectively said they were not sure, and the rest said they did not wish to get married. For the West Indian girls at that time, marriage seemed to be approached with less immediacy and more reservations. Like the white girls, if they did marry, they mostly thought this would happen by the time they were twenty-five. They did, however, incline slightly more towards the later ages. In keeping with their chosen sex preferences, they were very aware of the restrictions on life created by having children:

> I wouldn't get married now. Not until I'm about thirty I suppose. I want to live a bit first. Supposing you marry someone, got to live with them first, find out if you want to stay with them.

EVADNE

> Whenever anyone asks me if I want to get married, I say no, or maybe, but never yes. Don't want to get married, at least not yet. Want to be independent, I don't want to depend on somebody. Be free for a while I guess. That's what life is about, getting married and having children. I want to do something different. That's why I want to continue. You can have children and that's that. Looking at people gets you thinking sometimes.

BARBARA

For the girls from Asian families, marriage was approached in a different way. In Asian families, the birth of a son is far more cause for celebration than the birth of a daughter, and this stems largely from the economics of the marriage system. Marriage is highly respected and its sanctity is unquestioned. Divorce is deeply frowned upon, although in Britain it has become a slightly more common occurrence. If a marriage does recognizably break down and divorce is carried through, women are at a disadvantage compared to men. The option of remarriage, which is open to men, is a course disapproved of for women. Widows face similar discrimination. Marriage is a form of social contract. It is not based initially or primarily on love – a marriage is arranged first and the time for falling in love comes later.

The parents of a boy and a girl are responsible for the arrangement, and the most suitable choice is made by investigating backgrounds and family histories. Parents are very afraid of anything that will 'taint' their daughters and thereby lessen their chances of making a good match. This mainly explains girls' lack of freedom, since they are forced to remain separate and tucked away at home to avoid any opportunity for temptation. The main fear is contact with boys and men, and therefore Asian girls are not supposed to have any associations with them. This is more rigidly enforced for Muslim girls and makes life almost intolerable for some girls at school, who have to mix and do lessons with boys, while at the same time any rumour that they have been seen talking to boys may result in their being removed from school. For Asians living in Britain in the 1970s, the anonymity of the marriage arrangement had largely been removed and meetings were usually organized between the prospective marriage partners. The biggest consideration in many cases, however, was the financial one – the dowry. At the time of the first study, a boy or girl transported over from India to become husband or wife was considered a far better prospect than one living over here because he or she had not been 'vulgarized', and would be expected to be more dutiful and obedient. One of the Ealing girls commented then:

> If the girl stays here and nobody marries her then she goes to India and gets married down there. Their parents think that Indian boys are very good, better than London ones, because when they come from India they change down here and they're not what they used to be, you know, quiet and shy, but go out and parties and everything and they don't behave like the other boys, that's what they think.

RAJINDER

Although arranged marriage had become somewhat liberalized by the 1970s, and boys and girls usually could make the final decision, love marriages were still frowned upon and were, and still are to some extent, relatively unusual. They happened more between westernized or educated people like college graduates. But it is still not approved of to marry outside your religion or caste. Mixed marriages have increased, but are unusual. While it is possible to make some generalizations it should be remembered that girls from Asian families are not a homogeneous group. There will be differences which depend on things like religion: for instance, Sikh girls have a little more freedom than Muslim girls, and families will differ individually.

At the time of the first study, many Asian girls felt they could still exert little power over either the time of their marriage or the choice of husband. They might continue their education in an effort to postpone marriage, or reject their prospective husband, but since parents go to a lot of trouble to select a suitable boy, it might be difficult to justify. But although a lot of the Ealing girls complained about the inevitability of their marriage, some also acknowledged that their parents are usually concerned to make the best choice.

I will be eighteen when I go back to Pakistan and get married. My parents will stay here. I will have time to get to know him before I get married. I have met him. He's good, he's OK, two or three years older. If I didn't like him, just don't get married to him I suppose. But your parents don't just give you away to another person, he is very carefully chosen. You can't choose someone of your own. My friends will do the same ... If I stayed here, I don't want to get married – but my parents says I can't do [that]. That's what my cousins say – they don't want to get married, all of them – if they earn their own living they won't have to ask their parents for it and it's OK, but if you stay with your parents ... After we get married we can do what we like, our parents cannot tell us. But as long as you live with your parents, they will tell you.

NASEEM

I suppose I will get married. I don't know if I'll get married to an Indian, it all depends on the person. I would have to take some notice of my parents but they have said that I can choose my own man. My best friend's parents would choose her man because they think that they can choose the best person for her. They ask about how much land you have got, how many O levels and all that. I don't like that idea. Some girls go back after schooling to their own country, not to work at all, because they think that if you get married in India or Pakistan, all the boys are innocent.

MARJIT

Whatever the traditional advantages of an arranged marriage, the general unpopularity of marriage at this point in their lives, whether because of its imminence or the method of arrangement, was reflected in other parts of the earlier research where both getting married and having children were dismissed or considered unimportant by the Asian girls. For example, when girls were asked if they wanted to get married, only a quarter committed themselves to saying yes, half were unsure, and the rest said no. They consistently regarded school and a career as more important than marriage, and were less than enthusiastic about being housewives or having a lot of children. Yet family life was understandably of great importance in their lives and it is not surprising that many simultaneously anticipated future satisfactions in having a husband and family of their own. Their response contrasted with that of their white contemporaries, whose current enthusiasm for social life, boys, marriage and children tended to overshadow more studious pursuits.

Although it seemed as if the Asian girls were being denied the 'freedom' to marry who they chose, in general families are careful in their choice of husband, and it has to be questioned how far Western marriage provides a better option. Marriages based on love do not seem to last very long these days. And consider, for instance, how much time and mental energy is devoted by other 'freer' girls in the contemplation of their future 'love marriages'. This provides girls with plenty to distract them from developing more individual freedom of expression and interests, not to mention education. While arranged marriage is more circumscribed in nature, the romance of a love marriage ensures voluntary capture. In the 1970s at least, it was taken for granted as a positive, integral and almost inevitable part of the feminine role for which there is elaborate preparation and competition. Most girls could gain a wealth of experience through having boyfriends and practising with different sorts of relationships. Love can be dabbled in and tested, and every boyfriend assessed as a possible husband. Arranged marriage views love rather differently as something which can develop through marriage, rather than the reverse. Many of the other girls with whom the 1972 Ealing Asian girls shared their classrooms had access to the freedoms that the Asian girls like those I talked to yearned for. They could go out at night, have boyfriends, go to films, dances and parties. Parents still applied rules more strictly to them than to their brothers but compared to Asian girls these were minimal. But for many such girls, this precious freedom was not often extensively used to explore new areas of interest and individual possibility. It was mainly invested in a preoccupation with boys, love and romance, which seem to them like the most meaningful pursuits. In some respects, their so-called 'freedom' can ensnare them into the marriage trap.

The View from 1991

Clearly, significant changes have taken place in girls' attitudes to marriage over the last twenty years. In these two studies, the high proportion of the white Ealing girls who said in 1972 that they wanted to marry had fallen from 82 per cent to 45 per cent in 1991. This drop was taken up by the relatively high (46 per cent) of girls who declared that they were 'not sure' if they wanted to marry. Whereas almost no one in the 1970s said they did not want to marry, almost one in ten girls in the 1990s firmly asserted this. Corresponding trends were reflected in the age they thought they might get married, if they did marry: whereas a third of the girls in the earlier study estimated that they would be married by the time they were twenty, a mere 4 per cent gave this age in the later study. However, by the anticipated age of twenty-five, this difference was beginning to even out, and a total of 56 per cent of girls in 1991 predicted that they would be married by this age, compared with 75 per cent in 1972. The West Indian girls' views on wanting to marry did not significantly change, in that about half said yes to marriage at both times, and the majority of the rest were unsure. If they did get married, like the white girls, just over half expected to do this by the age of twenty-five, and practically all by the time they were thirty. Their views on marriage were also very similar.

These reflect social changes that have occurred in the general nature of marriage and divorce. Nowadays, marriage is far less secure than it used to be. One in five families is headed by a single parent, and in 1991 it was estimated that as many as 42 per cent of those people who marry will get divorced. (It is interesting that over 70 per cent of divorce petitions are filed by women, the majority citing the husband's 'unreasonable behaviour'.) In 1990 there was a 4·5 per cent decrease in the number of marriages (331,000 registered) compared to the previous year, and there had not been such a significant decline since 1980–81. Over the last decade, there has been an increase in the numbers of couples cohabiting: for instance, whereas in the period 1980–84, it was estimated that one in three of those marrying had lived together first, for the subsequent period 1985–88, this had risen to one in two. In 1990, 17 per cent of all 16–59-year-olds who were not married were cohabiting.

These changes were reflected in the attitudes expressed by a significant number of girls who considered that living with someone was preferable to getting married, and easier to get out of:

> I would want to get married but not too soon. I want to do things first, before you get tied down, say when I'm twenty-seven. My mum and dad aren't married and they've been together for twenty years. So if it is going to work out, it doesn't mean you have to get married first, it's just a piece of paper. It doesn't prove that you love someone more does it? If it doesn't work out you've got to go through divorce, but if you're not married you just split up.
>
> LUCY

> I don't know how I feel about marriage. When I was younger I always wanted to get married, but now I'd like to get married but when I'm a lot older. I read about divorce and everything and everyone who married young all seem to be getting divorced. My mum and dad married about four years ago, but they'd been together for about twenty years, I think it's better like that, because as soon as you get married it's like you own the person and they own you. If I do get married I'll be much older.
>
> JACKIE

Lucy's and Jackie's parents seem to be a recommendation for parental cohabitation. As also illustrated in the 1970s research, girls' experiences of the failed marriages of their parents have a negative effect on their own attitudes to getting married:

> I'm not getting married, not after my mum and dad – no way! I'd quite like to live with someone when I'm older but I don't know if I'll get married to them. I don't see the point in marriage, it's just a piece of paper, isn't it? I suppose it's nice to have a commitment, depends on the type of people. I've seen it

too much with my mum and dad, all the bad things. I suppose it's got good things as well ... If you could just live with someone and have a relationship that was really steady, it could just be like you were married. The thing is now it's so complicated, my mum and dad are separated with the divorce and half the money for the house and this and that. It's too much confusion, too much hassle.

LYN

The tendency to want to delay marriage for career reasons or simply having fun, still endorsed the idea that marriage is a restrictive practice.[8] Nina is also aware that she would like a marriage to work so that her children can have their father around:

I definitely want to get married, but I think I'd live with them for a while, so that I'd know it would work, and then get married. I wouldn't want my kids to grow up without a father, especially if they're sons. I've seen my brother grow up and can see a father needs to be around. So I'd make sure first, by living with them. But I think marriage brings a family together more, and you've got the same name. I'd get married, I think, late twenties – twenty-five to thirty, no earlier. I want to have fun, travel and work. Get something out of life first.

NINA

Some are well aware that girls now tend to deny that they are going to get married, or to say they will marry at an older age, but in reality they know things may be different if they meet the 'right' person:

I don't know about getting married, see what happens. You can't really say 'I'm not going to get married until whenever'. A lot of my friends say that. But if someone came along – you can't say what's going to happen. I'd like to, if the right person came along.

TERESA

As everybody says, I'm not going to get married, I'm going to stay young and single. But I know in the end I will get married, but I want a career first, I want to get out first, explore things, before I settle down. I'll keep my career, I'm determined to do that, and do part-time maybe. I'd get married in my thirties, late thirties. I don't know about children, but I know I will, it's a way of life really. You mature in your thirties, you're a completely different person. I'll want to do different things than I do now.

KATE

With more emphasis on equality and sharing in the home, it is not surprising to find at least one girl whose reservations about marriage are rooted in a fear that their husband may try to tell them what to do:

That's another reason I don't want to get married, if my husband was telling me what I should and shouldn't do. I'd rather think it out for myself. I'd rather not get married but I suppose I'll have to wait and see. If there was someone I really wanted to be with, I'd probably marry them, but I don't see why I couldn't be with them all the time and not be married to them – live with them.

ROSIE

Whereas in 1972 only a quarter of the Ealing girls from Asian families said they wanted to marry, this had increased to 55 per cent in 1991. In the first study just over half were unsure about marriage compared to just over a quarter in the second study, and the rest said they did not want to marry. In terms of age things had not changed much: one in five Asian girls in the earlier study thought they would be married by the age of twenty, and this proportion had fallen only slightly in the later one; while about 90 per cent in both studies thought they would be married by the age of twenty-five.

The system of arranged marriages is still prevalent amongst the Asian community, and not surprisingly marriage remained a salient issue for the Asian Ealing girls in 1991. Their feelings, however, did not emerge nearly as resentfully as in 1972. There were some who were very against arranged marriage, and it is not unknown for girls to run away from home to avoid this, but this reaction also implies desperately unhappy conditions at home. Most Asian parents, like other parents, want their children to be happy, and their daughters are aware of this. The idea that arranged marriages have been largely forced on protesting daughters who have to marry people they have not met or do not like is a myth.[9] Although in the past some families brought over prospective husbands or wives from their countries of origin for their daughters and sons respectively, this is no longer a frequent practice.

Many girls have seen that arranged marriages within their own families can and have worked out all right, like Madhu:

> I don't think my dad would mind, but my mum would want me to have an arranged marriage. But I would want that, it's to do with my religion and everything. I'd prefer to have an arranged marriage. I don't know why. I think they work out more than other marriages. My sisters' have all been arranged marriages and they've worked out.

The rules have also relaxed about meeting and going out with prospective partners, and both sides have the right of veto. Most of the Ealing Asian girls said they would probably have an arranged marriage. Many of them did not mind this arrangement at all; some stipulating their preference for marrying later rather than sooner, as they wanted to get their education finished first. Others thought their parents would not mind if they found their own partner, provided he was of the right caste.

> I think my parents are quite open on marriage. But they want me to marry an Asian guy the same caste and everything, it's quite complicated. My whole family would be totally disappointed if I married a black guy or a white man. My mum would be very upset although she says she'd accept it. I could get away with it but I know myself I wouldn't feel very comfortable because to me my family is very important and my culture. If I married a white or a black guy I know where I'd be left in the community and the same would go for my children. I don't look at white boys and think – 'Oh. I'd like to marry that kind of guy.' I always look at Indian guys.
>
> RAJWINDER

Shazia wants to be an engineer, and hopes that her future husband will have a favourable attitude towards this. Her mother is already looking to arrange marriage for her but Shazia wants to finish her studies first:

My mum asks me if I want an arranged marriage and I go, 'No'.
She goes, 'Well, the parents choose the best.' I go, 'You can
choose the husband and if I like him I will.' But if I found
somebody I liked who had a good family background then my
mum would probably agree to it. My mum says, 'You young
generation are bad. At your age we were stuck in the house not
allowed out.' We're allowed to go out and everything, we've got
more freedom. But Mum's looking for a husband for me now! I
say, 'Let me get my studies over and done with and at college
and everything then maybe at twenty-two or something.' She
says, 'You'll be too old by then.' Because down in Pakistan girls
get married when they're about thirteen.

Ushma wants to go to college or university and do fashion design.
If she doesn't do well at school she would like to join the police
force. Her mother is always telling her she should get a good career,
and this is what she wants to do. Although she will have an
arranged marriage, she stressed that she would never be made to
marry anyone against her will:

> The arranged marriages now are different. The parents will meet
> the boys' parents and after that you're allowed to go out as long
> as you want until you're ready. But while you're going out if
> anything goes wrong, they're really gutted about it. The family
> is let down and all that. But they let you meet the boy and you
> can go out with him. When they arrange it they give you the
> right to say no. Some of the arranged marriages aren't so bad.
> My mum would never force me into a marriage. There's no
> point, it would only end in divorce.

Although there is some incidence of divorce or separation in the
Asian community in Britain, it still invokes a high level of disapproval and negative social consequences for women. Geeta's mother
and father are divorced, and although the family is very close, life
has not been easy for them.

> My mum and dad are divorced. We were really young, we don't
> remember it. He used to beat my mum up and us too, so we
> didn't get on. So mum is bringing us up on her own. It's not
> acceptable for Asian people to get divorced. People really talk,

they give her a bad name. When my mum was getting divorced from my dad, my dad's brothers were always saying that no one would marry her daughters because she divorced her husband. They gave her so much grief. Recently people in school have been coming up to my sister and saying, 'Your mum's a slag.' And I'm going out with a boy and they all say, 'You're taking after your mum.' They never leave a lone woman alone. It's stupid. Since we were small we didn't get on with people. We had a really hard time because my mum was divorced and lived on her own. We had fights with our neighbours. Now, as we're growing up we're getting it sorted. It's like a disadvantage not having a father or not having a husband.

Marriage still looms large in the lives of Asian girls and women, but as far as most of those in the Ealing study were concerned, it was not going to put a stop to them studying and going for a good job or a career, nor continuing after marriage and children. Delaying marriage was possible, but not getting married at all was less of an option, and on this point most Asian parents would still agree.

In our family you're not meant to leave home until you get married. I'm against marriage altogether. My friends think I'm weird as well, because they all want to get married and they all want to get a good job. I want a career but I just feel I'll be happy if I'm on my own. But my parents feel I would have to get married no matter if I study or not.

HARWINDER

FAMILY LIFE – PRESENT AND FUTURE

In the 1972 study, girls talked about aspects of their home and family life, their relationships with their parents and ways in which they might like things to change, especially in their own future families. For instance, many young girls find their mother a greater source of empathy and understanding than their father. This is rooted at least partly in the close relationships that mothers have with children during their earliest years, and the mother–daughter identification that occurs as a result.[10] This empathy is strengthened by the accepted attitude towards women, which sees it as natural that they should talk freely about personal feelings and problems, but regards the same behaviour in a man as an admission of personal failure.[11] Women's traditional role in the home has made them more easily available to talk with than fathers, and mothers are girls' confidantes in many difficult situations. They act as a source of emotional reassurance while fathers are seen more as sources of information. The way parents are perceived and related to again reflects their different personalities and knowledge. Dad is often seen by daughters as distant and impersonal, factual and worldly-wise.[12] Mum is usually softer, more protective and more sympathetic to problems, although she too has to be tough in other ways.

> I find it easier to talk to mum compared to my dad – most people get on better with their mums than their dads. Girls I think will find that their mum will understand more because they've had to go through it all.
>
> HELEN

> If there's anything I wanna know and I know that he's got the answer, he'll tell me the answer. But I can talk about anything I like to me mum – she's not embarrassed to tell me the answer to any of the facts of life or anything like that and I'm not embarrassed to ask her because I know that she'll answer me and she won't say, 'That's best not talked about.'
>
> MICHELLE

In the nineties, as in the seventies, girls still tended to confide in their mothers more than their fathers, once more demonstrating that the role of fathers and their relationship with their daughters is more often characterized by distance than closeness. As one girl said:

> I'm closer to my mum, I talk to my mum about things I wouldn't talk to my dad about. Me and my mum are really similar people. It's not like a mother and daughter relationship, more like friends. It's good. We just talk about anything.

Family life has suffered increasing fragmentation over the last twenty years, and the rise in lone parent families – mainly lone mothers, but also a significant number of lone fathers – has meant that some fathers have had to take a more intimate role in their daughter's growing up. Karen had chosen to live with her father and stepmother, and it is her father to whom she goes to for intimate advice:

> I always speak to my dad more, and he told me everything – like how to use my first Tampax, he demonstrated how to do it. And safe sex and all that. I'll go, 'Dad, I need a new bra,' and he'll go out and get me one. It's funny, he has more of a way like that than my mum. He's not like a traditional dad. He used to be but he changed. He's a young dad, even though he's in his forties.
>
> LUCY

When asked in 1972 whether they would like their own future home and family to be like their present one, nearly half the girls gave a negative reply. Over a third of their dissatisfactions lay in the nature of family relationships which they wished to make closer, more united and understanding.

> I will talk more to my children about life and problems. I'd be a friend and mother.

> I would like it to be nice and peaceful and I will trust my children.

> I would make it feel more together and loving.

Others desired changes that revealed their frustration with old-fashioned ideas, and their intention to give children more freedom and independence. They also wanted better and more modern houses, instead of the old terraces and cramped flats in which many of them lived. Their hopes for the future sprang out of their conditions in the present and their optimism at that time about the possibility of change. But it is the wider social and economic conditions about which they complained, such as bad housing, that themselves affect and exacerbate the family tensions that many girls were determined to avoid. The housing and working conditions under which many black families, like many working class families, were living made the ideal happy family life even more complicated and difficult to achieve than it would be in more favourable circumstances. Some West Indian girls I spoke to were also very aware of stresses at home.

> I don't get on with my dad all that much . . . he's a train driver, works at nights so he's out in the daytime, so we don't see each other all that much. Can get on with my mum, like a house on fire. Sometimes have off-moments but that's soon patched over 'cause you've got to talk to her all the time . . . But I don't like talking to my mum and dad, they don't understand people. They think I talk in riddles so they don't listen to me. I don't care anyway. I keep everything to myself. Don't talk to nobody. I keep it to myself. I don't have to talk to anybody. I don't need to talk to anybody. I can solve my own problems. I only have problems sometimes, but I can solve them myself. I wouldn't tell 'em to my mum and dad for anything.
>
> GLORIA

Earlier writings about the situation of black people in Britain tended to pathologize the black family, instead of looking at the sources of problems within the discriminatory responses of our society and its institutions. Later writers have pointed out how black family relationships are not significantly different in aspects of affection, concern, conflicts, etc., from any other families.[13]

Some of the girls in 1972 were asked whether they would bring up a daughter of their own any differently from the way they had been brought up. They mentioned specific changes that they would make, for instance:

> I think I'd be fairly strict with her in some ways, for example school work. I'd like her to do well at school, but I don't think I'd insist on her going to university or staying on for A levels, although I suppose I'd like her to. I wouldn't be too strict about clothes, and I'd let her go out to work on Saturdays, but not in the evenings. But however much she may not want to do her homework, she ought to. But I don't think I'd be too strict.
>
> PENNY

The only thing I would not do is – I've had a load of responsibilities laid on to me and I don't mind 'em, but they just annoy me sometimes because in the holidays I look after me little sister and it stops me going out where I would really want to go, 'cause I'd have to take her and I can't afford to pay for her, and half the time me mum and dad can't afford to pay for her. I don't suppose I'd give [my daughter] as much to do as I've had to do, but otherwise there's nothing wrong in the way my mum's brought me up.

MICHELLE

In 1991, about the same proportion of girls as before (about half) said they would prefer their own home and family to be different from their present one. Many expressed the same reasons as those who in 1972 intended to give greater freedom to their own children; be less strict as parents; provide greater understanding; give their children more money; or have a larger or tidier house. However, the increase in lone parent families is reflected by some girls who specifically mentioned their desire to ensure that both parents are around for their children.

It will be better. Not so many rows and I would not let my children run me down and stress me out. I would try not to separate in marriage!

I will try and make sure the children have their father around as I grew up from the age of four without one and miss that. If this wasn't possible I would like my own family to be how mine is now.

Share the tasks, the man isn't going to take over. Not so hard on the children, give them more space.

I'd like to have about four children and be really close with them. I'd like them to confide in me, not like it is with me and my mother, I can't tell her anything. I'd like my children to be able to come to me, and I'd give them things I didn't have, because I know how they feel. And I'd bring them up all equal, boys and girls the same.

CATHERINE

Many of the feelings of the Ealing Asian girls in the earlier study about the restrictions in their lives also emerged in the ways Asian girls in 1991 thought they would treat their own children differently:

I will help my kids with all their problems and let them go out with friends more often.

I will give my children a little more freedom. They will be allowed to put their views about things forward.

I'd let my daughter do what she likes – what we can't do. Wear fancy clothes, wear make-up. Wouldn't like her to go out with boys. I would like her to choose her own husband.

I'd let her go out with boys definitely. I'd like her to tell me what she's doing and not like I do to my parents – say I'm going round to a friend's house when I'm not.

Things have not changed quite as much for Asian girls today as their predecessors in 1972 might have hoped. If we consider as before, that these girls' mothers could just about be the girls in the 1972 study, then as parents they had not made their daughters' lives significantly different from their own. Clearly some freedoms have been won, and individual families vary within the more specific characteristics of their particular religions. While the other girls in the research were split as to whether they would make their own home and family different from their own, the girls from Asian families came down slightly more (63 per cent) on the side of making them different. In keeping with their feelings described earlier, 35 per cent of these specifically mentioned giving their children more freedom. Other significant differences they hoped to make lay in giving children more care and understanding and talking with them; and treating girls and boys equally in the home.

Our generation will be a lot different. We'll let our kids go out with boys, we'll meet them, won't mind them coming round. We would warn about the birds and the bees. It's easier for us to talk about it. I don't think the Asian families now know the words to use. We'd probably end up laughing. But we know how to. It'll be easier for us. The next generation is going to have such an easy life – we'll let them do what they want. If our parents come along and say about their grandchildren, 'You shouldn't let them do that,' we'll say, 'They're our kids.'

USHMA

I would let her be more free and I'd like her to talk to me about her feelings. I don't want her to lock them away. When it comes to boys I'd like her to bring them home, I wouldn't mind. If she chooses someone of her own I'd like her to tell me first and to get to know him as well. If she didn't want to get married straight away I would agree to that. I'd like her to wait a few years, until they got to know each other. And if I had a boy and a girl I wouldn't want to treat them different.

MADHU

There are two religions in Sophia's family; her mother is French and a Christian and her father came from Kenya and is Muslim. This has affected her views on how she would bring up a daughter:

I'm going to bring her up as Muslim or as not a Muslim. I'm between the two: I celebrate Christmas, but when it comes to boys I'm suddenly Muslim. I want my kids to be one or the other. It's too hard. Christians and Muslims are so different, in cooking and culture. I don't want them to go through half and half. It's heartache. I've ended up in tears quite a lot because of it, mostly over boys. And I want to do drama and dance, but my dad doesn't like it.

Geeta's family is unusual in that her mother is a lone mother, and as described earlier, the family has experienced discrimination from other Asian people because of it. Whether or not this treatment and her position as head of her household has changed her mother's attitudes, she is not so strict with her daughters as other Asian mothers, as Geeta describes:

We're different from other families, I know that. My mum has her hair cut and she wears skirts and make-up. She says to us sometimes, 'You look bad, go and put some make-up on.' She wants us to have short hair. She wants us to wear what we like, do what we like. Others, it's like being in prison in your own home. It's not like that in our house. Our friends come round. Even boys come round and we talk and play, our mum and all.

It is very confusing to try to balance out changing beliefs and expectations of the past, present and future. They are not simply swapped around, but tend to coexist awkwardly. Like their white class-mates only more so, Asian girls were confronting a situation in which the perception of the traditionally accepted feminine role has become increasingly hazy.

FEMINISM AND WOMEN'S RIGHTS

Girls from working class and middle class backgrounds in the 1970s were destined to have longer working lives than previous generations due to social and economic changes that include better contraception and smaller families as well as their own increasing desire to have some sort of a career. The continuing acceptance of separate domestic roles for men and women, however, has consistently left women with the double load of work and home. Although ideas about sex discrimination and women's equality were publicly discussed, they did not deeply enter the consciousness of many girls at this time. However, the idea that women have rights which have been withheld from them is one with which that generation was growing up. Most girls in the early 1970s had heard of the Women's Liberation Movement, even if they had only absorbed its misrepresentation in the media and thought members of such a movement must be ridiculous or freaky. Some of the 1972 Ealing girls mentioned this subject spontaneously, at other times it came up as a natural extension of discussion. Their ideas and impressions were mixed – often unclear and fragmentary – a reflection of the way that they had been picked up. Aspects of feminism and the women's movement concerning equal pay and anti-discrimination were usually mentioned and approved of but at that time the Ealing girls were rather doubtful and confused about altering roles or personal relationships.

I think girls have got an advantage over the boys. Apart from women's lib which I think it's not very strong, it'll die out in a little bit, although I think some people will persevere and keep the standards up, something like that. But I don't really believe in women's lib.

Equal pay part – that's all right, but when it comes to marriage I think most women like to be dominated to a certain extent, and the man probably needs to feel important to dominate. They always do it like that and I think it's the best way. Most women think, 'Oh, I'm equal to a man' but they aren't in many respects. But when it comes to marriage I think, I suppose, you have to have discussions between them – the important matters. Not 'I want you to do this.'

Most of the others who talked of 'women's lib' were also prepared to sanction equal pay and opportunity but nothing more radical. Like many other people, they had taken in the media send-up about 'bra-burning' and rightly thought it was absurd. Unfortunately, they associated women's liberation with this image, which produced an artificial gap between the true ideas of the women's movement and their own embryonic stirrings. Their ideas were often somewhat contradictory:

I agree with some of it but not all of it. Some of it's stupid – burn the bra and all that. It's a waste of time because they're not getting anywhere. They should worry about getting equal pay and things like that. If a girl wants to drive a lorry, she should be allowed to. There's a lot of jobs that girls would like to do but just haven't got the chances. Should be allowed to do it if they wants to. There's a lot of boy's jobs that a girl could do better than a boy, but she's never had the chance to do it.

I agree with some of it like equal pay and equal opportunity in jobs, but I like men to be domineering and I don't like women always trying to be better than men.

Boys and girls are more equal than they used to be now. It's not that just the girls are taught how to cook and iron and all that, and the boys taught woodwork now. I think that's a good thing – up women's lib! I don't believe in girls not doing housework and going out to work. I wouldn't go as far as that – or burning your bras.

In 1972, some of them were visibly wrestling with their opinions, and trying to line up and work out the (il)logical reasons for some of the traditional ideas they were reluctant to part with, such as male dominance.

The changes that have taken place over the last two decades have been due in part to the efforts of feminists in publicizing and campaigning around issues of equality. Since then there has been an enormous amount written by feminists, on every area of women's lives. In the early 1970s, the women's movement in Britain was only a few years old. The Ealing girls at that time had a mixed response, many endorsing the idea of equality but rejecting the extreme behaviour they understood to be feminism. In the 1990s, attitudes to feminists and feminism were not as different as one might have expected, but there was resounding support for women's equality. One or two endorsed the traditional dominance of men, but they were the minority. Nina was one of them. She thought things had changed enough and supported more traditional divisions:

> I think it's all right now. I think we've got to the stage where people are accepting the fact that women can do it, and we don't need any more. I think men will get upset by the fact that we're trying to overpower them if we carry on. I think men will always be slightly the more powerful sex, I think that's the way they were made to be, brought up to be like that. A lot of men are stronger, not all men, but in build and in looking after the family and the woman, I think they're meant to be like that. I don't think the woman should look after the man and the family, it's better the other way round. I suppose that's the way I've been brought up as well, I think it's nice like that.

Everyone else was definitely in favour of equal roles at work and home, and for women standing up for their rights. However, many considered that positive changes in women's opportunities had already been brought about, and thought that feminism and women's liberation were now largely redundant. They were optimistic that equality had been achieved, and that nowadays women could do anything if they just put their minds to it:

> I think because there's much more [equality] now, I don't think we need to worry about it so much. We don't really because we get treated equally in this school, I don't know about out of school. Things like feminism and women's liberation, that's

cooled down. We're getting more chance anyway. There's nothing much to fight for. People can go into engineering now, we can be mayor, we can be prime minister, we can be virtually anything we want if we put our mind to it, so I think that's calmed down a lot.

KIM

I think feminism and women's liberation is still a bit relevant, but not as much as it used to be. I think both sexes have got equal chances now. Quite a while ago, if a man and woman were going for a job the chances were that the man would get it, but now I think they've got equal chances. I know the job I want to do [joining the RAF] and I've got to work much harder than the men do to show that I am as good as them. That will be something to do. I suppose it's not fair but I want more out of my life so I must show I am better and I can get up higher than they can.

CAROLINE

Unfortunately their beliefs about equality are ill-founded. Although some movement has been made in opening up men's and women's jobs to both sexes, job segregation, sex discrimination, and unequal pay still exist in many areas of work. The steady erosion of the power of the trade unions over the last two decades has also whittled away at some of the post-war advances made in working conditions for both women and men.

In both of these Ealing studies, as in the general population, girls and women tend to either express or implicitly endorse many feminist principles about women's role, status, equality and opportunity, while at the same time denying that they are feminists themselves. They identify feminists as 'other people', who have extreme ideas and who are usually anti-men. Lyn was of this opinion, while also describing how she saw these kinds of changes occurring in her own family:

I think some people go over the top with feminism and women's rights, they're a bit too much. But I think there is a need for it and I understand it all, but I think some people just take it a bit too far. Some women are really anti-men, saying men are dreadful. I don't think that's right. We did about the Suffragettes recently in history and I thought that was good . . . Things have definitely changed. I can see things have changed. I can see it in the generations in my family. My nan stays at home all the time and does the cooking for my grandad, but she likes it like that, she's old-fashioned and traditional. But then I can see with my mum and dad it wasn't quite like that. My mum was out a lot and my dad did cooking sometimes and my mum had a job. Yes. I can see that it's changed.

Lyn was aware that it was women who had demanded and made changes in their lives, and her own mother had been involved in a women's group in the past:

I think women air their feelings now, and stand up for themselves. They assert themselves more, they say what they want. I think if women hadn't said anything it would have just carried on with men doing what they wanted to do and not having much consideration for women, taking it for granted. My mum used to belong to a women's group. I can't remember what it was about, about sexism and things like that. My mum's really assertive, she goes for what she wants. I'd like to see more women having more senior jobs in politics and stuff. I think more women should aim to achieve higher things because some feel they can't because it's men-dominated.

In this context it was interesting that at least two girls specifically mentioned that women were no longer going for office work or secretarial jobs. As illustrated in chapter 4, what used to be a nice job for a girl is no longer good enough.

Feminism is not really relevant, more women are doing jobs that men do, stuff like that; and more men are staying in the house. I don't think it's the same as it was, it's changing. There's more women going for top jobs now. More women being barristers and stuff. (I think there's less going for office jobs now.)

EILEEN

Recently a lot of women have been getting to the top in the business world and whatever. That never used to happen. Women would just be at home and the men would go to work. I would say it has changed over the last five years or so, a bit. It should change more. Women should be right at the top. Not secretaries and stuff, only if they like secretarial jobs.

CATHERINE

Like Catherine, others did feel that more change was necessary, and that equality was a way off yet:

Girls are more aware now that they can do more, that they can do what boys do. If someone told me that I couldn't do something because I was a girl, I'd have a big row. I think women's rights and feminism are still relevant. Even though they're getting a few more jobs that they want, it's not really equal. You don't very often see a woman pilot or a woman plumber, but if they want to do it they can do it. It shouldn't matter what sex you are.

LEAH

The Ealing Asian girls in 1991 were similarly enthusiastic about equality.

Equality is very important. You're not happy unless you're treated equally. You go round thinking people are looking down on you. There was a girl who went into mechanics. You can't give that up because you think there will be men there who will give you a hard time. You have to stand up for it, work for it. Women and men should be treated equally.

USHMA

As someone looking in rather from the outside, it seemed to me that things were changing for Asian girls living here. Not linear change, but more according to individual, family, and religion and the size and location of the community. I was therefore very interested in the ways that Asian girls themselves felt that the situation had changed for girls. Here are some of their views:

Before, when they came over they would just go through school because it is the law but then they got them married off. I think quite recently, the last five or six years, girls have gone to university and they are finally showing that it's not just the boys who can do it, girls can do it as well. A lot of Asian parents think get the boy in and see that he works, get the girls through but it doesn't matter what comes out at the end. And a lot of girls at university have come out the other end and they're showing that we can do something, so it's good for us. It's like a fight really because you're Asian, and because you're a girl as well. To prove to anybody that you can do it. My parents aren't sexist or anything but a lot of Asian parents are. A boy is a boy. It's all hail when a boy is born, they have a celebration. Girls are born and they start crying basically. It makes me quite proud actually to think there are so many Indian people making the effort in school and so many girls as well. A lot of girls in our year can actually do something with their lives. I think as girls we have to do what we want and not let the boys try and push us over. It's important for us to stand up for ourselves. It is different for Indian girls, it's so much harder for us (than English girls) to do something good. I think girls in general, not just Asian girls, should be more aware of what's going on in the world. Maybe then they'd realize that we don't have to do this, we don't have to do that, we can do what we like. You should have a general knowledge of everything, not just what lipstick you want to wear. And I like my culture. I like being Indian. I like being me.

RAJWINDER

The thing with families now is that women know what they're doing. Before it was the man taking the lead. Now women can tell them to stick it. The women have learnt to stand up for themselves. A lot of Asian women have been through rough patches and have brought up their kids. Ladies go out to work now, they're people with careers. Ladies doing their own thing. Before men used to look down on the Asian women in families a lot and they had to stay at home and produce babies. Men went to work. Now it's more level. It's better now. Then, parents influenced their children a lot but now people are growing up to think for themselves whether they want to get married or not. Twenty years ago it was what was good for the family.

USHMA

Things have changed for girls. My mum tells me how they used to help and that and came straight home from school. We stay at school and we can go out and join clubs and things. We meet more people than they did. It's a lot different. I think it's better, we have more control over what we want to do. My mum and them just used to go home and help. Girls have changed in many ways. They now wear a lot of make-up and do their hair in different ways. In Sikh families we weren't allowed to cut our hair, but a lot of them do, you're not supposed to.

I think we have got some equality. Now women can work in places they want, I think they get most of what they want. Girls in Asian families haven't got what they want yet! I think that will take quite a long time. They need more persuading. But people like ourselves now, we can pass it down to our children and it will change. There are still some people who want to do the same as their parents, but most of them want to change, and that's good.

KAMALJIT

Although Kamaljit believes that change is good, we should also keep a critical perspective over what they are hoping to change. Any implication that it is inherently better to live life totally in the style of a Western girl or woman would be a mistake, and girls should be aware of potential drawbacks as well as advantages.

In promoting change in the situation of women in general, it is equally, or even more, important to promote change on the part of boys and men. The Asian girls thought that some Asian boys were changing a little bit, but if they are to fulfil the girls' expectations of them as future sharing husbands, they will need to change a lot more.

I enjoy school but there's a lot of discrimination, boys discriminating girls. As I do sociology there's a lot of group discussion and they say, 'Oh girls belong in the kitchen.' I go, 'No they don't. Times are changing now, these are the 1990s not 1975. Haven't you ever heard of women's liberation?' They all shut up. I say, 'Women are becoming more aware of themselves, that's the way it should be.' They don't know what to say then.

REHANA

I think boys' attitudes have changed but not enough. The intelligent boys realize that just because you're a girl doesn't mean you're thick. But the ones who aren't so intelligent think, 'She's a girl, she should stay at home and make the chapatis.'

RAJWINDER

Asian boys haven't changed a lot, just a little bit. They take the feelings of girls nowadays. A year ago we were talking about how girls and boys feel at home. The boys in the class actually took what we said and some of them have changed their views, so boys have changed.

KAMALJIT

For all girls in the 1990s the situation of their counterparts way back in the 1970s seemed very distant, and they had a sense that things must have been far worse then.

From what I've heard about girls in the seventies from people, I think the parents were much more strict in them days than what they are now. I think in them days girls left school, got married and pregnant and that was life. But now it's changing. I think it's getting better now for women.

TRACY

Another girl described her different perception of what life for girls in the 1970s must have been like:

Maybe when they got married it's a bit different. I think they'd want to get married a bit earlier. They'd be opposite to me. And children - I think they'd want more children than me. And I think jobs would be different, they'd want to go into nursing and that. I think they were very much into women's lib then - more than us.

KIM

Kim is right about girls' expectations of an earlier marriage, but the relatively small number of children desired remains about the same. She is also correct to some extent about more girls wanting to go into jobs like nursing. However, she is incorrect in her assumptions about girls in the 1970s and 'women's lib'. At that time they only paid lip service to women's liberation and were quite unsure about some of its demands. Today girls are much clearer about the sorts of demands they want, many of which still coincide with those demanded by the militant feminists of the 1970s. Girls from all backgrounds recognized that significant changes have occurred in women's lives, and although aware of continuing discrimination, believed that women's situation at work and in the home is improving. They will ultimately discover that although advances should not be underestimated, they have not been as great as girls imagine; they are often hard to sustain; some change is more in ideology than reality; and some of these advances are being eroded at this very moment.

The ways girls see themselves and their lives have altered with the social and economic changes of the intervening twenty years, reflecting changes in family structure and stability, and a rise in the status of women – at least in women's eyes. In my conclusion to the first edition I was suggesting that some girls were slow to part with traditional ideas about sex and gender differences such as the belief in male dominance. Nowadays, this suggestion is rejected by the majority of girls and women. Even those who are still sympathetic to this idea only endorse physical dominance, which is of less use in serving contemporary society. It does, however, still serve to deny true freedom and equality to women through the implicit threat of male sexual violence inside and outside the home. Even though the Ealing girls may deny any strong expression of feminism, I felt in 1991 that the girls in this later research appeared to have a greater sense of the equal importance of women, and their own individuality and independence, even if in some cases this has evolved out of the anticipated instability of their future family lives. 'Feminine' identity, as noted earlier, involves 'deeper self-investment than merely taking on a superficial role', and the Ealing girls in 1991 were beginning to more strongly define and invest in their own desires and needs outside the traditional role assigned to women. They are recognizing that at the end of the day, how they organize their lives to accommodate this may be down to them. In the present socio-economic climate this may prove a struggle, and they will need to draw on all the resources they can muster.

NOTES

CHAPTER 6

1. D. G. Brown, 'Sex-Role Preference in Young Children', *Psychological Monographs*, 70, 1956.
2. S. E. Clautour and T. W. Moore, 'Attitudes of 12-year-old Children to Present and Future Life Roles', *Human Development*, 12, 1969.
3. Figures from the 1971 census revealed that one in five women were the chief economic supporters of the household. Between 1971 and 1991 the percentage of families with independent children that were one-parent families more than doubled – from 8% in 1971 to 18% in 1991.
4. Ann Oakley, *Housewife*, Allen Lane, 1974.
5. The related pressures on young men to be seen as sexually successful and 'macho' is explored in Janet Holland *et al.*, *Wimps and Gladiators*, The Tufnell Press, 1992.
6. Sue Lees examines the effects of sexual reputation in *Sugar and Spice*, Penguin, 1993.
7. Research on girls and romance includes A. McRobbie, *'Jackie': An Ideology of Adolescent Femininity*, University of Birmingham, Centre for Contemporary Cultural Studies, 1978, and *Feminism and Youth Culture: from 'Jackie' to 'Just Seventeen'*, Macmillan, 1991; Sue Lees, op. cit.
8. See also Sue Lees, op. cit.
9. V. Amos and P. Parmar, 'Resistances and Responses: the Experiences of Black Girls in Britain', in A. McRobbie and T. McCabe, *Feminism for Girls: An Adventure Story*, Routledge & Kegan Paul, 1981; and A. Brah and R. Minhas in Gaby Weiner (ed.), *Just a Bunch of Girls*, Open University, 1985, also discuss the myth of arranged marriage in the lives of Asian girls.
10. Such as the theory of early socialization suggested by Nancy Chodorow and discussed in chapter 2.
11. D. Tannen, *You Just Don't Understand*, Virago, 1992.

12. The nature of the father–daughter relationship is explored further in Sue Sharpe, *Fathers and Daughters*, Routledge, 1994.
13. A. Brah and R. Minhas in Gaby Weiner, op. cit.

CHAPTER 7

OVERVIEW

Teenage girls in the early 1990s are 'Thatcher's children'. They have been brought up with a sense of expanding individualism and self enterprise in a period of increasingly severe economic recession. With role models like Madonna and Margaret Thatcher, they have learnt that there can be a variety of alternative expressions of femininity. But have their attitudes and expectations significantly changed over the past two decades? For fourteen- to fifteen-year-old girls at school in the beginning of the 1990s, the world of girls in 1972 seemed like a century away. For myself, researching their ideas and hopes at both times, their lives did not appear so far apart. Although there have clearly been many social and economic changes in the intervening two decades, I felt both a sense of difference and yet a strong familiarity about many of their attitudes and expectations.

When I did the original research in 1972, girls (and boys) could leave school at fifteen (the last year they were able to do this), and there was a reasonable chance of them getting a job. Teenagers of both sexes looked forward to a fuller landscape of employment opportunities than the relative wasteland of today. Throughout the post-war years, educational policy reports had emphasized equality of educational opportunity regardless of class, gender or race. The comprehensive system, hailed as a more equal system of education, did not seem to have provided a solution. In the early seventies, demands for women's equality were being raised by a growing women's liberation movement. 'Feminism' had entered the general vocabulary, and the next few years would see both the Sex Discrimination Act and the Equal Pay Act pass successfully through parliament.

The following years witnessed a steady decline in Britain's industrial base. Manufacturing industries disappeared, taking men out of the work-force. At the same time, service industries expanded, drawing women into the lower paid, lower status and part-time opportunities that opened up in many traditionally female areas of work such as the 'caring' professions. Banking and the financial sector also increased during the Thatcher years. But this expansion was short-lived and the economic recession of the early eighties deepened through the remaining years of the decade into the nineties, with a subsequent contraction in service industries. The impact of this recession was felt in previously secure occupations such as banks and insurance companies, causing unprecedented redundancies. With such high unemployment levels everywhere, reality for young people in Britain in the nineties is that they can easily spend many years after leaving school with little or no experience of work. The government's intention to provide training schemes for all those leaving school at sixteen or seventeen has fallen far short of its goal. With such bleak prospects, it was not surprising to find that working class girls' attitudes to leaving school and getting a job in 1991 had changed from those of their predecessors. Only a minority of the Ealing girls wanted to leave school at sixteen. The rest looked forward to moving up into the sixth form, or going to a sixth form college or further education college to take GCSEs, A levels, or other qualifications such as BTec. Whatever the nature of their feelings about being at school, they showed an awareness of the paucity of work opportunities and preferred to stay longer in education.

> Well, even if I fail GCSEs this year I'm going to carry on until I pass. As far as I'm concerned there's no point in leaving without qualifications because you're not going to get a job anyway. So while you're wasting your life at home, you might as well be getting more qualifications for a better job in the future.

> MARIE

In the seventies and eighties ideas and beliefs about equality of opportunities became more commonplace. It might reasonably be assumed that by the early 1990s, girls' job choices would show some change. In my early research, girls from four Ealing schools described job expectations covering about thirty occupations, most of which fell into the general realm of 'women's work'. Significantly, 40 per cent of these were in some sort of office work. The next most popular jobs were teacher, nurse, shop assistant or bank clerk:

these accounted for a quarter of their choices. When receptionist, telephonist, air hostess, hairdresser and children's nurse or nanny were added to these, this range of jobs accounted for three-quarters of their job expectations. Almost twenty years later, girls from the Ealing schools similarly cited about thirty jobs they expected to go into and, like the generation before them, these were predominantly in 'women's work'. Increased awareness of gender issues and rights and equality of opportunities did not seem to be reflected in expanding job expectations. There was, however, some significant change in their choices. For example, the expectation or desire to do office work had greatly fallen away. Hardly anyone specified wanting to be a secretary or to work in an office, and jobs like receptionist and telephonist were also missing. The disappearance of office work may be explained by several related changes. One is linked to the technological changes that have occurred in the business world, and the way jobs are defined. Secretarial work is now done using word processors and other computing machines, and the relevant lessons taught in school are now called business studies rather than typing and office skills. It also reflects a change in attitude towards careers for girls. Office work was once seen as 'a nice job for a girl', that is, the sort of girl who wants a 'clean, respectable' job until she gets married and gives up full-time work to have children. This criterion has become old-fashioned, and, seeing women actively involved in more exciting work, many young girls declare their intention of avoiding 'a boring office job'. The proportion of girls wanting to work in banking and insurance, however, did show an increase in parallel with the expansion in the financial sector during the past decade.

Unlike previously, these Ealing girls did not expect to become shop assistants or hairdressers and, more surprisingly, hardly anyone specifically wanted to be a nurse, although this desire could be disguised within those who wanted to work in the health services. Working with children, however, which had been a well represented choice in 1972, was even more popular nearly twenty years later. Unfortunately, this kind of employment is still as low paid and low status as it was in the 1970s. Despite a few men entering this field, it remains a 'caring' job predominantly carried out by women, in keeping with the traditional feminine stereotype. Other jobs named

similarly at both times include veterinary nurse, air hostess, policewoman, beautician, and radiographer. New areas of work mentioned
include photography, psychology, psychotherapy, graphic design,
conservation, and theatre and media studies, the teaching and
training related to which entered the school curriculum in the
intervening period. It is not clear at present to what extent these
kinds of subjects will be affected by the strictures of the National
Curriculum. There were some aspirations to take up professional
careers as doctors, lawyers, solicitors, and pharmacists, and, as in
1972, these were mainly expressed by the girls of Asian origin. It
was good to see some girls (two of whom were Asian girls)
expressing hopes to become car mechanics, engineers, or firefighters,
but their small number reflects the slow pace of movement away
from the traditional stereotype of women's work.

While work horizons had slightly changed but not significantly
broadened, some expansion was more apparent in girls' personal
horizons. They all placed a greater stress on equality with men, and
on their own needs. I constantly detected an increased expression of
assertiveness and confidence, and an emphasis on women's ability to
stand on their own feet. They almost unanimously endorsed the
importance of having a job or career, and in this respect emphasized
being able to support themselves if their marriage or relationship
broke down, and not having to depend on nor be dominated by,
men. In 1972, girls endorsed their preference to be a girl rather than
a boy, and those responding in 1991 were even more emphatic. At
neither time, however, did girls find it acceptable to define themselves as 'feminist'. In the early seventies, this label was attached to
the bra-burning image portrayed by the media. After more than
twenty years of feminist activity and campaigns; the establishment
of equal rights legislation; and positive changes in attitudes to
women in general, many girls in the 1990s remain reluctant to
identify themselves as feminist. The naïve association of feminism
solely with separatism and a rejection of men, or using the term to
define women viewed as too active in promoting women, is still
commonplace. They, like many women older than themselves, try
to disguise feminist pronouncements by the preface: 'I'm not a
feminist, but . . .', and there is a tendency to assume more change
has occurred than has actually taken place. It is interesting that each

generation in this research thought that it had progressed faster and further in this area, and that things were much improved for them compared to their mothers' day. In many respects this has not been the case.

> Feminism is still relevant but not so much now. I think things are changing a lot. In my dad's office it used to be the men doing the high-powered jobs and the women doing secretarial work. Now they've got men secretaries, some, and some women. There are still men in the high jobs but there are more women coming in . . . I think it will carry on changing. I hope so, it's a better way to work. I think men are more willing to accept women into the higher jobs . . . I don't think I'd call myself a feminist. I'm not one of those that says 'come on, you should be doing this, you should let women in.' They don't need women now to say there shouldn't be a divide because men've realized it now, everyone is changing. It's a lot better.
>
> TERESA

Girls in the early nineties recognized various social changes that have already made an impact on the lives of many of their friends and relatives. They assumed that nothing can be taken for granted, especially in employment and marriage, (although for Asian girls marriage was still very much on the agenda). Whether they wished to or not, they were aware that they should stay on at school for as long as they could, because if they left without some qualifications, there might be nothing for them in the world of work. Many rightly assumed that doing A levels would help them in a career, but that it was no longer a guarantee of work where there were few or no jobs. On the personal side, their less positive attitudes to marriage acknowledged the current high rates of family breakdown.

> I don't want to get married. I don't see the point in getting married. You could live with someone, then if it broke up then it's easier than going through divorce, half this and half that. Some people think it's traditional and you should do it, but I don't see any point in it. You can make a commitment without marriage.
>
> LISA

However, while these young women had absorbed some of life's social realities, they remained optimistic about other crucial expectations in which they might be disappointed. For example, they had understandably taken on the ideology of gender equality in education and employment. Many schools have anti-sexist and anti-racist policies and there is general endorsement of equal opportunities. In 1991, for the first time, more women than men applied for a university place, although evidence has always shown fewer women than men actually go to university. Women have not made many inroads into areas of work hitherto thought of as 'men's work'; and they still earn considerably less than men. Girls' hopes in education and employment may therefore be curtailed.

Like many of the 1972 girls, they also anticipated combining work and family life, and assumed that future husbands or partners would help equally with housework and child-care. Unfortunately, such hopes are difficult to translate into practice. In this respect it is interesting to observe the possibility that some of their own mothers could have been girls who participated in my earlier research, and to speculate on the implications of their current occupations. If we compare their mothers' work to that done by the 1972 girls' mothers, we find that there has been very little change. Both are employed in similar low paid, low status, and often part-time work in areas like cleaning, shop work, office work, health work and childminding. Without a radical upturn in the economy, employers are unlikely to expand their work-force in the near future nor offer conditions such as essential child-care to help women with family commitments. Girls' expectations and aspirations in the nineties are likely to come up against exactly the same barriers as their predecessors.

In the 1970s things seemed clearer and more obviously differentiated by gender. I could talk more confidently about girls' preoccupations with marriage, for instance, and about boys facing a continuous working life. Nowadays these issues are blurred. For example, both marriage and employment are unstable entities within which both sexes can take a whole variety of stances. It is tempting to say that women have achieved a certain amount of equality and this is why things are less clear-cut, but I think it is more complicated than this. I sense some of these changes are double edged, and that girls' expression of greater independence and assertiveness, for instance, has come through their perceived future need for self survival and the real possibility of ending up on their own, which is a rather negative aspect of an otherwise positive development. Double edges can cut both ways.

The restraining parameters of girl's and women's domestic and working lives have changed little in the last two decades, or they have merely been redrawn a little differently. But while these constraints remain, girls themselves have changed. Whatever the practical realities of their future lives, they have absorbed assumptions of equality and independence, and the ability to support themselves. Although such concerns can also be seen to reflect the increased emphasis on individualism characterizing the Thatcher/Major years, their other concerns remain more altruistic. Like their predecessors, the reasons they gave for choosing a possible job or career tended to endorse non-materialistic values such as helping or meeting people, rather than simply earning money. It is cheering to find that such human values have not been superseded, and that positive aspects of traditional femininity are retained. Perhaps it also reflects an awareness of the contradictory nature of society, which makes it hard for girls to gain access to the economic goals it idealizes. On the home front, despite some change in family organization due to factors like male unemployment, patriarchal values are still endorsed. The 'new man' has been more or less dismissed as rather a joke, and few men really share responsibility for home and family, either because they resist doing so, or because the structure of their work prevents this. Boys growing up today are being made increasingly aware of gender equality, but they are unlikely to make it a priority in their own lives. Young woman may be more aware and determined about their lives and aspirations, but they look forward to a future in which they are likely to end up juggling work and domestic life like their mothers before them.

With economic depression and high unemployment a feature of the early 1990s, it seems like a relative luxury to still be demanding more, wider and better opportunities for women in all areas of their lives, but it must continue. Any notion that we have already got them is a myth. We must sustain the momentum produced through positive changes in attitudes to women working and women's work, and the actual movement, however limited, of women into new areas of employment and higher positions. We also need to find or create strategies (as well as more and better child-care facilities) to enable women to balance family demands alongside work commitments. And we must also look seriously at how to change the upbringing and education of boys and men.[1] However much men may acknowledge women's rights and equality, this is rarely translated into behaviour. With their backs against the wall, many men are put into the position of defending what they have rather than opening it up to provide equal opportunities. So far it has been girls and women who have changed their perceptions and attitudes, made demands in their personal and working lives, adapted themselves in many ways, and are left doing far more than their fair share in the belief that this at least is a better use of their talents. Perhaps the sense of individualism nurtured in 'Thatcher's children' could have a positive spin-off in supplying the self-determination that will help young women to demand and create these equal opportunities for themselves and for the benefit of others.

CHAPTER 7

1. More attention has been given to this subject with the publication of various books on masculinity and on boys in particular, such as Angela Phillips, *The Trouble With Boys*, Pandora, 1993; and Carol Lee, *Talking Tough: the Fight for Masculinity*, Arrow Books, 1993.

INDEX

A levels, 36, 100, 101, 104, 117, 132,
    139, 165, 195, 196, 299
ability, upbringing and, 121–4
abortion, 50
Adie, Kate, 191–2
adolescence, 241
advertising, 44, 66
AEU (Amalgamated Engineering
    Union), 31
Afro-Caribbeans, see West Indian girls
    and women
aggression, 79–81, 120, 124, 252
ambition, 80
Amos, V., 293
analytic thought, 122–3
Anderson, Miss, 19
Andrews, Irene Osgood, 55, 56
anthropology, 59–61, 62, 202
APEX, 38, 56
apprenticeships, 17, 180, 195
Arapesh tribe, 59, 205
Archer, J., 90
Arnot, M., 153, 199
arranged marriages, 266–70, 273–5
arts, as 'girls' subject', 132
Asian girls and women
    attitudes to education, 12, 97–100,
        102–3, 104
    attitudes to girls in men's work,
        187–8
    boyfriends, 262–4
    boys' and girls' subjects, 134, 137
    combining work with family life,
        225–9
    family life, 280–83
    and feminism, 288–91
    gender preferences, 244, 249, 250, 252,
        254, 255–6, 257–9

housework, 108, 235–6
importance of work, 99–100, 219–20
job expectations, 156–7, 158, 159–60,
    298
marriage, 98–9, 104, 265, 266–70,
    273–6, 299
    in mixed schools, 147–8
    and motherhood, 205
    office work, 163
    parental encouragement, 123–4
    and racism, 144
    working mothers, 172–3, 174–5, 176
    Youth Training Scheme, 197
assertiveness, 80, 121, 129, 220, 251, 298,
    300–301
Association of Laundrymen, 21–2
ATS (Auxiliary Territorial Service),
    26n, 27
Australian aborigines, 205

Bacon, M.K., 60, 89
Bangladesh, 98
banking, 158–9, 296, 297
Barry, H., 60, 89
Bass, B. M., 90
Beach, F., 89
beauty, 66, 77
behaviour, control in schools, 128
Benet, M., 238
Benn, C., 152
Benney, M., 56
Beveridge, William, 29
Beveridge Report, 56
Biddle, J., 90
birth control, 25n, 35
Bookhagen, C., 238
Bowlby, John, 34, 208, 237
boyfriends, 118, 131, 259–64

305

Discover more about our forthcoming books through Penguin's FREE newspaper...

Penguin
Quarterly

It's packed with:

- exciting features
- author interviews
- previews & reviews
- books from your favourite films & TV series
- exclusive competitions & much, much more...

READ MORE IN PENGUIN

In every corner of the world, on every subject under the sun, Penguin represents quality and variety – the very best in publishing today.

For complete information about books available from Penguin – including Puffins, Penguin Classics and Arkana – and how to order them, write to us at the appropriate address below. Please note that for copyright reasons the selection of books varies from country to country.

In the United Kingdom: Please write to *Dept. JC, Penguin Books Ltd, FREEPOST, West Drayton, Middlesex UB7 0BR*

If you have any difficulty in obtaining a title, please send your order with the correct money, plus ten per cent for postage and packaging, to *PO Box No. 11, West Drayton, Middlesex UB7 0BR*

In the United States: Please write to *Penguin USA Inc., 375 Hudson Street, New York, NY 10014*

In Canada: Please write to *Penguin Books Canada Ltd, 10 Alcorn Avenue, Suite 300, Toronto, Ontario M4V 3B2*

In Australia: Please write to *Penguin Books Australia Ltd, 487 Maroondah Highway, Ringwood, Victoria 3134*

In New Zealand: Please write to *Penguin Books (NZ) Ltd, 182–190 Wairau Road, Private Bag, Takapuna, Auckland 9*

In India: Please write to *Penguin Books India Pvt Ltd, 706 Eros Apartments, 56 Nehru Place, New Delhi 110 019*

In the Netherlands: Please write to *Penguin Books Netherlands B.V., Keizersgracht 231 NL–1016 DV Amsterdam*

In Germany: Please write to *Penguin Books Deutschland GmbH, Friedrichstrasse 10–12, W–6000 Frankfurt/Main 1*

In Spain: Please write to *Penguin Books S. A., C. San Bernardo 117–6° E–28015 Madrid*

In Italy: Please write to *Penguin Italia s.r.l., Via Felice Casati 20, I–20124 Milano*

In France: Please write to *Penguin France S. A., 17 rue Lejeune, F–31000 Toulouse*

In Japan: Please write to *Penguin Books Japan, Ishikiribashi Building, 2–5–4, Suido, Bunkyo-ku, Tokyo 112*

In Greece: Please write to *Penguin Hellas Ltd, Dimocritou 3, GR–106 71 Athens*

In South Africa: Please write to *Longman Penguin Southern Africa (Pty) Ltd, Private Bag X08, Bertsham 2013*

READ MORE IN PENGUIN

WOMEN'S INTEREST

A History of Their Own Bonnie S. Anderson and Judith P. Zinsser
Volumes One and Two

This is an original and path-breaking European history, the first to approach the past from the perspective of women. 'A richly textured account that leaves me overwhelmed with admiration for our foremothers' ability to survive with dignity' – *Los Angeles Times Book Review*

Our Bodies Ourselves Angela Phillips and Jill Rakusen
A Health Book by and for Women

'The bible of the women's health movement' – *Guardian*. 'The most comprehensive guide we've seen for women' – *Woman's World*. 'Every woman in the country should be issued with a copy free of charge' – *Mother & Baby*

Women's Experience of Sex Sheila Kitzinger

Sheila Kitzinger explores the subject in a way that other books rarely aspire to – she places sex in the context of life and writes about women's feelings concerning their bodies, and the many different dimensions of sexual experience, reflecting the way individual attitudes can change between adolescence and later years.

The Past Is Before Us Sheila Rowbotham

'An extraordinary, readable distillation of what [Sheila Rowbotham] calls an "account of ideas in the women's movement in Britain" ... This is a book written from the inside, but with a clarity that recognizes the need to unravel ideas without abandoning the excitements and frustrations that every political movement brings with it' – *Sunday Times*